DANGEROUS GOODS

DANGEROUS GOODS

A guide to exemptions from The Carriage of Dangerous Goods by Road Regulations

ROGER WRAPSON

KOGAN
PAGE

Publisher's note
Every possible effort has been made to ensure that the information contained in this book is accurate at the time of going to press, and the publishers and authors cannot accept responsibility for any errors or omissions, however caused. No responsibility for loss or damage occasioned to any person acting, or refraining from action, as a result of the material in this publication can be accepted by the editor, the publisher or any of the authors.

First published in Great Britain in 2009 by Kogan Page Limited

Kogan Page Limited
120 Pentonville Road
London N1 9JN
United Kingdom
www.koganpage.com

© Roger Wrapson, 2009

British Library Cataloguing in Publication Data

A CIP record for this book is available from the British Library.

ISBN 978 0 7494 5634 4

Typeset by JS Typesetting Ltd, Porthcawl, Mid Glamorgan
Printed and bound in India by Replika Press Pvt Ltd

Acknowledgements

Thanks are due to various officers from the Dangerous Goods Branch of the Department of Transport and from the Health and Safety Executive who not only provided inspiration, but more importantly, provided the motivation and enthusiasm for the subject of *Dangerous Goods*.

My grateful thanks go to my many colleagues and friends at the Road Haulage Association who freely gave me their help, support, encouragement and advice over a number of years when I was the Senior Manager.

Thanks are also due to my long suffering and very able secretary Tina Gill at the RHA who supported me at my time at the Road Haulage Association.

Thanks are also due to the Dangerous Goods and Special Cargoes section of the Transport Division of UN ECE in Geneva for help in unravelling some copyright issues.

Finally, thanks must go to my dear wife Judy who, while not understanding the issues, put up with my absence when away at meetings and with proof reading and writing at peculiar times, and to my daughter Eleanor who as Super Secretary in her own right, helped with various formatting issues of text and table.

Preface

In spite of every diligence in its production errors may well appear. Indeed it's important to remember that this is a living, working document and that while the text contains the author's own interpretation on the regulations this may well change in use. While it is to be hoped that regulation, interpretation and enforcement go hand in hand (the author is aware that the various agencies go to great lengths to ensure this is the case), situations can, and do, arise, where this is not immediately obvious. I am aware that where enforcement is queried that, not unexpectedly, the enforcement action will reflect the element of risk. Dangerous goods, while able to take advantage of exemptions from regulation, do not lose any of their properties that make them dangerous.

The reader should also mark his personal calendar to reflect that, in any case, the Dangerous Goods Regulations are updated every two years and rules and interpretation may change.

Introduction

Since 2004 dangerous goods in the UK have been carried under ADR European Agreement concerning the International Carriage of Dangerous Goods by Road as enacted for the UK as The Carriage of Dangerous Goods and Use of Transportable Pressure Equipment Regulations – known as the Carriage Regulations. The ADR European agreement is updated every two years and the carriage regulations follow suit. In this book we refer variously to the Regulations, Carriage Regulations, or the Dangerous Goods Regulations when we mean the regulations concerning the carriage of dangerous goods by road. We have also incorporated the 2009 updates where they are relevant.

This book is designed to help you decide if the goods you are about to carry are subject to the Carriage Regulations. It presents the exemptions that could apply (if any) if the goods were packed according to the dangerous goods table.

It should be noted that if none of the exemptions contained here apply then the majority of chemical products can still be moved, but will require movement subject to all the requirements of the carriage regulations.

The author would be the first to admit that this book doesn't immediately constitute a gripping bedtime read; however, transport operators would be well advised to read all sections in order to get a feel for the transport of dangerous goods and some of its subtle nuances. Apart from that this book is designed as a reference book for those unfamiliar with the world of dangerous goods.

This book represents the best guess you the operator are going to get to the exemptions available under the dangerous goods regulations, but the author cannot accept any liability for any legal action caused as a result of using information contained or implied in this book. It provides no substitute for reading the Regulations themselves, nor for consulting a Dangerous Goods Safety Advisor or your Trade Association. The carriage of dangerous goods in any quantities is a serious business, requiring skill and judgement on your part and on the part of your driver(s). Even when the carriage regulations do not apply the product is still 'dangerous' and awareness training is still required for your driver and ancillary staff.

An exemption from the regulations does not alter a product's ability to injure or even cause death and while the regulations are designed to reduce risk, the human element is ever present as victim or perpetrator, accidental or deliberate. Be vigilant, be circumspect and, best of all, be informed.

Methodology

In this book we are only considering the Carriage Regulations where they affect packaged goods. Apart from setting out the mantra that a Tank or Tanker is always a Tank or Tanker we make no attempt to deal with that side of dangerous goods transport.

The regulations allow a number of exemptions, which we have attempted to set out here. The carriage of dangerous goods is beset by opinions and misinformation which we hope to correct and we also hope to put some flesh on the bones of statements from your customer(s) to the effect that – for instance – their goods are not considered dangerous under the regulations.

You may be aware that dangerous goods have strange names that don't mean much to the average transporter – what is the difference between Calcium Chlorate and Calcium Chlorite – and are we sure we have the right Calcium derivative? For that reason all dangerous goods are assigned a UN Number and frequently further identified with a Packing Group. Armed with these two bits of information we can conquer the (dangerous goods) world! Without it we are at best making vague assumptions which could have serious consequences. It is your customer's responsibility to supply you with this information and if it's not forthcoming my advice is to walk away from the job – you can't afford to take the risk.

We have already referred to packaged goods in the opening paragraph. This frequently, but not invariably, means product in UN-approved packaging with the UN mark and the clever code which tells you what the package is suitable for. This package also needs to be 'clearly and durably marked' with the UN number of the goods contained within a diamond shaped area at least

100 mm × 100 mm. It is your customer's responsibility to do all this but, as is inevitable in transport, your responsibility to make sure he's done it.

The dangerous goods table incorporates changes brought about in the 2009 version of ADR and where possible we have identified some interpretation of the regulations which helps the cause.

Anyone involved in international dangerous goods transport should be aware that this interpretation may well be confined to the UK enforcement authorities only. It is also important to recognise that some countries have their own additional requirements over and above the requirements of ADR and their enforcement authorities will, for instance, impose an on-the-spot fine for displaying an orange plate when it *wasn't* necessary with as much enthusiasm as imposing a fine for not displaying an orange plate when it is necessary!

While you may be able to take advantage of exemptions from the regulations, you need to be aware that your journey may also be subject to separate additional regulations. These include the IMDG Regulations which you will also be subject to for carriage by sea, the Regulations that Le Shuttle imposes on the carriage of dangerous goods, and regulations imposed by operators of road tunnels etc, both within the United Kingdom and in Europe.

You should be aware by now that all drivers of vehicles less than 3.5 tonnes gross, which were originally exempt from the VTC (ADR Licence) requirements, are required to hold such qualification from 1st January 2007 – but only when their loads are over the relevant thresholds to make them subject to the full weight of the ADR requirements. Thus if you are able to take advantage of an exception no ADR Licence is needed.

SECURITY

Various well publicised terrorist activities around the world make it clear that there are forces at work which look to impose their point of view on others by any means possible. Dangerous goods have been perceived as being vulnerable in this area and security measures are included in the regulations.

As a responsible Road Haulage Operator you will in any case go to great lengths to ensure that the load arrives at its destination in as good order as possible and that there is no possibility of the goods having been intercepted or pilfered in any way. However, the regulations require that you are able to demonstrate this 'good housekeeping' should the VOSA enforcement man come knocking.

The regulations require that all persons engaged in the carriage of dangerous goods shall consider the security requirements... commensurate with their responsibilities, dangerous goods shall only be offered for carriage to carriers that are appropriately identified; storage areas including vehicle depots shall be properly secured, well lit, and not accessible to the general public.

Inevitably you will need to consider security training and refresher training, security awareness, methods to reduce risks, and security plans (if appropriate) commensurate with the responsibilities and duties of individuals.

You should be aware that there are dangerous goods that are considered particularly attractive to terrorists and these have uprated security requirements as High Consequence Dangerous Goods. It is my hope that responsible consignors will not offer such goods to Operators who are inexperienced and for the sake of simplicity and clarity I have omitted details of these goods – should you have any concerns in this area you are recommended to contact the HSE Dangerous Goods website at www.hse.gov.uk/cdg/manual or your Trade Association.

Information on Security, including a video aimed at making drivers aware of security issues, is available at: www.dft.gov.uk/pgr/security/subdangerousgoods.

Load security

The Carriage Regulations require that all loads of Dangerous Goods are suitably restrained to prevent the load from moving or being ejected to the danger and discomfort of other road users. It doesn't matter that the goods may have already travelled from A to B without moving – the Regulations require that all dangerous goods are secured by 'appropriate means' ie using suitable and visible load restraints. In the case of a curtain-sided vehicle the curtains might not be considered as appropriate means, particularly if the curtains are not load bearing. So in case you are stopped in a roadside check, it's important that appropriate load restraints are in use.

Some countries in Europe, notably Belgium, require load restraints at all times and do not allow the carriage of drums in curtain-sided trailers.

DANGEROUS GOODS SAFETY ADVISOR

It is a paradox that exemptions contained within this book enable you to operate quite legitimately without the services of a Dangerous Goods Safety

Advisor (DGSA), and yet you will probably be unable to ascertain where you stand regarding dangerous goods you've been offered for carriage without one.

It is at this point that this book should help. However, there is no reason why you shouldn't appoint your own DGSA even if under the regulations you don't need to. I also mention it because you may be asked for details of your DGSA, and it is important to know why you don't need one if asked if you have one.

So, as a (very) general rule of thumb – if the goods you carry are subject to the carriage regulations, you will need to appoint a DGSA. He or she doesn't have to be an employee – they can work on a consultancy basis, but there must be a formal agreement that can be produced on demand.

The DGSA is not just there to answer questions; they have duties to perform – monitoring compliance, training, equipment, and security, and investigating accidents or serious infringements, while preparing an annual report on the undertakings of dangerous goods activities.

GENERAL EXEMPTIONS

Before we get underway it is useful to know that there are some general exemptions that may apply to your operation.

The provisions of ADR do not apply to:

1. The carriage of machinery or equipment that contains dangerous goods in their internal or operational equipment, provided measures have been taken to prevent leakage.
2. Carriage undertaken by organisations that is ancillary to their main activity, in quantities of no more than 450 litres per packaging and within the maximum load threshold. This exemption, by its nature, is vague and it is not recommended that much reliance is placed on it, but in the case, for instance, of a driver taking dangerous goods with him to use himself in a machine or process, this exemption can be used.
   This exemption does not include carriage that represents supply or external or internal distribution.
3. The carriage of dangerous goods by private individuals where the goods are packaged for retail sale and intended for their personal or domestic use – or for leisure or sporting activities, provided measures have been taken

to prevent leakage under normal conditions. This has been amended for the 2009 Regulations onwards to: when the goods are flammable liquids carried in refillable receptacles filled by, or for, a private individual, the total quantity may not exceed 60 litres per receptacle and only 240 litres per transport unit. There may be other Regulations which limit still further the quantity a private individual can carry on his own vehicle. 'Packaged for retail sale' is quite specific and excludes Intermediate Bulk Containers, Large Packaging or Tanks.

4. Carriage undertaken by Emergency Services, including carriage by break-down vehicles of vehicles involved in accidents, or those which have broken down, and contain dangerous goods.

5. Carriage by Emergency Services intended to save human lives.

Fuel

The provisions of ADR do not apply to the carriage of:

1. Fuel contained in the tanks of vehicles performing a transport operation and used for its propulsion or the operation of any of its equipment.

    The fuel may be carried in fixed fuel tanks, directly connected to the vehicle's engine and/or auxiliary equipment, or may be carried in portable fuel containers.

    The total capacity of the fixed tanks shall not exceed 1500 litres per vehicle and the capacity of a tank fitted to a trailer shall not exceed 500 litres. A maximum of 60 litres per vehicle may be carried in portable fuel containers. Therefore, the fuel tank(s) on your truck mustn't exceed 1500 litres and if you're carrying any spare fuel in a drum or can this mustn't exceed 60 litres.

2. Fuel contained in the tanks of vehicles or other means of conveyance (eg boats), carried as a load. Any fuel cocks between the engine and fuel tank shall be closed unless it is essential for the equipment to remain operational.

3. Gases contained in the tanks of vehicles performing a transport operation and destined for its propulsion or operation of any of its equipment, eg refrigerating equipment.

4. Gases contained in fuel tanks of vehicles transported. The fuel cock shall be closed and electrical contact open.

5. Gases contained in equipment used for operation of the vehicle – fire extinguishes etc.

    Measures shall be taken to prevent spillage and this exemption does not apply to Class 7.

There are also exemptions available for:

- Vehicles with less than four wheels and a design speed of 25 km/hr or less.
- Vehicles that run on rails.
- Mobile Machinery – not defined and therefore should be used with caution.
- Agricultural or Forestry Tractor. The NFU has produced a paper on this which defines when a tractor can be considered an agricultural tractor and therefore is able to use this exemption.

LIMITED QUANTITY EXEMPTION

It is possible to use this exemption when values are shown in the dangerous goods table. It requires that the goods are packed in suitable combination packages, ie inner and outer packages in the quantities shown. I liken the concept of combination packages to goods being carried in jam jars (the inner) and packed in a cardboard box (the outer). The values carried in the inners and the values of gross weight (or otherwise) must match or be less than the values in the table.

There are requirements for the quality and type of such packages which are the consignor's responsibility. It is not necessary to use UN-approved packages and it is anticipated that you as a haulier will not be involved in the packaging aspect of the consignment, other than to ensure that the goods are in combination packages (inners and outers) and that they are suitable for purpose. If in doubt ask, and if you note any packaging failure in service, report this immediately to the consignor and ask for rectification for future consignments.

Each package should be clearly marked with the UN number of the goods, preceded by the letters 'UN' and in the case of different goods with different UN numbers within a single package, the UN number and the letters 'LQ'. These markings shall be displayed within a diamond shaped area surrounded by a line at least 100 mm x 100 mm.

The regulations do require orientation arrows on packages.

From 2009 vehicles, wagons and containers require new markings of 'LTD QTY' in black letters not less than 65 mm high on a white background. The location of the marking is the same as for orange-coloured plates or placards. Alternatively, if sea transport is also involved, marking according to the IMDG Code is acceptable.

However, for road transport the requirement for marking a transport unit or container will only apply to loads of limited quantities in excess of 8 tonnes gross weight on transport units with a tare weight in excess of 12 tonnes, and if orange-coloured plates (or placards on the container) are not already displayed.

Where LQ0 is shown there is no Limited Quantity exemption available for this product and you can't carry it without the full ramifications of the dangerous goods regulations applying – although an exemption may exist elsewhere.

So, where the quantities carried within the inner packaging and the quantities for the outer packages (complete with 'inners') do not exceed the values given against the relevant UN number and Packing Group (if any) then any amount of the product so packed can be carried without the requirements of the carriage regulations being observed apart from one important consideration – the driver (and you his employer) need to be able to show that he has received Awareness Training relevant to the product(s) being carried and knows what to do in an emergency.

Subject to the maximum limits shown against the relevant UN number in the dangerous goods table, dangerous goods may be packed together with other articles or substances, provided they will not react dangerously in the event of a leakage.

A pallet (or similar), or a box or crate containing several packages secured to it or in it – an 'Overpack' – must have all packages conforming to the LQ requirements above and the Overpack must be marked as above unless markings representative of all dangerous goods contained are visible.

You might decide that it would be a wise move to carry a fire extinguisher and first aid kit; this is entirely your operating decision – there is no legal requirement to carry this equipment where the Limited Quantity exemption applies. Under this exemption the driver doesn't need to hold a VTC ('ADR Licence') nor does the vehicle need to display orange plates.

Summary

Under this part of the regulations you are wholly exempt from all requirements (apart from awareness training) if the innermost packaging (the receptacle) and the outer packaging are within prescribed limits – as enumerated in the dangerous goods table. If all the packages of the consignment conform to these requirements then you can have a 40 ft trailer load of the goods and still not be subject to the regulations.

EXCEPTED QUANTITIES

For the 2009 Regulations a new category of exemption has been introduced, that of Excepted Quantities. This is similar in principle to the air freight excepted quantities which allows small quantities of dangerous goods for specific purposes to move without being subject to the regulations, excepting awareness training for your driver, and making the customer aware of the very specific packing requirements.

While the specific requirements for the values of the 'inner' and 'outer' packaging are clearly set out in the dangerous goods table, it has to be remembered that there are requirements for compliance of the packaging used. The inner packaging can be plastic (for liquids 0.2 mm min), or glass, porcelain, stoneware, earthenware or metal and the lid must be securely retained with wire, tape or leak-proof threaded cap.

Each 'inner' needs to be contained in intermediate cushioning material which is capable of retaining the contents of the 'inner' and none of the packaging or cushioning material shall react dangerously with the contents.

The intermediate packaging must be securely packed in strong, rigid outer packaging of a reasonable size to accommodate all necessary markings and there are specific tests for the suitability of packages used.

Packages must be marked with the specific 'Excepted Quantity' mark (dimensions 100 mm x 100 mm minimum) and the name of the consignor or consignee shall be included within the mark (unless shown elsewhere on the package).

The maximum number of excepted quantity packages in any consignment shall be 1,000.

Accompanying documents for goods carried as excepted quantities (including CMR notes and consignment notes) will include the statement 'dangerous goods in excepted quantities' and the number of packages.

Because of the very specific packing requirements for excepted quantities it is unlikely that the haulier would be able to make the decision to carry under this exemption in preference to any other. The process of consignment needs to be started further up the chain. However, with the aid of the dangerous goods table the haulier can work with the consignor to identify the best method of carriage.

EXEMPTIONS RELATED TO QUANTITIES CARRIED PER VEHICLE

Also known as the 'Small Load' exemption or 'Load Max' in the dangerous goods table.

This rather grand heading simply means exemptions because of the small quantities of dangerous goods in total carried on the vehicle and refers you to the relevant column in the table in this book. You will note that this exemption is not available for all products and differs between products. It does, however, allow for the carriage of, for instance, a limited number of gas cylinders, and other dangerous goods, by tradesmen where it's not clear if any other exemption could apply. It can also be used in situations where your customer has not packed the goods to take advantage of the Limited Quantity exemptions.

These exemptions apply when the total amount of dangerous goods carried on a vehicle is within a prescribed limit.

When the quantity of dangerous goods carried on a vehicle does not exceed the value shown in the table, they may be carried in packages on a vehicle but the following WILL apply:

Packing

It is necessary that all the packaging conforms to the UN requirements and carries the UN marks.

Training

The driver will need to be able to demonstrate that he has received – and understood – awareness training which relates to the goods being carried.

Documents to be carried on the vehicle

The Transport Document – this can be the consignment note providing it contains the following information:

- The UN number preceded by the letters UN, The proper shipping name, supplemented when applicable with the trade name, for substances of Class 1 the classification code, for radioactive material of Class 7 the Class number 7, for substances of other classes the label model number, when assigned the Packing Group preceded by the letters PG.

- The number and description of the packages, the total quantity of each item of dangerous goods bearing a different UN number, address of the consignor, address of the consignee and any declaration as required by the terms of any special agreement (if applicable).

Fire extinguishers

Trucks carrying dangerous goods under this exemption need to be equipped with one portable fire extinguisher for flammability classes A, B and C, with a minimum capacity of 2 kg dry powder.

The portable fire extinguisher shall be fitted with a seal to verify that it has not been used. In addition it must carry a compliance mark to a recognised standard and an inscription indicating the date of the next inspection or maximum permissible period of use.

Load restraint

As outlined on page 5 it is important that the load is demonstrably properly restrained on the vehicle.

Smoking is prohibited in the vicinity of the vehicle and inside the vehicle.
    Where the value given is 'Unlimited' in the table, any amount of this product can be carried under this exemption provided the requirements above are observed.
    Be aware also however, that if for any reason you exceed these thresholds, you will become subject to the full ramifications of ADR, including the need for the driver to hold an 'ADR Licence', to appoint a Dangerous Goods Safety Advisor and to carry mandatory equipment etc.

The available exemptions which relate to quantities carried are in fact partial exemptions – but the requirements that you do have to comply with as above are not particularly onerous.

Dangerous goods are assigned a transport category as shown in the dangerous goods table. When goods on the vehicle all fall under the same transport category, the exemption can be applied up to the value shown.

For a consignment made up of differing transport categories the following methodology should be used:

Multiply the quantity of goods in Transport Category 1 (if any) by 50.
Multiply the quantity of goods in Transport Category 11 (if any) by 3.
Add these together and add to this the quantity of goods in Transport Category 111.
To be able to use this exemption the total must not exceed 1,000.

Summary

So – this exemption looks rather more complex than the Limited Quantity exemption, but can be useful where the goods exceed the other thresholds. In all cases the driver will need awareness training and will need to carry a 2 kg (minimum) fire extinguisher. He will need to keep his wits about him to ensure the exemption thresholds are not exceeded, particularly with mixed loads. If he can do this then, for instance, orange plates and VTC ('ADR Licences') are not needed.

SPECIAL PROVISIONS

There are exemptions by virtue of the Special Provisions (SP) (right-hand column of the table). For the sake of brevity I have only included those special provisions that provide an exemption from the Carriage Regulations. It is important that the tables are read in their entirety in order that the full picture is gained – for instance, while there may be values given under the Limited Quantity and 'Load Max' exemptions, it is possible that there may be total exemptions given under Special Provisions if some requirements can be complied with. If none of the other values give exemption it is possible that Special Provisions will.

The right-hand columns of the dangerous goods tables contain reference numbers for special provisions (SPs) appropriate to individual products. For the sake of comprehensiveness we have included all reference numbers but only included in the key those that refer to carriage exemptions. Thus you will be able to see that batteries are exempt from the carriage regulations provided that certain conditions are met while in the case of other special provisions we thought it enough that you would be aware that other SPs existed which were more relevant to how the product was carried rather than if you could carry it at all.

Special Provisions applicable to certain articles or substances

32 This substance is not subject to the requirements of ADR when in any other form.

37 This substance is not subject to the requirements of ADR when coated.

38 This substance is not subject to the requirements of ADR when it contains not more than 0.1 per cent calcium carbide.

39 This substance is not subject to the requirements of ADR when it contains less than 30 per cent or not less than 90 per cent silicon.

45 Antimony sulphides and oxides which contain not more than 0.5 per cent of arsenic calculated on the total mass are not subject to the requirements of ADR.

47 Ferricyanides and ferrocyanides are not subject to the requirements of ADR.

59 These substances are not subject to the requirements of ADR when they contain not more than 50 per cent magnesium.

62 This substance is not subject to the requirements of ADR when it contains not more than 4 per cent sodium hydroxide.

65 Hydrogen peroxide aqueous solutions with less than 8 per cent hydrogen peroxide are not subject to the requirements of ADR.

119 Refrigerating machines include machines or other appliances which have been designed for the specific purpose of keeping food or other items at a low temperature in an internal compartment, and air conditioning units. Refrigerating machines and refrigerating machine components are not subject to the provisions of ADR if they contain less than 12 kg of gas in Class 2, Group A or O according to 2.2.2.1.3, or if they contain less than 12 litres ammonia solution (UN No. 2672).

135 The dihydrated sodium salt of dichloroisocyanuric acid is not subject to the requirements of ADR.

138 p-Bromobenzl cyanide is not subject to the requirements of ADR.

141 Products which have undergone sufficient heat treatment so that they present no hazard during carriage are not subject to the requirements of ADR.

142 Solvent extracted soya bean meal containing not more than 1.5 per cent oil and 11 per cent moisture, which is substantially free of flammable solvent, is not subject to the requirements of ADR.

144 An aqueous solution containing not more than 24 per cent alcohol by volume is not subject to the requirements of ADR.

145 Alcoholic beverages of packing group III, when carried in receptacles of 250 litres or less, are not subject to the requirements of ADR.

168 Asbestos which is immersed or fixed in a natural or artificial binder (such as cement, plastics, asphalt, resins or mineral ore) in such a way that no escape of hazardous quantities of respirable asbestos fibres can occur during carriage is not subject to the requirements of ADR. Manufactured articles containing asbestos and not meeting this provision are nevertheless not subject to the requirements of ADR when packed so that no escape of hazardous quantities of respirable asbestos fibres can occur during carriage.

169 Phthalic anhydride in the solid state and tetrahydrophthalic anhydrides, with not more than 0.05 per cent maleic anhydride, are not subject to the requirements of ADR. Phthalic anhydride molten at a temperature above its flash-point, with not more than 0.05 per cent maleic anhydride, shall be classified under UN No. 3256.

177 Barium sulphate is not subject to the requirements of ADR.

188 Lithium cells and batteries offered for carriage are not subject to other provisions of ADR if they meet the following:
   (a) For a lithium or lithium alloy cell, the lithium content is not more than 1 g, and for a lithium-ion cell, the lithium-equivalent content is not more than 1.5 g.
   (b) For a lithium metal or lithium alloy battery the aggregate lithium content is not more than 2 g, and for a lithium-ion battery, the aggregate lithium-equivalent content is not more than 8 g.
   (c) Each cell or battery is of the type proved to meet the requirements of each test in the *Manual of Tests and Criteria*, Part III, sub-section 38.3.

(d) Cells and batteries are separated so as to prevent short circuits and are packed in strong packaging, except when installed in equipment.

(e) Except when installed in equipment, each package containing more than 24 lithium cells or 12 lithium batteries shall in addition meet the following requirements:

    (i) Each package shall be marked indicating that it contains lithium batteries and that special procedures should be followed in the event of the package being damaged.

    (ii) Each shipment shall be accompanied with a document indicating that packages contain lithium batteries and that special procedures should be followed in the event of a damaged package.

    (iii) Each package is capable of withstanding a 1.2 m drop test in any orientation without damage to cells or batteries contained therein, without shifting the contents so as to allow battery to battery (or cell to cell) contact and without release of contents.

    (iv) Except in the case of lithium batteries packed with equipment, packages may not exceed 30 kg gross mass.

As used above and elsewhere in ADR, 'lithium content' means the mass of lithium in the anode of a lithium metal or lithium alloy cell, except in the case of a lithium-ion cell the 'lithium-equivalent content' in grams is calculated to be 0.3 times the rated capacity in ampere-hours.

190   Aerosol dispensers shall be provided with protection against inadvertent discharge. Aerosols with a capacity not exceeding 50 ml containing only non-toxic constituents are not subject to the requirements of ADR.

191   Receptacles, small, with a capacity not exceeding 50 ml, containing only non-toxic constituents are not subject to the requirements of ADR.

208   The commercial grade of calcium nitrate fertilizer, when consisting mainly of a double salt (calcium nitrate and ammonium nitrate) containing not more than 10 per cent ammonium nitrate and at least 12 per cent water of crystallisation, is not subject to the requirements of ADR.

216   Mixtures of solids which are not subject to the requirements of ADR and flammable liquids may be carried under this entry without first applying the classification criteria of Class 4.1, provided there is no free liquid visible at the time the substance is loaded or at the time the packaging, vehicle or container is closed. Sealed packets containing less than 10 ml of a packing group II or III flammable liquid absorbed into a

solid material are not subject to ADR provided there is no free liquid in the packet.

226 Formulations of this substance containing not less than 30 per cent non-volatile, non-flammable phlegmatizer are not subject to the requirements of ADR.

238 Non-spillable batteries are not subject to the requirements of ADR if, at a temperature of 55 °C, the electrolyte will not flow from a ruptured or cracked case and there is no free liquid to flow and if, as packaged for carriage, the terminals are protected from short circuit.

241 The formulation shall be prepared so that it remains homogeneous and does not separate during carriage. Formulations with low nitrocellulose contents and not showing dangerous properties when tested for their liability to detonate, deflagrate or explode when heated under defined confinement by tests of Test series 1 (a), 2 (b) and 2 (c) respectively in the *Manual of Tests and Criteria*, Part 1 and not being a flammable solid when tested in accordance with test No.1 in the *Manual of Tests and Criteria*, Part III, sub-section 33.2.1.4 (chips, if necessary, crushed and sieved to a particle size of less than 1.25 mm) are not subject to the requirements of ADR.

242 Sulphur is not subject to the requirements of ADR when it has been formed to a specific shape (eg Prills, granules, pellets, pastilles or flakes).

249 Ferrocerium, stabilised against corrosion, with a minimum iron content of 10 per cent, is not subject to the requirements of ADR.

251 The entry CHEMICAL KIT or FIRST AID KIT is intended to apply to boxes, cases etc containing small quantities of various dangerous goods which are used for medical, analytical or testing purposes.
  Components shall not react dangerously. The total quantity of dangerous goods in any one kit shall not exceed either 1 l or 1 kg. The packing group assigned to the kit as a whole shall be the most stringent packing group assigned to any individual substance in the kit.
  Kits carried on board vehicles for first-aid or operating purposes are not subject to the requirements of ADR.

252 Provided the ammonium nitrate remains in solution under all conditions of carriage, aqueous solutions of ammonium nitrate, with not more than 0.2 per cent combustible material, in a concentration not exceeding 80 per cent, are not subject to the requirements of ADR.

283   Articles containing gas, intended to function as shock absorbers, including impact energy-absorbing devices, or pneumatic springs are not subject to the requirements of ADR provided:

    (a)   Each article has a gas space capacity not exceeding 1.6 litres and a charge pressure not exceeding 280 bar where the product of the capacity (litres) and charge pressure (bars) does not exceed 80 (ie 0.5 litres gas space and 160 bar charge pressure, 1 litre gas space and 80 bar charge pressure, 1.6 litres gas space and 50 bar charge pressure, 0.28 litres gas space and 280 bar charge pressure).

    (b)   Each article has a minimum burst pressure of four times the charge pressure at 20 °C for products not exceeding 0.5 litres gas space capacity and five times charge pressure for products greater than 0.5 litres gas space capacity.

    (c)   Each article is manufactured from material which will not fragment upon rupture.

    (d)   Each article is manufactured in accordance with a quality assurance standard acceptable to the competent authority.

    (e)   The design type has been subjected to a fire test demonstrating that the article relieves its pressure by means of a fire-degradable seal or other pressure relief device, such that the article will not fragment and that the article does not rocket.

286   Nitrocellulose membrane filters covered by this entry, each with a mass not exceeding 0.5 g, are not subject to the requirements of ADR when contained individually in an article or a sealed packet.

289   Air bags or seat-belts installed in vehicles or in completed vehicle components such as steering columns, door panels, seats, etc, are not subject to the requirements of ADR.

291   Flammable liquefied gases shall be contained within refrigerating machine components. These components shall be designed and tested to at least three times the working pressure of the machinery. The refrigerating machines shall be designed and constructed to contain the liquefied gas and preclude the risk of bursting or cracking of the pressure retaining components during normal conditions of carriage. Refrigerating machines and refrigerating machine components are not subject to the requirements of ADR if they contain less than 12 kg of gas.

304   Batteries, dry, containing corrosive electrolyte which will not flow out of the battery if the battery case is cracked are not subject to the requirements of ADR provided the batteries are securely packed and protected

against short-circuits. Examples of such batteries are: alkali-manganese, zinc-carbon, nickel-metal hydride and nickel cadmium batteries.

305   These substances are not subject to the requirements of ADR when in concentrations of not more than 50 mg/kg.

533   UN No. 1198 formaldehyde solutions, flammable, are substances of Class 3. Formaldehyde solutions, non-flammable, with less than 25 per cent formaldehyde are not subject to the requirements of ADR.

543   UN No. 1005 ammonia, anhydrous, UN No. 3318 ammonia solution with more than 50 per cent ammonia and UN No. 2073 ammonia solution, with more than 35 per cent but not more than 50 per cent ammonia, are substances of Class 2. Ammonia solutions with not more than 10 per cent ammonia are not subject to the requirements of ADR.

546   UN No. 2009 zirconium, dry, finished sheets, strip or coiled wire, in thicknesses of less than 18 μm, is a substance of Class 4.2. Zirconium, dry, finished sheets, strip or coiled wire, in thicknesses of 254 μm or more, is not subject to the requirements of ADR.

584   This gas is not subject to the requirements of ADR when:
      – it is in the gaseous state;
      – it contains not more than 0.5 per cent air;
      – it is contained in metal capsules (sodors, sparklets) free from defects which may impair their strength;
      – the leak proofness of the closure of the capsule is ensured;
      – a capsule contains not more than 25 g of this gas;
      – a capsule contains not more than 0.75 g of this gas per cm^3 of capacity.

585   Cinnabar is not subject to the requirements of ADR.

586   Hafnium, titanium and zirconium powders shall contain a visible excess of water. Hafnium, titanium and zirconium powders, wetted, mechanically produced, of a particle size of 53 μm and over, or chemically produced, of a particle size of 840 μm and over, are not subject to the requirements of ADR.

587   Barium stearate and barium titanate are not subject to the requirements of ADR.

588   Solid hydrated forms of aluminium bromide and aluminium chloride are not subject to the requirements of ADR.

589 Calcium hypochlorite mixtures, dry, containing not more than 10 per cent available chlorine are not subject to the requirements of ADR.

590 Ferric chloride hexahydrate is not subject to the requirements of ADR.

591 Lead sulphate with not more than 3 per cent free acid is not subject to the requirements of ADR.

592 Uncleaned empty packaging (including empty IBCs and large packaging), empty tank-vehicles, empty demountable tanks, empty portable tanks, empty tank-containers and empty small containers which have contained this substance are not subject to the requirements of ADR.

593 This gas, intended for the cooling of, for example, medical or biological specimens, if contained in double wall receptacles which comply with the provisions of packing instruction P203 (11) of 4.1.4.1. is not subject to the requirements of ADR.

594 The following articles, manufactured and filled according to the regulations of the manufacturing state and packaged in strong outer packaging, are not subject to the requirements of ADR.
   – UN No. 1044 fire extinguishers provided with protection against inadvertent discharge;
   – UN No. 3164 articles, pressurised pneumatic or hydraulic, designed to withstand stresses greater than the internal gas pressure by virtue of transmission of force, intrinsic strength or construction.

596 Cadmium pigments, such as cadmium sulphides, cadmium sulphoselenides and cadmium salts of higher fatty acids (eg cadmium stearate), are not subject to the requirements of ADR.

597 Acetic acid solutions with not more than 10 per cent pure acid by mass, are not subject to the requirements of ADR.

598 The following are not subject to the requirements of ADR:
   (a) New storage batteries when:
      – they are secured in such a way that they cannot slip, fall or be damaged;
      – they are provided with carrying devices, unless they are suitably stacked, eg on pallets;
      – there are no dangerous traces of alkalis or acids on the outside;
      – they are protected against short circuits.

(b) Used storage batteries when:
- their cases are undamaged;
- they are secured in such a way that they cannot leak, slip, fall or be damaged, eg by stacking on pallets;
- there are no dangerous traces of alkalis or acids on the outside of the articles;
- they are protected against short circuits.

'Used storage batteries' means storage batteries carried for re-cycling at the end of their normal service life.

599 Manufactured articles or instruments containing not more than 1 kg of mercury are not subject to the requirements of ADR.

600 Vanadium pentoxide, fused and solidified, is not subject to the require-ments of ADR.

601 Pharmaceutical products ready for use, eg cosmetics, drugs and med-icines, which are substances manufactured and packed in packaging of a type intended for retail sale or distribution for personal or household consumption are not subject to the requirements of ADR.

646 Carbon made by steam activation process is not subject to the re-quirements of ADR.

647 The carriage of vinegar and acetic acid food grade with not more than 25 per cent pure acid by mass is subject only to the following requirements:
(a) Packaging, including IBCs and large packaging, and tanks shall be manufactured from stainless steel or plastic material which is permanently resistant to corrosion of vinegar/acetic acid food grade.
(b) Packaging, including IBCs and large packaging, and tanks shall be subjected to a visual inspection by the owner at least once a year. The results of the inspections shall be recorded and the records kept for at least one year. Damaged packaging, including IBCs and large packaging, and tanks shall not be filled.
(c) Packaging, including IBCs and large packaging, and tanks shall be filled in a way that no product is spilled or adheres to the outer surface.
(d) Seals and closures shall be resistant to vinegar/acetic acid food grade. Packaging, including IBCs and large packaging, and tanks shall be hermetically sealed by the packer or the filler so that under normal conditions of carriage there will be no leakage.

(e)   Combination packaging with inner packaging made of glass or plastic (see packing instruction P001 in 4.1.4.1) which fulfil the general packing requirements of 4.1.1.1, 4.1.1.2, 4.1.1.4, 4.1.1.5, 4.1.1.6, 4.1.1.7 and 4.1.1.8 may be used.

The other provisions of ADR do not apply.

648   Articles impregnated with this pesticide, such as fibreboard plates, paper strips, cotton-wool balls, sheets of plastics material, in hermetically closed wrappings, are not subject to the provisions of ADR.

650   Waste consisting of packaging residues, solidified residues and liquid residues of paint may be carried under the conditions of packing group II; the waste may also be packed and carried as follows:
(a)   The waste may be packed in accordance with packing instruction P002 of 4.1.4.1 or to packing instruction IBC06 of 4.1.4.2.
(b)   The waste may be packed in flexible IBC's of types 13H3, 13H4 and 13H5 in overpacks with complete walls.
(c)   Testing of packaging and IBCs indicated under (a) or (b) may be carried out in accordance with the requirements of Chapters 6.1 or 6.5, as appropriate, in relation to solids, at the packing group II performance level.
      The tests shall be carried out on packagings and IBCs, filled with a representative sample of the waste, as prepared for carriage.
(d)   Carriage in bulk in sheeted vehicles, closed containers or sheeted large containers, all with complete walls is allowed. The body of vehicles or containers shall be leak-proof or rendered leak-proof, for example by means of a suitable and sufficiently stout inner lining.
(e)   If the waste is carried under the conditions of this special provision, the goods shall be declared in accordance with 5.4.1.1.3 in the transport document, as follows: 'WASTE, UN 1263 PAINT, 3, II'.

653   The carriage of this gas in cylinders with a maximum capacity of 0.5 litres, is not subject to the other provisions of ADR if the following conditions are met:
–   The provisions for construction and testing of cylinders are observed.
–   The cylinders are contained in outer packaging which at least meet the requirements of Part 4 for combination packaging. The general provisions of packing of 4.1.1.1, 4.1.1.2 and 4.1.15 to 4.1.1.7 shall be observed.
–   The cylinders are not packed together with other dangerous goods.
–   The total gross mass of a package does not exceed 30 kg.

– Each package is clearly and durably marked with 'UN 1013'. This marking is displayed within a diamond-shaped area surrounded by a line that measures at least 100 mm × 100 mm

USING THE DANGEROUS GOODS REFERENCE TABLE

The regulations controlling the carriage of dangerous goods by road do offer some exemptions or partial exemptions from the full weight of the regulations and this book seeks to identify and quantify what they are, when they exist. It has to be understood that there are some chemical products which are so 'anti-social' that no exemptions are available and in such cases the full requirements of the regulations will have to be observed. Such information is beyond the remit of this book and it is recommended that a dangerous goods professional is engaged to move such products if your operation is not itself geared up to do this.

For the purposes of identifying dangerous goods exemptions and exceptions – the object of this book – it has already been established that we need to know the 'UN Number' of the product to be carried. This is the identifying number allocated to the dangerous goods by the United Nations. You will not be surprised to learn that this is the first column in the book's dangerous goods tables. It has to be your starting point in order to identify the correct product so ask your customer for this number and don't pass go until you have it. It is your customer's responsibility to supply you with this information, so don't be afraid to ask for it. You might also need to know the 'Packing Group' to further identify the goods and the extent of danger they represent.

The second column contains the name of the chemical substance – for this exercise it's purpose is to confirm that we've got the right UN number. It also contains information, where necessary, for the purposes of identifying exemptions etc, and the Packing Group, identified as PG1, PG11 or PG111. PG1 is the most dangerous and PG111 the least. Amounts carried, or if they can be carried at all (for many chemicals) will depend on this classification.

The third column identifies the quantities (if any) that can be carried under the 'Excepted Quantity' exemption and you are referred to that section to see how it works. It should be noted that this new concept – introduced in the 2009 regulations – requires the chemical products to be packed in quantities as in the table, or less. A nil value means that no exemption is available under this specific exemption. If this is the case don't give up immediately because it may well be that an exemption is available under another heading – so keep on reading.

The fourth and fifth columns of Receptacle Size and Package Gross under the umbrella heading of LQ Packages and the sixth and seventh headings of Receptacle Size and Package Gross under LQ Shrink Wrapped Trays contain the packing methodology to use the Limited Quantity exemption – where appropriate.

You are referred to the section on the Limited Quantity exemption which details the requirements to be able to use this exemption. The columns contain details for double packing chemicals – firstly in an inner container and secondly in an outer. I use the analogy of jam jars in a cardboard box. The jam jars are the 'receptacle' and with the correct quantity packed in the cardboard box form the 'package'. Both the quantity contained in each individual receptacle (column four) and the total weight of receptacles, chemical and box, need to match or be less than the value in the columns.

As a further complication chemical 'packages' can be carried as 'shrink wrapped trays' – not as individual pallets but as any number of trays on a pallet. Again the trays and the goods shrink wrapped in receptacles have to conform to the values shown.

The good news is that if your packages of dangerous goods conform to these values then you can have as many of these packages as you like on the vehicle without having to conform to the regulations.

The eighth column headed 'Limited Quantity Value/Transport Category' is what I think is usually described as 'for office use only'. It enables the author to work out how he arrived at the values shown.

The ninth column is for the other exemption known rather grandly as 'exemptions related to quantities carried per vehicle' or how much dangerous goods you've got on a vehicle. You are referred to the relevant chapter for details. This can be a useful exemption where your consignor has not been too focused on the correct packaging to take advantage of the other exemptions but you need to be aware that you can come unstuck using this exemption unless you have your wits about you. This is because it refers to an exemption where there are only limited amounts of dangerous goods on a vehicle. Thus you can have several consignments that individually meet this exemption but when the consignments are assembled all together as a load, exceed the load threshold and in such a case the full ramifications of the regulations will apply.

The tenth and final column headed Special Provisions give reference numbers which may provide an exemption for specific products that the earlier exemptions are unable to supply. You are referred to the section on this which enumerates the Special Provisions.

So armed with the appropriate UN number for your goods and the correct Packing Group where appropriate, you can find the entry. You may find that you have a range of options where you can select the appropriate exemption and ensure the necessary requirements are met or you may find that your options are limited. In some cases carriage under only one exemption is possible, or alternatively no exemption exists – in which case the goods can only be carried with the full requirements of the dangerous goods regulations.

Dangerous Goods Table

UN	Substance	Excepted Quantities	LQ Packages		LQ Shrink Wrapped Trays		Limited Quantity Value/Transport Category	Max Load	Special Provisions
			Receptacle Size	Package Gross	Receptacle Size	Package Gross			
0004	AMMONIUM PICTRATE	Nil	Nil	Nil	Nil	Nil	LQ0/1	20	
0005	CARTRIDGES FOR WEAPONS 1.1F	Nil	Nil	Nil	Nil	Nil	LQ0/1	20	
0006	CARTRIDGES FOR WEAPONS 1.1E	Nil	Nil	Nil	Nil	Nil	LQ0/1	20	
0007	CARTRIDGES FOR WEAPONS 1.2F	Nil	Nil	Nil	Nil	Nil	LQ0/1	20	
0009	AMMUNITION INCENDIARY 1.2G	Nil	Nil	Nil	Nil	Nil	LQ0/1	20	
0010	AMMUNITION INCENDIARY 1.3G	Nil	Nil	Nil	Nil	Nil	LQ0/1	20	
0012	CARTRIDGES FOR WEAPONS	Nil	Nil	Nil	Nil	Nil	LQ0/4	Unlimited	
0014	CARTRIDGES FOR WEAPONS, BLANK	Nil	Nil	Nil	Nil	Nil	LQ0/4	Unlimited	
0015	AMMUNITION, SMOKE 1.2G	Nil	Nil	Nil	Nil	Nil	LQ0/1	20	
0016	AMMUNITION, SMOKE 1.3G	Nil	Nil	Nil	Nil	Nil	LQ0/1	20	
0018	AMMUNITION, TEAR PRODUCING 1.2G	Nil	Nil	Nil	Nil	Nil	LQ0/1	20	
0019	AMMUNITION, TEAR PRODUCING 1.3G	Nil	Nil	Nil	Nil	Nil	LQ0/1	20	
0020	AMMUNITION, TOXIC 1.2K	Carriage	Prohibited	Nil	-	-	Carriage		Prohibited
0021	AMMUNITION, TOXIC 1.3K	Carriage	Prohibited	Nil	-	-	Carriage		Prohibited
0027	BLACK POWDER (GUNPOWDER)	Nil	Nil	Nil	Nil	Nil	LQ0/1	20	
0028	BLACK POWDER (GUNPOWDER) COMPRESSED	Nil	Nil	Nil	Nil	Nil	LQ0/1	20	

0029	DETONATORS - NON ELECTRIC	Nil	Nil	Nil	Nil	LQ0/1	20
0030	DETONATORS - ELECTRIC	Nil	Nil	Nil	Nil	LQ0/1	20
0033	BOMBS 1.1F	Nil	Nil	Nil	Nil	LQ0/1	20
0034	BOMBS 1.1D	Nil	Nil	Nil	Nil	LQ0/1	20
0035	BOMBS 1.2D	Nil	Nil	Nil	Nil	LQ0/1	20
0037	BOMBS PHOTO FLASH 1.1F	Nil	Nil	Nil	Nil	LQ0/1	20
0038	BOMBS PHOTO FLASH 1.1D	Nil	Nil	Nil	Nil	LQ0/1	20
0039	BOMBS PHOTO FLASH 1.2G	Nil	Nil	Nil	Nil	LQ0/1	20
0042	BOOSTERS	Nil	Nil	Nil	Nil	LQ0/1	20
0043	BURSTERS	Nil	Nil	Nil	Nil	LQ0/1	20
0044	PRIMERS, CAP TYPE	Nil	Nil	Nil	Nil	LQ0/4	Unlimited
0048	CHARGES DEMOLITION	Nil	Nil	Nil	Nil	LQ0/1	20
0049	CARTRIDGES FLASH 1.1G	Nil	Nil	Nil	Nil	LQ0/1	20
0050	CARTRIDGES FLASH 1.3G	Nil	Nil	Nil	Nil	LQ0/1	20
0054	CARTRIDGES SIGNAL	Nil	Nil	Nil	Nil	LQ0/1	20
0055	CASES, CARTRIDGE, EMPTY, WITH PRIMER	Nil	Nil	Nil	Nil	LQ0/4	Unlimited
0056	CHARGES, DEPTH	Nil	Nil	Nil	Nil	LQ0/1	20
0059	CHARGES, SHAPED	Nil	Nil	Nil	Nil	LQ0/1	20
0060	CHARGES, SUPPLEMENTARY, EXPLOSIVE	Nil	Nil	Nil	Nil	LQ0/1	20
0065	CORD, DETONATING	Nil	Nil	Nil	Nil	LQ0/1	20

UN	Substance	Excepted Quantities	LQ Packages Receptacle Size	LQ Packages Gross Package	LQ Shrink Wrapped Trays Receptacle Size	LQ Shrink Wrapped Trays Gross Package	Limited Quantity Value/Transport Category	Max Load	Special Provisions
0066	CORD, IGNITER	Nil	Nil	Nil	Nil	Nil	LQ0/2	333	
0070	CUTTERS, CABLE, EXPLOSIVE	Nil	Nil	Nil	Nil	Nil	LQ0/4	Unlimited	
0072	CYCLOTRIMETHYLENE-TRINITRAMINE, WETTED	Nil	Nil	Nil	Nil	Nil	LQ0/1	20	266
0073	DETONATORS FOR AMMUNITION	Nil	Nil	Nil	Nil	Nil	LQ0/1	20	
0074	DIAZODINITROPHENOL, WETTED	Nil	Nil	Nil	Nil	Nil	LQ0/0	Nil	266
0075	DIETHYLENEGLYCOL DINITRATE, DESENSITISED	Nil	Nil	Nil	Nil	Nil	LQ0/1	20	266
0076	DINITROPHENOL 1.1D	Nil	Nil	Nil	Nil	Nil	LQ0/1	20	
0077	DINITROPHENOL 1.3C	Nil	Nil	Nil	Nil	Nil	LQ0/1	20	
0078	DINITRORESORCINOL	Nil	Nil	Nil	Nil	Nil	LQ0/1	20	
0079	HEXANITRODIPHENYL-AMINE	Nil	Nil	Nil	Nil	Nil	LQ0/1	20	
0081	EXPLOSIVE, BLASTING, TYPE A	Nil	Nil	Nil	Nil	Nil	LQ0/1	50 kg max	616, 617
0082	EXPLOSIVE, BLASTING, TYPE B	Nil	Nil	Nil	Nil	Nil	LQ0/1	20	617
0083	EXPLOSIVE, BLASTING, TYPE C	Nil	Nil	Nil	Nil	Nil	LQ0/1	20	267, 617
0084	EXPLOSIVE, BLASTING, TYPE D	Nil	Nil	Nil	Nil	Nil	LQ0/1	50 kg	Max
0092	FLARES, SURFACE	Nil	Nil	Nil	Nil	Nil	LQ0/1	20	

0093	FLARES, ARIEL	Nil	Nil	Nil	LQ0/1	20	
0094	FLASH POWDER	Nil	Nil	Nil	LQ0/1	20	
0099	FRACTURING DEVICES, EXPLOSIVE	Nil	Nil	Nil	LQ0/1	20	
0101	FUSE, NON-DETONATING	Nil	Nil	Nil	LQ0/1	20	
0102	CORD (FUSE) DETONATING	Nil	Nil	Nil	LQ0/1	20	
0103	FUSE, IGNITER	Nil	Nil	Nil	LQ0/2	333	
0104	CORD (FUSE) DETONATING, MILD EFFECT	Nil	Nil	Nil	LQ0/2	333	
0105	FUSE, SAFETY	Nil	Nil	Nil	LQ0/4	Unlimited	
0106	FUSES, DETONATING	Nil	Nil	Nil	LQ0/1	20	
0107	FUSES, DETONATING	Nil	Nil	Nil	LQ0/1	20	
0110	GRENADES, PRACTICE	Nil	Nil	Nil	LQ0/4	Unlimited	
0113	GUANYLNITROSAMINO-GUANYLIDENE HYDRAZINE, WETTED	Nil	Nil	Nil	LQ0/0	Nil	266
0114	GUANYLNITROSAMINO-GUANYLTETRAZENE (TETRAZINE), WETTED	Nil	Nil	Nil	LQ0/0	Nil	266
0118	HEXOLITE (HEXOTOL)	Nil	Nil	Nil	LQ0/1	20	
0121	IGNITERS	Nil	Nil	Nil	LQ0/1	20	
0124	JET PERFORATING GUNS, CHARGED	Nil	Nil	Nil	LQ0/1	20	
0129	LEAD AZIDE, WETTED	Nil	Nil	Nil	LQ0/0	Nil	266
0130	LEAD STYPHNATE (LEAD TRINITRORESORCINATE), WETTED	Nil	Nil	Nil	LQ0/0	Nil	266
0131	LIGHTERS, FUSE	Nil	Nil	Nil	LQ0/4	Unlimited	

UN	Substance	Excepted Quantities	LQ Packages Receptacle Size	LQ Packages Package Gross	LQ Shrink Wrapped Trays Receptacle Size	LQ Shrink Wrapped Trays Package Gross	Limited Quantity Value/Transport Category	Max Load	Special Provisions
0132	DEFLAGRATING METAL SALTS OF AROMATIC NITRODERIVATIVES N.O.S.	Nil	Nil	Nil	Nil	Nil	LQ0/1	20	274
0133	MANNITOL HEXANITRATE (NITROMANNITE), WETTED	Nil	Nil	Nil	Nil	Nil	LQ0/1	20	266
0135	MERCURY FULMINATE, WETTED	Nil	Nil	Nil	Nil	Nil	LQ0/0	Nil	266
0136	MINES 1.1F	Nil	Nil	Nil	Nil	Nil	LQ0/1	20	
0137	MINES 1.1D	Nil	Nil	Nil	Nil	Nil	LQ0/1	20	
0138	MINES 1.2D	Nil	Nil	Nil	Nil	Nil	LQ0/1	20	
0143	NITROGLYCERIN, DESENSITISED	Nil	Nil	Nil	Nil	Nil	LQ0/1	20	266, 271
0144	NITROGLYCERIN SOLUTION IN ALCOHOL	Nil	Nil	Nil	Nil	Nil	LQ0/1	20	500
0146	NITROSTARCH	Nil	Nil	Nil	Nil	Nil	LQ0/1	20	
0147	NITRO UREA	Nil	Nil	Nil	Nil	Nil	LQ0/1	20	
0150	PENTAERYTHRITE TENTRANITRATE, WETTED	Nil	Nil	Nil	Nil	Nil	LQ0/1	20	266
0151	PENOLITE	Nil	Nil	Nil	Nil	Nil	LQ0/1	20	
0153	TRINITROANILINE (PICRAMIDE)	Nil	Nil	Nil	Nil	Nil	LQ0/1	20	
0154	TRINITROPHENOL (PICRIC ACID)	Nil	Nil	Nil	Nil	Nil	LQ0/1	20	

0155	TRINITROCHLORO-BENZENE (PICRIC ACID)	Nil	Nil	Nil	Nil	LQ0/1	20	
0159	POWDER CAKE, WETTED	Nil	Nil	Nil	Nil	LQ0/1	20	266
0160	POWDER, SMOKELESS 1.1C	Nil	Nil	Nil	Nil	LQ0/1	20	
0161	POWDER, SMOKELESS 1.3C	Nil	Nil	Nil	Nil	LQ0/1	20	
0167	PROJECTILES 1.1F	Nil	Nil	Nil	Nil	LQ0/1	20	
0168	PROJECTILES 1.1D	Nil	Nil	Nil	Nil	LQ0/1	20	
0169	PROJECTILES 1.2D	Nil	Nil	Nil	Nil	LQ0/1	20	
0171	AMMUNITION ILLUMINATING	Nil	Nil	Nil	Nil	LQ0/1	20	
0173	RELEASE DEVICES, EXPLOSIVE	Nil	Nil	Nil	Nil	LQ0/4	Unlimited	
0174	RIVETS, EXPLOSIVE	Nil	Nil	Nil	Nil	LQ0/4	Unlimited	
0180	ROCKETS 1.1F	Nil	Nil	Nil	Nil	LQ0/1	20	
0181	ROCKETS 1.1E	Nil	Nil	Nil	Nil	LQ0/1	20	
0182	ROCKETS 1.2E	Nil	Nil	Nil	Nil	LQ0/1	20	
0183	ROCKETS 1.3C	Nil	Nil	Nil	Nil	LQ0/1	20	
0186	ROCKET MOTORS	Nil	Nil	Nil	Nil	LQ0/1	20	
0190	SAMPLES, EXPLOSIVE	Nil	Nil	Nil	Nil	LQ0/0	Nil	16, 274
0191	SIGNAL DEVICES HAND	Nil	Nil	Nil	Nil	LQ0/2	333	
0192	SIGNALS, RAILWAY TRACK 1.1G	Nil	Nil	Nil	Nil	LQ0/1	20	
0193	SIGNALS, RAILWAY TRACK 1.4S	Nil	Nil	Nil	Nil	LQ0/4	Unlimited	
0194	SIGNALS, DISTRESS, SHIP 1.1G	Nil	Nil	Nil	Nil	LQ0/1	20	

UN	Substance	Excepted Quantities	LQ Packages Receptacle Size	LQ Packages Package Gross	LQ Shrink Wrapped Trays Receptacle Size	LQ Shrink Wrapped Trays Package Gross	Limited Quantity Value/Transport Category	Max Load	Special Provisions
0195	SIGNALS, DISTRESS, SHIP 1.3G	Nil	Nil	Nil	Nil	Nil	LQ0/1	20	
0196	SIGNALS, SMOKE 1.1G	Nil	Nil	Nil	Nil	Nil	LQ0/1	20	
0197	SIGNALS, SMOKE 1.4G	Nil	Nil	Nil	Nil	Nil	LQ0/2	333	
0204	SOUNDING DEVICES, EXPLOSIVE	Nil	Nil	Nil	Nil	Nil	LQ0/1	20	
0207	TETRANITROANILINE	Nil	Nil	Nil	Nil	Nil	LQ0/1	20	
0208	TRINITROPHENYLMETHYL NATRAMINE	Nil	Nil	Nil	Nil	Nil	LQ0/1	20	
0209	TRINITROTOLUENE (TNT)	Nil	Nil	Nil	Nil	Nil	LQ0/1	20	
0212	TRACERS FOR AMMUNITION	Nil	Nil	Nil	Nil	Nil	LQ0/1	20	
0213	TRINITROANISOLE	Nil	Nil	Nil	Nil	Nil	LQ0/1	20	
0214	TRINITROBENZENE	Nil	Nil	Nil	Nil	Nil	LQ0/1	20	
0215	TRINITROBENZOLIC ACID	Nil	Nil	Nil	Nil	Nil	LQ0/1	20	
0216	TRINITRO-M-CRESOL	Nil	Nil	Nil	Nil	Nil	LQ0/1	20	
0217	TRINITRONAPHTHALENE	Nil	Nil	Nil	Nil	Nil	LQ0/1	20	
0218	TRINITROPHENETOLE	Nil	Nil	Nil	Nil	Nil	LQ0/1	20	
0219	TRINITRORESORCINOL	Nil	Nil	Nil	Nil	Nil	LQ0/1	20	
0220	UREA NITRATE	Nil	Nil	Nil	Nil	Nil	LQ0/1	20	

0221	WARHEADS, TORPEDO	Nil	Nil	Nil	Nil	Nil	LQ0/1	20	
0222	AMMONIUM NITRATE	Nil	Nil	Nil	Nil	Nil	LQ0/1	20	
0224	BARIUM AZIDE	Nil	Nil	Nil	Nil	Nil	LQ0/0	Nil	
0225	BOOSTERS WITH DETONATOR	Nil	Nil	Nil	Nil	Nil	LQ0/1	20	
0226	CYCLOTETRAMETHYLENE TETRANITRAMINE	Nil	Nil	Nil	Nil	Nil	LQ0/1	20	266
0234	SODIUM DINITRO-O-CRESOLATE	Nil	Nil	Nil	Nil	Nil	LQ0/1	20	
0235	SODIUM PICRAMATE	Nil	Nil	Nil	Nil	Nil	LQ0/1	20	
0236	ZIRCONIUM PICRAMATE	Nil	Nil	Nil	Nil	Nil	LQ0/1	20	
0237	CHARGES SHAPED	Nil	Nil	Nil	Nil	Nil	LQ0/2	333	
0238	ROCKETS, LINE THROWING 1.2G	Nil	Nil	Nil	Nil	Nil	LQ0/1	20	
0240	ROCKETS, LINE THROWING 1.3G	Nil	Nil	Nil	Nil	Nil	LQ0/1	20	
0241	EXPLOSIVE, BLASTING TYPE E	Nil	Nil	Nil	Nil	Nil	LQ0/1	50 kg max	617
0242	CHARGES, PROPELLING, FOR CANNON	Nil	Nil	Nil	Nil	Nil	LQ0/1	20	
0243	AMMUNITION, INCENDIARY 1.2H	Nil	Nil	Nil	Nil	Nil	LQ0/1	20	
0244	AMMUNITION, INCENDIARY 1.3H	Nil	Nil	Nil	Nil	Nil	LQ0/1	20	
0245	AMMUNITION, SMOKE 1.2H	Nil	Nil	Nil	Nil	Nil	LQ0/1	20	
0246	AMMUNITION, SMOKE 1.3H	Nil	Nil	Nil	Nil	Nil	LQ0/1	20	
0247	AMMUNITION, INCENDIARY 1.3J	Nil	Nil	Nil	Nil	Nil	LQ0/1	20	
0248	CONTRIVANCES, WATER ACTIVATED 1.2L	Nil	Nil	Nil	Nil	Nil	LQ0/0	Nil	274
0249	CONTRIVANCES, WATER ACTIVATED 1.3L	Nil	Nil	Nil	Nil	Nil	LQ0/0	Nil	274

UN	Substance	Excepted Quantities	LQ Packages Receptacle Size	LQ Packages Gross Package	LQ Shrink Wrapped Trays Receptacle Size	LQ Shrink Wrapped Trays Gross Package	Limited Quantity Value/Transport Category	Max Load	Special Provisions
0250	ROCKET MOTORS WITH HYPERGOLITHIC LIQUIDS	Nil	Nil	Nil	Nil	Nil	LQ0/0	Nil	
0254	AMMUNITION, ILLUMINATING	Nil	Nil	Nil	Nil	Nil	LQ0/1	20	
0255	DETONATORS, ELECTRIC	Nil	Nil	Nil	Nil	Nil	LQ0/2	333	
0257	FUSES, DETONATING	Nil	Nil	Nil	Nil	Nil	LQ0/2	333	
0266	OCTOLITE (OCTOL)	Nil	Nil	Nil	Nil	Nil	LQ0/1	20	
0267	DETONATORS, NON ELECTRIC	Nil	Nil	Nil	Nil	Nil	LQ0/2	333	
0268	BOOSTERS WITH DETONATOR	Nil	Nil	Nil	Nil	Nil	LQ0/1	20	
0271	CHARGES, PROPELLING 1.1C	Nil	Nil	Nil	Nil	Nil	LQ0/1	20	
0272	CHARGES, PROPELLING 1.3C	Nil	Nil	Nil	Nil	Nil	LQ0/1	20	
0275	CARTRIDGES, POWER DEVICE 1.3C	Nil	Nil	Nil	Nil	Nil	LQ0/1	20	
0276	CARTRIDGES, POWER DEVICE 1.4C	Nil	Nil	Nil	Nil	Nil	LQ0/2	333	
0277	CARTRIDGES, OIL WELL 1.3C	Nil	Nil	Nil	Nil	Nil	LQ0/1	20	
0278	CARTRIDGES, OIL WELL 1.4C	Nil	Nil	Nil	Nil	Nil	LQ0/2	333	
0279	CHARGES, PROPELLING FOR CANNON	Nil	Nil	Nil	Nil	Nil	LQ0/1	20	
0280	ROCKET MOTORS 1.1C	Nil	Nil	Nil	Nil	Nil	LQ0/1	20	

0281	ROCKET MOTORS 1.2C	Nil	Nil	Nil	Nil	Nil	LQ0/1	20
0282	NITROGUANIDINE (PICRITE)	Nil	Nil	Nil	Nil	Nil	LQ0/1	20
0283	BOOSTERS	Nil	Nil	Nil	Nil	Nil	LQ0/1	20
0284	GRENADES 1.1D	Nil	Nil	Nil	Nil	Nil	LQ0/1	20
0285	GRENADES 1.2D	Nil	Nil	Nil	Nil	Nil	LQ0/1	20
0286	WARHEADS, ROCKET 1.1D	Nil	Nil	Nil	Nil	Nil	LQ0/1	20
0287	WARHEADS, ROCKET 1.2D	Nil	Nil	Nil	Nil	Nil	LQ0/1	20
0288	CHARGES, SHAPED	Nil	Nil	Nil	Nil	Nil	LQ0/1	20
0289	CORD, DETONATING 1.4D	Nil	Nil	Nil	Nil	Nil	LQ0/2	333
0290	CORD, (FUSE) DETONATING 1.1D	Nil	Nil	Nil	Nil	Nil	LQ0/1	20
0291	BOMBS	Nil	Nil	Nil	Nil	Nil	LQ0/1	20
0292	GRENADES 1.1F	Nil	Nil	Nil	Nil	Nil	LQ0/1	20
0293	GRENADES 1.2F	Nil	Nil	Nil	Nil	Nil	LQ0/1	20
0294	MINES	Nil	Nil	Nil	Nil	Nil	LQ0/1	20
0295	ROCKETS	Nil	Nil	Nil	Nil	Nil	LQ0/1	20
0296	SOUNDING DEVICES, EXPLOSIVE	Nil	Nil	Nil	Nil	Nil	LQ0/1	20
0297	AMMUNITION, ILLUMINATING	Nil	Nil	Nil	Nil	Nil	LQ0/2	333
0299	BOMBS, PHOTOFLASH	Nil	Nil	Nil	Nil	Nil	LQ0/1	20
0300	AMMUNITION, INCENDIARY	Nil	Nil	Nil	Nil	Nil	LQ0/2	333
0301	AMMUNITION, TEAR PRODUCING	Nil	Nil	Nil	Nil	Nil	LQ0/2	333

UN	Substance	Excepted Quantities	LQ Packages		LQ Shrink Wrapped Trays		Limited Quantity Value/Transport Category	Max Load	Special Provisions
			Receptacle Size	Package Gross	Receptacle Size	Package Gross			
0303	AMMUNITION, SMOKE	Nil	Nil	Nil	Nil	Nil	LQ0/2	333	
0305	FLASH POWDER	Nil	Nil	Nil	Nil	Nil	LQ0/1	20	
0306	TRACERS FOR AMMUNITION	Nil	Nil	Nil	Nil	Nil	LQ0/2	333	
0312	CARTRIDGES, SIGNAL	Nil	Nil	Nil	Nil	Nil	LQ0/2	333	
0313	SIGNALS, SMOKE	Nil	Nil	Nil	Nil	Nil	LQ0/1	20	
0314	IGNITERS 1.2G	Nil	Nil	Nil	Nil	Nil	LQ0/1	20	
0315	IGNITERS 1.3G	Nil	Nil	Nil	Nil	Nil	LQ0/1	20	
0316	FUSES, IGNITING 1.3G	Nil	Nil	Nil	Nil	Nil	LQ0/1	20	
0317	FUSES, IGNITING 1.4G	Nil	Nil	Nil	Nil	Nil	LQ0/2	333	
0318	GRENADES, PRACTICE	Nil	Nil	Nil	Nil	Nil	LQ0/1	20	
0319	PRIMERS, TUBULAR 1.3G	Nil	Nil	Nil	Nil	Nil	LQ0/1	20	
0320	PRIMERS, TUBULAR 1.4G	Nil	Nil	Nil	Nil	Nil	LQ0/2	333	
0321	CARTRIDGES FOR WEAPONS	Nil	Nil	Nil	Nil	Nil	LQ0/1	20	
0322	ROCKET MOTORS	Nil	Nil	Nil	Nil	Nil	LQ0/0	Nil	
0323	CARTRIDGES, POWER DEVICE	Nil	Nil	Nil	Nil	Nil	LQ0/4	Unlimited	
0324	PROJECTILES	Nil	Nil	Nil	Nil	Nil	LQ0/1	20	

UN No.	Name							
0325	IGNITERS	Nil	Nil	Nil	Nil	LQ0/2	333	
0326	CARTRIDGES FOR WEAPONS, BLANK 1.1C	Nil	Nil	Nil	Nil	LQ0/1	20	
0327	CARTRIDGES FOR WEAPONS, BLANK 1.3C	Nil	Nil	Nil	Nil	LQ0/1	20	
0328	CARTRIDGES FOR WEAPONS, INERT PROJECTILE	Nil	Nil	Nil	Nil	LQ0/1	20	
0329	TORPEDOES 1.1E	Nil	Nil	Nil	Nil	LQ0/1	20	
0330	TORPEDOES 1.1F	Nil	Nil	Nil	Nil	LQ0/1	20	
0331	EXPLOSIVE, BLASTING TYPE B	Nil	Nil	Nil	Nil	LQ0/1	50 kg max	617
0332	EXPLOSIVE, BLASTING TYPE E	Nil	Nil	Nil	Nil	LQ0/1	50 kg max	617
0333	FIREWORKS 1.1G	Nil	Nil	Nil	Nil	LQ0/1	20 kg (UK only 50 kg)	645
0334	FIREWORKS 1.2G	Nil	Nil	Nil	Nil	LQ0/1	20 kg (UK only 50 kg)	645
0335	FIREWORKS 1.3G	Nil	Nil	Nil	Nil	LQ0/1	20 kg (UK only 50 kg)	645
0336	FIREWORKS 1.4G	Nil	Nil	Nil	Nil	LQ0/2	333 kg (UK only 500 kg)	645
0337	FIREWORKS 1.4S	Nil	Nil	Nil	Nil	LQ0/4	Unlimited	645
0338	CARTRIDGES FOR WEAPONS, BLANK 1.4C	Nil	Nil	Nil	Nil	LQ0/2	333	
0339	CARTRIDGES FOR WEAPONS, INERT 1.4C	Nil	Nil	Nil	Nil	LQ0/2	333	

UN	Substance	Excepted Quantities	LQ Packages		LQ Shrink Wrapped Trays		Limited Quantity Value/Transport Category	Max Load	Special Provisions
			Receptacle Size	Package Gross	Receptacle Size	Package Gross			
0340	NITROCELLULOSE 1.1D	Nil	Nil	Nil	Nil	Nil	LQ0/1	20	
0341	NITROCELLULOSE 1.1D	Nil	Nil	Nil	Nil	Nil	LQ0/1	20	
0342	NITROCELLULOSE, WETTED 1.3C	Nil	Nil	Nil	Nil	Nil	LQ0/1	20	105
0343	NITROCELLULOSE, PLASTICISED	Nil	Nil	Nil	Nil	Nil	LQ0/1	20	105
0344	PROJECTILES 1.4D	Nil	Nil	Nil	Nil	Nil	LQ0/2	333	
0345	PROJECTILES 1.4S	Nil	Nil	Nil	Nil	Nil	LQ0/4	Unlimited	
0346	PROJECTILES 1.2D	Nil	Nil	Nil	Nil	Nil	LQ0/1	20	
0347	PROJECTILES 1.4D	Nil	Nil	Nil	Nil	Nil	LQ0/2	333	
0348	CARTRIDGES 1.4F	Nil	Nil	Nil	Nil	Nil	LQ0/2	333	
0349	ARTICLES, EXPLOSIVE N.O.S. 1.4S	Nil	Nil	Nil	Nil	Nil	LQ0/4	Unlimited	178, 274
0350	ARTICLES, EXPLOSIVE N.O.S. 1.4B	Nil	Nil	Nil	Nil	Nil	LQ0/2	333	178, 274
0351	ARTICLES, EXPLOSIVE N.O.S. 1.4C	Nil	Nil	Nil	Nil	Nil	LQ0/2	333	178, 274
0352	ARTICLES, EXPLOSIVE N.O.S. 1.4D	Nil	Nil	Nil	Nil	Nil	LQ0/2	333	178, 274
0353	ARTICLES, EXPLOSIVE N.O.S. 1.4G	Nil	Nil	Nil	Nil	Nil	LQ0/2	333	178, 274
0354	ARTICLES, EXPLOSIVE N.O.S. 1.1L	Nil	Nil	Nil	Nil	Nil	LQ0/0	Nil	178, 274
0355	ARTICLES, EXPLOSIVE N.O.S. 1.2L	Nil	Nil	Nil	Nil	Nil	LQ0/0	Nil	178, 274

0356	ARTICLES, EXPLOSIVE N.O.S. 1.3L	Nil	Nil	Nil	Nil	LQ0/0	Nil	178, 274
0357	SUBSTANCES, EXPLOSIVE, N.O.S. 1.1L	Nil	Nil	Nil	Nil	LQ0/0	Nil	178, 274
0358	SUBSTANCES, EXPLOSIVE, N.O.S. 1.2L	Nil	Nil	Nil	Nil	LQ0/0	Nil	178, 274
0359	SUBSTANCES, EXPLOSIVE, N.O.S. 1.3L	Nil	Nil	Nil	Nil	LQ0/0	Nil	178, 274
0360	DETONATOR ASSEMBLIES, NON ELECTRIC 1.1B	Nil	Nil	Nil	Nil	LQ0/1	20	
0361	DETONATOR ASSEMBLIES, NON ELECTRIC 1.4B	Nil	Nil	Nil	Nil	LQ0/2	333	
0362	AMMUNITION, PRACTICE	Nil	Nil	Nil	Nil	LQ0/2	333	
0363	AMMUNITION, PROOF	Nil	Nil	Nil	nil	LQ0/2	333	
0364	DETONATORS FOR AMMUNITION 1.2B	Nil	Nil	Nil	Nil	LQ0/1	20	
0365	DETONATORS FOR AMMUNITION 1.4B	Nil	Nil	Nil	Nil	LQ0/2	333	
0366	DETONATORS FOR AMMUNITION 1.4S	Nil	Nil	Nil	Nil	LQ0/4	Unlimited	
0367	FUSES, DETONATING	Nil	Nil	Nil	Nil	LQ0/4	Unlimited	
0368	FUSES, IGNITING	Nil	Nil	Nil	Nil	LQ0/4	Unlimited	
0369	WARHEADS, ROCKET WITH BURSTING CHARGE	Nil	Nil	Nil	Nil	LQ0/1	20	
0370	WARHEADS, ROCKET WITH BURSTING OR EXPELLING CHARGE 1.4D	Nil	Nil	Nil	Nil	LQ0/2	333	
0371	WARHEADS, ROCKET WITH BURSTING OR EXPELLING CHARGE 1.4F	Nil	Nil	Nil	Nil	LQ0/2	333	
0372	GRENADES, PRACTICE, HAND OR RIFLE	Nil	Nil	Nil	Nil	LQ0/1	20	

UN	Substance	Excepted Quantities	LQ Packages		LQ Shrink Wrapped Trays		Limited Quantity Value/Transport Category	Max Load	Special Provisions
			Receptacle Size	Package Gross	Receptacle Size	Package Gross			
0373	SIGNAL DEVICES HAND	Nil	Nil	Nil	Nil	Nil	LQ0/4	Unlimited	
0374	SOUNDING DEVICES, EXPLOSIVE 1.1D	Nil	Nil	Nil	Nil	Nil	LQ0/1	20	
0375	SOUNDING DEVICES, EXPLOSIVE 1.2D	Nil	Nil	Nil	Nil	Nil	LQ0/1	20	
0376	PRIMERS TUBULAR	Nil	Nil	Nil	Nil	Nil	LQ0/4	Unlimited	
0377	PRIMERS CAP TYPE 1.1B	Nil	Nil	Nil	Nil	Nil	LQ0/1	20	
0378	PRIMERS CAP TYPE 1.4B	Nil	Nil	Nil	Nil	Nil	LQ0/2	333	
0379	CASES, CARTRIDGE, EMPTY, WITH PRIMER	Nil	Nil	Nil	Nil	Nil	LQ0/2	333	
0380	ARTICLES, PYROPHORIC	Nil	Nil	Nil	Nil	Nil	LQ0/0	Nil	
0381	CARTRIDGES, POWER DEVICE	Nil	Nil	Nil	Nil	Nil	LQ0/1	20	
0382	COMPONENTS, EXPLOSIVE TRAIN N.O.S. 1.2B	Nil	Nil	Nil	Nil	Nil	LQ0/1	20	178, 274
0383	COMPONENTS, EXPLOSIVE TRAIN N.O.S. 1.4B	Nil	Nil	Nil	Nil	Nil	LQ0/2	333	178, 274
0384	COMPONENTS, EXPLOSIVE TRAIN N.O.S. 1.4S	Nil	Nil	Nil	Nil	Nil	LQ0/4	Unlimited	178, 274
0385	5-NITROBENZOTRIAZOL	Nil	Nil	Nil	Nil	Nil	LQ0/1	20	
0386	TRINITROBENZENE-SULPHONIC ACID	Nil	Nil	Nil	Nil	Nil	LQ0/1	20	

0387	TRINITROFLUORENONE	Nil	Nil	Nil	Nil	Nil	LQ0/1	20	
0388	TRINITROTOLUENE (TNT) AND TRINITROBENZENE MIXTURE OR TRINITROTOLUENE (TNT) AND HEXANITROSTILBENE MIXTURE	Nil	Nil	Nil	Nil	Nil	LQ0/1	20	
0389	TRINITROTOLUENE (TNT) MIXTURE CONTAINING TRINITROBENZENE AND HEXANITROSTILBENE	Nil	Nil	Nil	Nil	Nil	LQ0/1	20	
0390	TRITONAL	Nil	Nil	Nil	Nil	Nil	LQ0/1	20	
0391	CYCLOTRIMETHYLENE-TRINITRAMINE (CYCLONITE, HEXOGEN, RDX) AND CYCLOTETRAMETHYLENE-TETRANITRAMINE (HMX, OCTOGEN) MIXTURE, WETTED	Nil	Nil	Nil	Nil	Nil	LQ0/1	20	266
0392	HEXANITROSTILBENE	Nil	Nil	Nil	Nil	Nil	LQ0/1	20	
0393	HEXOTONAL	Nil	Nil	Nil	Nil	Nil	LQ0/1	20	
0394	TRINITRORESORCINOL (STYPHONIC ACID), WETTED	Nil	Nil	Nil	Nil	Nil	LQ0/1	20	
0395	ROCKET MOTORS, LIQUID FUELLED 1.2J	Nil	Nil	Nil	Nil	Nil	LQ0/1	20	
0396	ROCKET MOTORS, LIQUID FUELLED 1.3J	Nil	Nil	Nil	Nil	Nil	LQ0/1	20	
0397	ROCKETS, LIQUID FUELLED 1.1J	Nil	Nil	Nil	Nil	Nil	LQ0/1	20	
0398	ROCKETS, LIQUID FUELLED 1.2J	Nil	Nil	Nil	Nil	Nil	LQ0/1	20	
0399	BOMBS WITH FLAMMABLE LIQUID 1.1J	Nil	Nil	Nil	Nil	Nil	LQ0/1	20	
0400	BOMBS WITH FLAMMABLE LIQUID 1.2J	Nil	Nil	Nil	Nil	Nil	LQ0/1	20	
0401	DIPICRYL SULPHIDE	Nil	Nil	Nil	Nil	Nil	LQ0/1	20	

UN	Substance	Excepted Quantities	LQ Packages		LQ Shrink Wrapped Trays		Limited Quantity Value/Transport Category	Max Load	Special Provisions
			Receptacle Size	Package Gross	Receptacle Size	Package Gross			
0402	AMMONIUM PERCHLORATE	Nil	Nil	Nil	Nil	Nil	LQ0/1	20	152
0403	FLARES, AERIAL 1.4G	Nil	Nil	Nil	Nil	Nil	LQ0/2	333	
0404	FLARES, AERIAL 1.4S	Nil	Nil	Nil	Nil	Nil	LQ0/4	Unlimited	
0405	CARTRIDGES, SIGNAL	Nil	Nil	Nil	Nil	Nil	LQ0/4	Unlimited	
0406	DINITROSOBENZENE	Nil	Nil	Nil	Nil	Nil	LQ0/1	20	
0407	TETRAZOL-1-ACETIC ACID	Nil	Nil	Nil	Nil	Nil	LQ0/2	333	
0408	FUSES, DETONATING 1.1D	Nil	Nil	Nil	Nil	Nil	LQ0/1	20	
0409	FUSES, DETONATING 1.2D	Nil	Nil	Nil	Nil	Nil	LQ0/1	20	
0410	FUSES, DETONATING 1.4D	Nil	Nil	Nil	Nil	Nil	LQ0/2	333	
0411	PENTAERYTHRITE TETRANITRATE	Nil	Nil	Nil	Nil	Nil	LQ0/1	20	131
0412	CARTRIDGES FOR WEAPONS	Nil	Nil	Nil	Nil	Nil	LQ0/2	333	
0413	CARTRIDGES FOR WEAPONS, BLANK	Nil	Nil	Nil	Nil	Nil	LQ0/1	20	
0414	CARTRIDGES, PROPELLING, FOR CANNON	Nil	Nil	Nil	Nil	Nil	LQ0/1	20	
0415	CHARGES, PROPELLING	Nil	Nil	Nil	Nil	Nil	LQ0/1	20	
0417	CARTRIDGES FOR WEAPONS, INERT PROJECTILE	Nil	Nil	Nil	Nil	Nil	LQ0/1	20	
0418	FLARES, SURFACE 1.1G	Nil	Nil	Nil	Nil	Nil	LQ0/1	20	

0419	FLARES, SURFACE 1.2G	Nil	Nil	Nil	Nil	LQ0/1	20	
0420	FLARES, AERIAL 1.1G	Nil	Nil	Nil	Nil	LQ0/1	20	
0421	FLARES, AERIAL 1.2G	Nil	Nil	Nil	Nil	LQ0/1	20	
0424	PROJECTILES, INERT WITH TRACER 1.3G	Nil	Nil	Nil	Nil	LQ0/1	20	
0425	PROJECTILES, INERT WITH TRACER 1.4G	Nil	Nil	Nil	Nil	LQ0/2	333	
0426	PROJECTILES WITH BURSTER OR EXPELLING CHARGE 1.2F	Nil	Nil	Nil	Nil	LQ0/1	20	
0427	PROJECTILES WITH BURSTER OR EXPELLING CHARGE 1.4F	Nil	Nil	Nil	Nil	LQ0/2	333	
0428	ARTICLES, PYROTECHNIC 1.1G	Nil	Nil	Nil	Nil	LQ0/1	20	
0429	ARTICLES, PYROTECHNIC 1.2G	LQ0	Nil	Nil	Nil	LQ0/1	20	
0430	ARTICLES, PYROTECHNIC 1.3G	Nil	Nil	Nil	Nil	LQ0/1	20	
0431	ARTICLES, PYROTECHNIC 1.4G	Nil	Nil	Nil	Nil	LQ0/2	333	
0432	ARTICLES, PYROTECHNIC 1.4S	Nil	Nil	Nil	Nil	LQ0/4	Unlimited	
0433	POWDER CAKE	Nil	Nil	Nil	Nil	LQ0/1	20	266
0434	PROJECTILES 1.2G	Nil	Nil	nil	Nil	LQ0/1	20	
0435	PROJECTILES 1.4G	Nil	Nil	Nil	Nil	LQ0/2	333	
0436	ROCKETS 1.2C	Nil	Nil	Nil	Nil	LQ0/1	20	
0437	ROCKETS 1.3C	Nil	Nil	Nil	Nil	LQ0/1	20	
0438	ROCKETS 1.4C	Nil	Nil	Nil	Nil	LQ0/2	333	
0439	CHARGES, SHAPED 1.2D	Nil	Nil	Nil	Nil	LQ0/1	20	

UN	Substance	Excepted Quantities	LQ Packages		LQ Shrink Wrapped Trays		Limited Quantity Value/Transport Category	Max Load	Special Provisions
			Receptacle Size	Package Gross	Receptacle Size	Package Gross			
0440	CHARGES, SHAPED 1.4D	Nil	Nil	Nil	Nil	Nil	LQ0/2	333	
0441	CHARGES, SHAPED 1.4S	Nil	Nil	Nil	Nil	Nil	LQ0/4	Unlimited	
0442	CHARGES, EXPLOSIVE, COMMERCIAL 1.1D	Nil	Nil	Nil	Nil	Nil	LQ0/1	20	
0443	CHARGES, EXPLOSIVE, COMMERCIAL 1.2D	Nil	Nil	Nil	Nil	Nil	LQ0/1	20	
0444	CHARGES, EXPLOSIVE, COMMERCIAL 1.4D	Nil	Nil	Nil	Nil	Nil	LQ0/2	333	
0445	CHARGES, EXPLOSIVE, COMMERCIAL 1.4S	Nil	Nil	Nil	Nil	Nil	LQ0/4	Unlimited	
0446	CASES, COMBUSTIBLE, EMPTY 1.4C	Nil	Nil	Nil	Nil	Nil	LQ0/2	333	
0447	CASES, COMBUSTIBLE, EMPTY 1.3C	Nil	Nil	Nil	Nil	Nil	LQ0/1	20	
0448	5-MERCAPTOTETRAZOL-1-ACETIC ACID	Nil	Nil	Nil	Nil	Nil	LQ0/2	333	
0449	TORPEDOES, LIQUID FUELLED 1.1J	Nil	Nil	Nil	Nil	Nil	LQ0/1	20	
0450	TORPEDOES, LIQUID FUELLED 1.3J	Nil	Nil	Nil	Nil	Nil	LQ0/1	20	
0451	TORPEDOES 1.1D	Nil	Nil	Nil	Nil	Nil	LQ0/1	20	
0452	GRENADES, PRACTICE	Nil	Nil	Nil	Nil	Nil	LQ0/2	333	
0453	ROCKETS, LINE-THROWING	Nil	Nil	Nil	Nil	Nil	LQ0/2	333	
0454	IGNITERS	Nil	Nil	Nil	Nil	Nil	LQ0/4	Unlimited	
0455	DETONATORS, NON ELECTRIC	Nil	Nil	Nil	Nil	Nil	LQ0/4	Unlimited	

UN	Name						LQ	Quantity	Special provisions
0456	DETONATORS, ELECTRIC	Nil	Nil	Nil	Nil	Nil	LQ0/4	Unlimited	
0457	CHARGES, BURSTING, PLASTICS BONDED 1.1D	Nil	Nil	Nil	Nil	Nil	LQ0/1	20	
0458	CHARGES, BURSTING, PLASTICS BONDED 1.2D	Nil	Nil	Nil	Nil	Nil	LQ0/1	20	
0459	CHARGES, BURSTING, PLASTICS BONDED 1.4D	Nil	Nil	Nil	Nil	Nil	LQ0/2	333	
0460	CHARGES, BURSTING, PLASTICS BONDED 1.4S	Nil	Nil	Nil	Nil	Nil	LQ0/4	Unlimited	
0461	COMPONENTS, EXPLOSIVE TRAIN N.O.S. 1.1B	Nil	Nil	Nil	Nil	Nil	LQ0/1	20	178, 274
0462	ARTICLES, EXPLOSIVE N.O.S. 1.1C	Nil	Nil	Nil	Nil	Nil	LQ0/1	20	178, 274
0463	ARTICLES, EXPLOSIVE N.O.S. 1.1D	Nil	Nil	Nil	Nil	Nil	LQ0/1	20	178, 274
0464	ARTICLES, EXPLOSIVE N.O.S. 1.1E	Nil	Nil	Nil	Nil	Nil	LQ0/1	20	178, 274
0465	ARTICLES, EXPLOSIVE N.O.S. 1.1F	Nil	Nil	Nil	Nil	Nil	LQ0/1	20	178, 274
0466	ARTICLES, EXPLOSIVE N.O.S. 1.2C	Nil	Nil	Nil	Nil	Nil	LQ0/1	20	178, 274
0467	ARTICLES, EXPLOSIVE N.O.S. 1.2D	Nil	Nil	Nil	Nil	Nil	LQ0/1	20	178, 274
0468	ARTICLES, EXPLOSIVE N.O.S. 1.2E	Nil	Nil	Nil	Nil	Nil	LQ0/1	20	178, 274
0469	ARTICLES, EXPLOSIVE N.O.S. 1.2F	Nil	Nil	Nil	Nil	Nil	LQ0/1	20	178, 274
0470	ARTICLES, EXPLOSIVE N.O.S. 1.3C	Nil	Nil	Nil	Nil	Nil	LQ0/1	20	178, 274
0471	ARTICLES, EXPLOSIVE N.O.S. 1.4E	Nil	Nil	Nil	Nil	Nil	LQ0/2	333	178, 274
0472	ARTICLES, EXPLOSIVE N.O.S. 1.4F	Nil	Nil	Nil	Nil	Nil	LQ0/2	333	178, 274

UN	Substance	Excepted Quantities	LQ Packages		LQ Shrink Wrapped Trays		Limited Quantity Value/Transport Category	Max Load	Special Provisions
			Receptacle Size	Package Gross	Receptacle Size	Package Gross			
0473	SUBSTANCES, EXPLOSIVE N.O.S. 1.1A	Nil	Nil	Nil	Nil	Nil	LQ0/0	Nil	178, 274
0474	SUBSTANCES, EXPLOSIVE N.O.S. 1.1C	Nil	Nil	Nil	Nil	Nil	LQ0/1	20	178, 274
0475	SUBSTANCES, EXPLOSIVE N.O.S. 1.1D	Nil	Nil	Nil	Nil	Nil	LQ0/1	20	178, 274
0476	SUBSTANCES, EXPLOSIVE N.O.S. 1.1G	Nil	Nil	Nil	Nil	Nil	LQ0/1	20	178, 274
0477	SUBSTANCES, EXPLOSIVE N.O.S. 1.3C	Nil	Nil	Nil	Nil	Nil	LQ0/1	20	178, 274
0478	SUBSTANCES, EXPLOSIVE N.O.S. 1.3G	Nil	Nil	Nil	Nil	Nil	LQ0/1	20	178, 274
0479	SUBSTANCES, EXPLOSIVE N.O.S. 1.4C	Nil	Nil	Nil	Nil	Nil	LQ0/2	333	178, 274
0480	SUBSTANCES, EXPLOSIVE N.O.S. 1.4D	Nil	Nil	Nil	Nil	Nil	LQ0/2	333	178, 274
0481	SUBSTANCES, EXPLOSIVE N.O.S. 1.4S	Nil	Nil	Nil	Nil	Nil	LQ0/4	Unlimited	178, 274
0482	SUBSTANCES, EXPLOSIVE, VERY INSENSITIVE	Nil	Nil	Nil	Nil	Nil	LQ0/1	50 kg max	178, 274
0483	CYCLOTRIMETHYLENE-TRINITRAMINE	Nil	Nil	Nil	Nil	Nil	LQ0/1	20	
0484	CYCLOTETRAMETHYLENE-TETRA-NITRAMINE	Nil	Nil	Nil	Nil	Nil	LQ0/1	20	
0485	SUBSTANCES, EXPLOSIVE N.O.S.	Nil	Nil	Nil	Nil	Nil	LQ0/2	333	178, 274
0486	ARTICLES, EXPLOSIVE, EXTREMELY INSENSITIVE	Nil	Nil	Nil	Nil	Nil	LQ0/2	333	
0487	SIGNALS, SMOKE	Nil	Nil	Nil	Nil	Nil	LQ0/1	20	

No.	Name					LQ		
0488	AMMUNITION, PRACTICE	Nil	Nil	Nil	Nil	LQ0/1	20	
0489	DINITROGLYCOLURIL	Nil	Nil	Nil	Nil	LQ0/1	20	
0490	NITROTRIAZOLONE	Nil	Nil	Nil	Nil	LQ0/1	20	
0491	CHARGES, PROPELLING	Nil	Nil	Nil	Nil	LQ0/2	333	
0492	SIGNALS, RAILWAY TRACK, EXPLOSIVE 1.3G	Nil	Nil	Nil	Nil	LQ0/1	20	
0493	SIGNALS, RAILWAY TRACK, EXPLOSIVE 1.4G	Nil	Nil	Nil	Nil	LQ0/2	333	
0494	JET PERFORATING GUNS, CHARGED	Nil	Nil	Nil	Nil	LQ0/2	333	
0495	PROPELLANT, LIQUID	Nil	Nil	Nil	Nil	LQ0/1	20	224
0496	OCTONAL	Nil	Nil	Nil	Nil	LQ0/1	20	
0497	PROPELLANT, LIQUID	Nil	Nil	Nil	Nil	LQ0/1	20	224
0498	PROPELLANT, SOLID 1.1C	Nil	Nil	Nil	Nil	LQ0/1	20	
0499	PROPELLANT, SOLID 1.3C	Nil	Nil	Nil	Nil	LQ0/1	20	
0500	DETONATOR ASSEMBLIES, NON ELECTRIC	Nil	Nil	Nil	Nil	LQ0/4	Unlimited	
0501	PROPELLANT, SOLID 1.4C	Nil	Nil	Nil	Nil	LQ02	333	
0502	ROCKETS	Nil	Nil	Nil	Nil	LQ0/1	20	
0503	AIR BAG INFLATORS OR AIR BAG MODULES, OR SEAT BELT PRETENSIONERS	Nil	Nil	Nil	Nil	LQ0/2	333	235 289
0504	1H-TETRAZOLE	Nil	Nil	Nil	Nil	LQ0/1	20	
0505	SIGNALS, DISTRESS, SHIP	Nil	Nil	Nil	Nil	LQ0/2	333	

UN	Substance	Excepted Quantities	LQ Packages		LQ Shrink Wrapped Trays		Limited Quantity Value/Transport Category	Max Load	Special Provisions
			Receptacle Size	Package Gross	Receptacle Size	Package Gross			
0506	SIGNALS, DISTRESS, SHIP	Nil	Nil	Nil	Nil	Nil	LQ0/4	Unlimited	
0507	SIGNALS, SMOKE	Nil	Nil	Nil	Nil	Nil	LQ0/4	Unlimited	
0508	I-HYDROXY -BENZOTRIAZOLE, ANHYDROUS	Nil	Nil	Nil	Nil	Nil	LQ0/1	20	
1001	ACETYLENE, DISSOLVED	Nil	Nil	Nil	Nil	Nil	LQ0/2	333	
1002	AIR, COMPRESSED	30/1000	120 ml	30 kg	120 ml	20 kg	LQ1/3	1000	292
1003	AIR, REFRIGERATED LIQUID	Nil	Nil	Nil	Nil	Nil	LQ0/3	1000	
1005	AMMONIA, ANHYDROUS	Nil	Nil	Nil	Nil	Nil	LQ0/1	50 kg max	23
1006	ARGON, COMPRESSED	30/1000	120 ml	30 kg	120 ml	20 kg	LQ1/3	1000	
1008	BORON TRIFLUORIDE, COMPRESSED	Nil	Nil	Nil	Nil	Nil	LQ0/1	20	
1009	BROMOTRIFLUOROMETHANE (REFRIGERANT GAS R13B1)	30/1000	120 ml	30 kg	120 ml	20 kg	LQ1/3	1000	
1010	BUTADIENES, STABILISED	Nil	Nil	Nil	Nil	Nil	LQ0/2	333	618
1011	BUTANE	Nil	Nil	Nil	Nil	Nil	LQ0/2	333	
1012	BUTYLENES	Nil	Nil	Nil	Nil	Nil	LQ0/2	333	
1013	CARBON DIOXIDE	30/1000	120 ml	30 kg	120 ml	20 kg	LQ1/3	1000	584, 653
1016	CARBON MONOXIDE, COMPRESSED	Nil	Nil	Nil	Nil	Nil	LQ0/1	20	

1017	CHLORINE	Nil	Nil	Nil	Nil	Nil	LQ0/1	50 kg max
1018	CHLORODIFLUOROMETHANE (REFRIGERANT GAS R22)	30/1000	120 ml	30 kg	120 ml	20 kg	LQ1/3	1000
1020	CHLOROPENTAFLUOROETHANE (REFRIGERANT GAS R115)	30/1000	120 ml	30 kg	120 ml	20 kg	LQ1/3	1000
1021	1-CHLORO-1,2,2,2,-TETRAFLUOROETHANE (REFRIGERANT GAS R124)	30/1000	120 ml	30 kg	120 ml	20 kg	LQ1/3	1000
1022	CHLOROTRIFLUOROMETHANE (REFRIGERANT GAS R13)	30/1000	120 ml	30 kg	120 ml	20 kg	LQ1/3	1000
1023	COAL GAS, COMPRESSED	Nil	Nil	Nil	Nil	Nil	LQ0/1	20
1026	CYANOGEN	Nil	Nil	Nil	Nil	Nil	LQ0/1	20
1027	CYCLOPROPANE	Nil	Nil	Nil	Nil	Nil	LQ0/2	333
1028	DICHLORODIFLUOROMETHANE (REFRIGERANT GAS R12)	30/1000	120 ml	30 kg	120 ml	20 kg	LQ1/3	1000
1029	DICHLOROFLUOROMETHANE (REFRIGERANT GAS R21)	30/1000	120 ml	30 kg	120 ml	20 kg	LQ1/3	1000
1030	1,1-DIFLUOROETHANE (REFRIGERANT GAS R152A)	Nil	Nil	Nil	Nil	Nil	LQ0/2	333
1032	DIMETHYLAMINE, ANHYDROUS	Nil	Nil	Nil	Nil	Nil	LQ0/2	333
1033	DIMETHYL ETHER	Nil	Nil	Nil	Nil	Nil	LQ0/2	333
1035	ETHANE	Nil	Nil	Nil	Nil	Nil	LQ0/2	333
1036	ETHYLAMINE	Nil	Nil	Nil	Nil	Nil	LQ0/2	333
1037	ETHYL CHLORIDE	Nil	Nil	Nil	Nil	Nil	LQ0/2	333

UN	Substance	Excepted Quantities	LQ Packages		LQ Shrink Wrapped Trays		Limited Quantity Value/Transport Category	Max Load	Special Provisions
			Receptacle Size	Package Gross	Receptacle Size	Package Gross			
1038	ETHYLENE, REFRIGERATED LIQUID /	Nil	Nil	Nil	Nil	Nil	LQ0/2	333	
1039	ETHYL METHYL ETHER	Nil	Nil	Nil	Nil	Nil	LQ0/2	333	
1040	ETHYLENE OXIDE (WITH OR WITHOUT NITROGEN)	Nil	Nil	Nil	Nil	Nil	LQ0/1	20	
1041	ETHYLENE OXIDE AND CARBON DIOXIDE MIXTURE WITH MORE THAN 9% BUT NOT MORE THAN 87% ETHYLENE OXIDE	Nil	Nil	Nil	Nil	Nil	LQ0/2	333	
1043	FERTILIZER AMMONIATING SOLUTION WITH FREE AMMONIA	Not in	General	Use	–	–	–	–	642
1044	FIRE EXTINGUISHERS WITH COMPRESSED OR LIQUEFIED GAS	Nil	Nil	Nil	Nil	Nil	LQ0/3	1000	225, 594
1045	FLUORINE, COMPRESSED	Nil	Nil	Nil	Nil	Nil	LQ0/1	20	
1046	HELIUM, COMPRESSED	30/1000	120 ml	30 kg	120 ml	20 kg	LQ1/3	1000	
1048	HYDROGEN BROMIDE, ANHYDROUS	Nil	Nil	Nil	Nil	Nil	LQ0/1	20	
1049	HYDROGEN, COMPRESSED	Nil	Nil	Nil	Nil	Nil	LQ0/2	333	
1050	HYDROGEN CHLORIDE, ANHYDROUS	Nil	Nil	Nil	Nil	Nil	LQ0/1	20	
1051	HYDROGEN CYANIDE, STABILISED CONTAINING LESS THAN 3% WATER	Nil	Nil	Nil	Nil	Nil	LQ0/0	Nil	603
1052	HYDROGEN FLUORIDE, ANHYDROUS	Nil	Nil	Nil	Nil	Nil	LQ0/1	20	

No.	Substance									
1053	HYDROGEN SULPHIDE	Nil	Nil	Nil	Nil	Nil	Nil	LQ0/1	20	
1055	ISOBUTYLENE	Nil	Nil	Nil	Nil	Nil	Nil	LQ0/2	333	
1056	KRYPTON, COMPRESSED	30/1000	120 ml	30 kg	120 ml	Nil	20 kg	LQ1/3	1000	
1057	LIGHTERS OR LIGHTER REFILLS, CONTAINING FLAMMABLE GAS	Nil	Nil	Nil	Nil	Nil	Nil	LQ0/2	333	201, 654
1058	LIQUEFIED GASES, NON-FLAMMABLE, CHARGED WITH NITROGEN, CARBON DIOXIDE OR AIR	30/1000	120 ml	30 kg	120 ml	Nil	20 kg	LQ1/3	1000	
1060	METHYLACETYLENE AND PROPADIENE MIXTURE, STABILISED	Nil	Nil	Nil	Nil	Nil	Nil	LQ0/2	333	581
1061	METHYLAMINE, ANHYDROUS	Nil	Nil	Nil	Nil	Nil	Nil	LQ0/2	333	
1062	METHYL BROMIDE, WITH NOT MORE THAN 2% CHLOROPICRIN	Nil	Nil	Nil	Nil	Nil	Nil	LQ0/1	20	23
1063	METHYL CHLORIDE (REFRIGERANT GAS R40)	Nil	Nil	Nil	Nil	Nil	Nil	LQ0/2	333	
1064	METHYL MERCAPTAN	Nil	Nil	Nil	Nil	Nil	Nil	LQ0/1	20	
1065	NEON, COMPRESSED	30/1000	120 ml	30 kg	120 ml	Nil	20 kg	LQ1/3	1000	
1066	NITROGEN, COMPRESSED	30/1000	120 ml	30 kg	120 ml	Nil	20 kg	LQ1/3	1000	
1067	DINITROGEN TETROXIDE, (NITROGEN DIOXIDE)	Nil	Nil	Nil	Nil	Nil	Nil	LQ0/1	20	
1069	NITROSYL CHLORIDE	Nil	Nil	Nil	Nil	Nil	Nil	LQ0/1	20	
1070	NITROUS OXIDE	Nil	Nil	Nil	Nil	Nil	Nil	LQ0/3	1000	584
1071	OIL GAS, COMPRESSED	Nil	Nil	Nil	Nil	Nil	Nil	LQ0/1	20	

UN	Substance	Excepted Quantities	LQ Packages Receptacle Size	LQ Packages Package Gross	LQ Shrink Wrapped Trays Receptacle Size	LQ Shrink Wrapped Trays Package Gross	Limited Quantity Value/Transport Category	Max Load	Special Provisions
1072	OXYGEN, COMPRESSED	Nil	Nil	Nil	Nil	Nil	LQ0/3	1000	
1073	OXYGEN, REFRIGERATED LIQUID	Nil	Nil	Nil	Nil	Nil	LQ0/3	1000	
1075	PETROLEUM GASES, LIQUEFIED	Nil	Nil	Nil	Nil	Nil	LQ0/2	333	274, 583, 639
1076	PHOSGENE	Nil	Nil	Nil	Nil	Nil	LQ0/1	20	
1077	PROPYLENE	Nil	Nil	Nil	Nil	Nil	LQ0/2	333	
1078	REFRIGERANT GAS, N.O.S.	30/1000	120 ml	30 kg	120 ml	20 kg	LQ1/3	1000	274, 582
1079	SULPHUR DIOXIDE	Nil	Nil	Nil	Nil	Nil	LQ0/1	20	
1080	SULPHUR HEXAFLUORIDE	30/1000	120 ml	30 kg	120 ml	20 kg	LQ1/3	1000	
1081	TETRAFLUOROETHYLENE, STABILISED	Nil	Nil	Nil	Nil	Nil	LQ0/2	333	
1082	TRIFLUOROCHLOROETHYLENE, STABILISED	Nil	Nil	Nil	Nil	Nil	LQ0/1	20	
1083	TRIMETHYLAMINE, ANHYDROUS	Nil	Nil	Nil	Nil	Nil	LQ0/2	333	
1085	VINYL BROMIDE, STABILISED	Nil	Nil	Nil	Nil	Nil	LQ0/2	333	
1086	VINYL CHLORIDE, STABILISED	Nil	Nil	Nil	Nil	Nil	LQ0/2	333	
1087	VINYL METHYL ETHER, STABILISED	Nil	Nil	Nil	Nil	Nil	LQ0/2	333	
1088	ACETAL	30/500	3 litres	30 kg	1 litre	20 kg	LQ4/2	333	

No.	Name							
1089	ACETALDEHYDE	30/500	500 ml	1 litre	Not	Allowed	LQ3/1	20
1090	ACETONE	30/300	3 litres	30 kg	1 litre	20 kg	LQ4/2	333
1091	ACETONE OILS	30/500	3 litres	30 kg	1 litre	20 kg	LQ4/2	333
1092	ACROLEIN, STABILISED	1/300	Nil	Nil	Nil	Nil	LQ0/1	20
1093	ACRYLONITRILE, STABILISED	Nil	Nil	Nil	Nil	Nil	LQ0/1	20
1098	ALLYL ALCOHOL	1/300	Nil	Nil	Nil	Nil	LQ0/1	20
1099	ALLYL BROMIDE	Nil	Nil	Nil	Nil	Nil	LQ0/1	20
1100	ALLYL CHLORIDE	Nil	Nil	Nil	Nil	Nil	LQ0/1	20
1104	AMYL ACETATES	30/1000	5 litres	30 kg	5 litres	20 kg	LQ7/3	1000
1105	PENTANOLS, PG2	30/500	3 litres	30 kg	1 litre	20 kg	LQ4/2	333
1105	PENTANOLS, PG3	30/1000	5 litres	30 kg	5 litres	20 kg	LQ7/3	1000
1106	AMYLAMINE, PG2	30/500	3 litres	30 kg	1 litre	20 kg	LQ4/2	333
1106	AMYLAMINE, PG3	30/1000	5 litres	30 kg	5 litres	20 kg	LQ7/3	1000
1107	AMYL CHLORIDE	30/500	3 litres	30 kg	1 litre	20 kg	LQ4/2	333
1108	1-PENTENE (N-AMYLENE)	30/300	500 ml	1 litre	Not	Allowed	LQ3/1	20
1109	AMYL FORMATES	30/1000	5 litres	30 kg	5 litres	20 kg	LQ7/3	1000
1110	N-AMYL METHYL KETONE	30/1000	5 litres	30 kg	5 litres	20 kg	LQ7/3	1000
1111	AMYL MERCAPTAN	30/500	3 litres	30 kg	1 litre	20 kg	LQ4/2	333
1112	AMYL NITRATE	30/1000	5 litres	30 kg	5 litres	20 kg	LQ7/3	1000
1113	AMYL NITRITE	30/500	3 litres	30 kg	1 litre	20 kg	LQ4/2	333

UN	Substance	Excepted Quantities	LQ Packages		LQ Shrink Wrapped Trays		Limited Quantity Value/Transport Category	Max Load	Special Provisions
			Receptacle Size	Gross Package	Receptacle Size	Gross Package			
1114	BENZENE	30/500	3 litres	30 kg	1 litre	20 kg	LQ4/2	333	
1120	BUTANOLS, FLASH POINT LESS THAN 23 °C, PG11	30/500	3 litres	30 kg	1 litre	20 kg	LQ4/2	333	
1120	BUTANOLS, FLASH POINT 23 °C OR ABOVE, PG111	30/1000	5 litres	30 kg	5 litres	20 kg	LQ7/3	1000	
1123	BUTYL ACETATES, PG11	30/500	3 litres	30 kg	1 litre	20 kg	LQ4/2	333	
1123	BUTYL ACETATES, PG111	30/1000	5 litres	30 kg	5 litres	20 kg	LQ7/3	1000	
1125	N-BUTYLAMINE	30/500	3 litres	30 kg	1 litre	20 kg	LQ4/2	333	
1126	1-BROMOBUTANE	30/500	3 litres	30 kg	1 litre	20 kg	LQ4/2	333	
1127	CHLOROBUTANES	30/500	3 litres	30 kg	1 litre	20 kg	LQ4/2	333	
1128	N-BUTYL FORMATE	30/500	3 litres	30 kg	1 litre	20 kg	LQ4/2	333	
1129	BUTYRALDEHYDE	30/500	3 litres	30 kg	1 litre	20 kg	LQ4/2	333	
1130	CAMPHOR OIL	30/1000	5 litres	30 kg	5 litres	20 kg	LQ7/3	1000	
1131	CARBON DISULPHIDE	Nil	Nil	Nil	Nil	Nil	LQ0/1	20	
1133	ADHESIVES, PG1	30/300	500 ml	1 litre	Not	Allowed	LQ3/1	20	
1133	ADHESIVES, PG11	30/300	5 litres	20 litres	1 litre	20 litres & 20 kg	LQ6/2	333	640 C&D
1133	ADHESIVES, PG111	30/1000	5 litres	30 kg	5 litres	20 kg	LQ7/3	1000	640E-H

UN No	Name								
1134	CHLOROBENZENE	30/1000	5 litres	30 kg	5 litres	20 kg	LQ7/3	1000	
1135	ETHYLENE CHLOROHYDRIN	1/300	Nil	Nil	Nil	Nil	LQ0/1	20	
1136	COAL TAR DISTILLATES, FLAMMABLE, PG11	30/500	3 litres	30 kg	1 litre	20 kg	LQ4/2	333	
1136	COAL TAR DISTILLATES, FLAMMABLE, PG111	30/1000	5 litres	30 kg	5 litres	20 kg	LQ7/3	1000	
1139	COATING SOLUTION, PG1	30/300	500 ml	1 litre	Not	Allowed	LQ3/1	20	
1139	COATING SOLUTION, PG11	30/500	5 litres	20 litres	1 litre	20 kg	LQ6/2	333	640C-D
1139	COATING SOLUTION, PG111	30/1000	5 litres	30 kg	5 litres	20 kg	LQ7/3	1000	640E-H
1143	CROTONALDEHYDE, STABILISED	1/300	Nil	Nil	Nil	Nil	LQ0/1	20	324
1144	CROTONYLENE	30/300	500 ml	1 litre	Not	Allowed	LQ3/1	20	
1145	CYCLOHEXANE	30/500	3 litre	30 kg	1 litre	20 kg	LQ4/2	333	
1146	CYCLOPENTANE	30/500	3 litres	30 kg	1 litre	20 kg	LQ4/2	333	
1147	DECAHYDRONAPHTHALENE	30/1000	5 litres	30 kg	5 litres	20 kg	LQ7/3	1000	
1148	DIACETONE ALCOHOL, FLASH POINT LESS THAN 23 °C, PG11	30/500	3 litres	30 kg	1 litre	20 kg	LQ4/2	333	
1148	DIACETONE ALCOHOL, FLASH POINT 23 °C OR ABOVE, PG111	30/1000	5 litres	30 kg	5 litres	20 kg	LQ7/3	1000	
1149	DIBUTYL ETHERS	30/1000	5 litres	30 kg	5 litres	20 kg	LQ7/3	1000	
1150	1,2-DICHLOROETHYLENE	30/500	3 litres	30 kg	1 litre	20 kg	LQ4/2	333	
1152	DICHLOROPENTANES	30/1000	5 litres	30 kg	5 litres	20 kg	LQ7/3	1000	
1153	ETHYLENE GLYCOL DIETHYL ETHER, FLASH POINT LESS THAN 23 °C, PG11	30/500	3 litres	30 kg	1 litre	20 kg	LQ4/2	333	

UN	Substance	Excepted Quantities	LQ Packages		LQ Shrink Wrapped Trays		Limited Quantity Value/Transport Category	Max Load	Special Provisions
			Receptacle Size	Gross Package	Receptacle Size	Gross Package			
1153	ETHYLENE GLYCOL DIETHYL ETHER, FLASH POINT 23 °C OR MORE, PG111	30/1000	5 litres	30 kg	5 litres	20 kg	LQ7/3	1000	
1154	DIETHYLAMINE	30/500	3 litres	30 kg	1 litre	20 kg	LQ4/2	333	
1155	DIETHYL ETHER (ETHYL ETHER)	30/300	500 ml	1 litre	Not	Allowed	LQ3/1	20	
1156	DIETHYL KETONE	30/500	3 litres	30 kg	1 litre	20 kg	LQ4/2	333	
1157	DIISOBUTYL KETONE	30/1000	5 litres	30 kg	5 litres	20 kg	LQ7/3	1000	
1158	DIISOPROPYLAMINE	30/500	3 litres	30 kg	1 litre	20 kg	LQ4/2	333	
1159	DIISOPROPYL ETHER	30/500	3 litres	30 kg	1 litre	20 kg	LQ4/2	333	
1160	DIMETHYLAMINE, AQUEOUS SOLUTION	30/500	3 litres	30 kg	1 litre	20 kg	LQ4/2	333	
1161	DIMETHYL CARBONATE	30/500	3 litres	30 kg	1 litre	20 kg	LQ4/2	333	
1162	DIMETHYLDICHLOROSILANE	30/500	3 litres	30 kg	1 litre	20 kg	LQ4/2	333	
1163	DIMETHYLHYDRAZINE, UNSYMMETRICAL	1/300	Nil	Nil	Nil	Nil	LQ0/1	20	
1164	DIMETHYL SULPHIDE	30/500	3 litres	30 kg	1 litre	20 kg	LQ4/2	333	
1165	DIOXANE	30/500	3 litres	30 kg	1 litre	20 kg	LQ4/2	333	
1166	DIOXOLANE	30/500	3 litres	30 kg	1 litre	20 kg	LQ4/2	333	
1167	DIVINYL ETHER, STABILISED	30/300	500 ml	1 litre	Not	Allowed	LQ3/1	20	
1169	EXTRACTS, AROMATIC, LIQUID, PG1	30/300	500 ml	1 litre	Not	Allowed	LQ3/1	20	

1169	EXTRACTS, AROMATIC, LIQUID, PG11	30/500	5 litres	30 kg	1 litre	20 kg	LQ6/2	333	601, 640C-D
1169	EXTRACTS, AROMATIC, LIQUID, PG111	30/1000	5 litres	30 kg	5 litres	20 kg	LQ7/3	1000	601, 640E-H
1170	ETHANOL (ETHYL ALCOHOL) OR ETHANOL SOLUTION (ETHYL ALCOHOL SOLUTION), PG11	30/500	3 litres	30 kg	1 litre	20 kg	LQ4/2	333	144, 601
1170	ETHANOL (ETHYL ALCOHOL) OR ETHANOL SOLUTION (ETHYL ALCOHOL SOLUTION), PG111	30/1000	5 litres	30 kg	5 litres	20 kg	LQ7/3	1000	144, 601
1171	ETHYLENE GLYCOL MONOETHYL ETHER	30/1000	5 litres	30 kg	5 litres	20 kg	LQ7/3	1000	
1172	ETHYLENE GLYCOL MONOETHYL ETHER ACETATE	30/1000	5 litres	30 kg	5 litres	20 kg	LQ7/3	1000	
1173	ETHYL ACETATE	30/500	3 litres	30 kg	1 litre	20 kg	LQ4/2	333	
1175	ETHYLBENZENE	30/500	3 litres	30 kg	1 litre	20 kg	LQ4/2	333	
1176	ETHYL BORATE	30/500	3 litres	30 kg	1 litre	20 kg	LQ4/2	333	
1177	2-ETHYLBUTYL ACETATE	30/1000	5 litres	30 kg	5 litres	20 kg	LQ7/3	1000	
1178	2-ETHYLBUTYRALDEHYDE	30/500	3 litres	30 kg	1 litre	20 kg	LQ4/2	333	
1179	ETHYL BUTYL ETHER	30/500	3 litres	30 kg	1 litre	20 kg	LQ4/2	333	
1180	ETHYL BUTYRATE	30/1000	5 litres	30 kg	5 litres	20 kg	LQ7/3	1000	
1181	ETHYL CHLOROACETATE	1/500	500 ml	2 litres	100 ml	2 litres	LQ17/2	333	
1182	ETHYL CHLOROFORMATE	1/300	Nil	Nil	Nil	Nil	LQ0/1	20	
1183	ETHYLDICHLOROSILANE	Nil	Nil	Nil	Nil	Nil	LQ0/0	Nil	
1184	ETHYLENE DICHLORIDE	30/500	Nil	Nil	Nil	Nil	LQ0/2	333	
1185	ETHYLENEIMINE, STABILISED	1/300	Nil	Nil	Nil	Nil	LQ0/1	20	

UN	Substance	Excepted Quantities	LQ Packages Receptacle Size	LQ Packages Gross Package	LQ Shrink Wrapped Trays Receptacle Size	LQ Shrink Wrapped Trays Gross Package	Limited Quantity Value/Transport Category	Max Load	Special Provisions
1188	ETHYLENE GLYCOL MONOMETHYL ETHER	30/1000	5 litres	30 kg	5 litres	20 kg	LQ7/3	1000	
1189	ETHYLENE GLYCOL MONOMETHYL ETHER ACETATE	30/1000	5 litres	30 kg	5 litres	20 kg	LQ7/3	1000	
1190	ETHYL FORMATE	30/500	3 litres	30 kg	1 litre	20 kg	LQ4/2	333	
1191	OCTYL ALDEHYDES	30/1000	5 litres	30 kg	5 litres	20 kg	LQ7/3	1000	
1192	ETHYL LACTATE	30/1000	5 litres	30 kg	5 litres	20 kg	LQ7/3	1000	
1193	ETHYL METHYL KETONE (METHYL ETHYL KETONE)	30/500	3 litres	30 kg	1 litre	20 kg	LQ4/2	333	
1194	ETHYL NITRITE SOLUTION	Nil	Nil	Nil	Nil	Nil	LQ0/1	20	
1195	ETHYL PROPIONATE	30/500	3 litres	30 kg	1 litre	20 kg	LQ4/2	333	
1196	ETHYLTRICHLOROSILANE	30/500	3 litres	30 kg	1 litre	20 kg	LQ4/2	333	
1197	EXTRACTS, FLAVOURING, LIQUID, PG1	30/300	500 ml	1 litre	Not	Allowed	LQ3/1	20	
1197	EXTRACTS, FLAVOURING, LIQUID, PG11	30/500	5 litres	30 kg	1 litre	20 kg	LQ6/2	333	
1197	EXTRACTS, FLAVORING, LIQUID, PG111	30/1000	5 litres	30 kg	5 litres	20 kg	LQ7/3	1000	601,640E-H
1198	FORMALDEHYDE SOLUTION, FLAMMABLE	30/1000	5 litres	30 kg	5 litres	20 kg	LQ7/3	1000	
1199	FURALDEHYDES	1/500	Nil	Nil	Nil	Nil	LQ0/2	333	
1201	FUSEL OIL, PG11	30/500	3 litres	30 kg	1 litre	20 kg	LQ4/2	333	
1201	FUSEL OIL, PG111	30/1000	5 litres	30 kg	5 litres	20 kg	LQ7/3	1000	

UN No.	Name								
1202	GAS OIL OR DIESEL FUEL OR HEATING OIL, LIGHT	30/1000	5 litres	30 kg	5 litres	20 kg	LQ7/3	1000	640K,L,M
1203	MOTOR SPIRIT OR GASOLINE OR PETROL	30/500	3 litres	30 kg	1 litre	20 kg	LQ4/2	333	534, 243
1204	NITROGLYCERIN SOLUTION IN ALCOHOL, WITH NOT MORE THAN 1% NITROGLYCERIN	Nil	Nil	Nil	Nil	Nil	LQ0/2	333	
1206	HEPTANES	30/500	3 litres	30 kg	1 litre	20 kg	LQ4/2	333	
1207	HEXALDEHYDE	30/1000	5 litres	30 kg	5 litres	20 kg	LQ7/3	1000	
1208	HEXANES	30/500	3 litres	30 kg	1 litre	20 kg	LQ4/2	333	
1210	PRINTING INK, PG1	30/300	500 ml	1 litre	Not	Allowed	LQ3/1	20	163
1210	PRINTING INK, PG11	30/500	5 litres	20 litres	1 litre	20 kg	LQ6/2	333	163, 640C-D
1210	PRINTING INK, PG111	30/1000	5 litres	30 kg	5 litres	20 kg	LQ7/3	1000	163, 640D-H
1212	ISOBUTANOL (ISOBUTYL ALCOHOL)	30/1000	5 litres	30 kg	5 litres	20 kg	LQ7/3	1000	
1213	ISOBUTYL ACETATE	30/500	3 litres	30 kg	1 litre	20 kg	LQ4/2	333	
1214	ISOBUTYLAMINE	30/500	3 litres	30 kg	1 litre	20 kg	LQ4/2	333	
1216	ISOOCTENE	30/500	3 litres	30 kg	1 litre	20 kg	LQ4/2	333	
1218	ISOPRENE, STABILISED	30/300	500 ml	1 litre	Not	Allowed	LQ3/1	20	
1219	ISOPROPANOL (ISOPROPYL ALCOHOL)	30/500	3 litres	30 kg	1 litre	20 kg	LQ4/2	333	601
1220	ISOPROPYL ACETATE	30/500	3 litres	30 kg	1 litre	20 kg	LQ4/2	333	
1221	ISOPROPYLAMINE	Nil	500 ml	1 litre	Not	Allowed	LQ3/1	20	
1222	ISOPROPYL NITRATE	30/500	3 litres	30 kg	1 litre	20 kg	LQ4/2	333	
1223	KEROSENE	30/1000	5 litres	30 kg	5 litres	20 kg	LQ7/3	1000	

UN	Substance	Excepted Quantities	LQ Packages Receptacle Size	LQ Packages Package Gross	LQ Shrink Wrapped Trays Receptacle Size	LQ Shrink Wrapped Trays Package Gross	Limited Quantity Value/Transport Category	Max Load	Special Provisions
1224	KETONES, LIQUID, N.O.S., PG11	30/500	3 litres	30 kg	1 litre	20 kg	LQ4/2	333	274, 640 C-D
1224	KETONES, LIQUID, N.O.S., PG111	30/1000	5 litres	30 kg	5 litres	20 kg	LQ7/3	1000	274
1228	MERCAPTANS, LIQUID, FLAMMABLE, TOXIC, N.O.S., OR MERCAPTAN MIXTURE, LIQUID, FLAMMABLE, TOXIC, N.O.S., PG11	30/500	Nil	Nil	Nil	Nil	LQ0/2	333	274
1228	MERCAPTANS, LIQUID, FLAMMABLE, TOXIC, N.O.S., OR MERCAPTAN MIXTURE, LIQUID, FLAMMABLE, TOXIC, N.O.S., PG111	30/1000	5 litres	30 kg	5 litres	20 kg	LQ7/3	1000	274
1229	MESITYL OXIDE	30/1000	5 litres	30 kg	5 litres	20 kg	LQ7/3	1000	
1230	METHANOL	30/500	Nil	Nil	Nil	Nil	LQ0/2	333	279
1231	METHYL ACETATE	30/500	3 litres	30 kg	1 litre	20 kg	LQ4/2	333	
1233	METHYLAMYL ACETATE	30/1000	5 litre	30 kg	5 litres	20 kg	LQ7/3	1000	
1234	METHYLAL	30/500	3 litres	30 kg	1 litre	20 kg	LQ4/2	333	
1235	METHYLAMINE, AQUEOUS SOLUTION	30/500	3 litres	30 kg	1 litre	20 kg	LQ4/2	333	
1237	METHYL BUTYRATE	30/500	3 litres	30 kg	1 litre	20 kg	LQ4/2	333	
1238	METHYL CHLOROFORMATE	1/300	Nil	Nil	Nil	Nil	LQ0/1	20	
1239	METHYL CHLOROMETHYL ETHER	1/300	Nil	Nil	Nil	Nil	LQ0/1	20	

UN	Name								
1242	METHYLDICHLOROSILANE	Nil	Nil	Nil	Nil	Nil	LQ0/0	Nil	
1243	METHYL FORMATE	30/300	500 ml	1 litre	Not	Allowed	LQ3/1	20	
1244	METHYLHYDRAZINE	1/300	Nil	Nil	Nil	Nil	LQ0/1	20	
1245	METHYL ISOBUTYL KETONE	30/500	3 litres	30 kg	1 litre	20 kg	LQ4/2	333	
1246	METHYL ISOPROPENYL KETONE, STABILISED	30/500	3 litres	30 kg	1 litre	20 kg	LQ4/2	333	
1247	METHYL METHACRYLATE MONOMER, STABILISED	30/500	3 litres	30 kg	1 litre	20 kg	LQ4/2	333	
1248	METHYL PROPIONATE	30/500	3 litres	30 kg	1 litre	20 kg	LQ4/2	333	
1249	METHYL PROPYL KETONE	30/500	3 litres	30 kg	1 litre	20 kg	LQ4/2	333	
1250	METHYLTRICHLOROSILANE	30/500	3 litres	30 kg	1 litre	20 kg	LQ4/2	333	
1251	METHYL VINYL KETONE, STABILISED	1/300	Nil	Nil	Nil	Nil	LQ0/1	20	
1259	NICKEL CARBONYL	1/300	Nil	Nil	Nil	Nil	LQ0/1	20	
1261	NITROMETHANE	30/500	3 litres	30 kg	1 litre	20 kg	LQ4/2	333	
1262	OCTANES	30/500	3 litres	30 kg	1 litre	20 kg	LQ4/2	333	
1263	PAINT OR PAINT RELATED MATERIAL, PG1	30/300	500 ml	1 litre	Not	Allowed	LQ3/1	20	163 & 650
1263	PAINT OR PAINT RELATED MATERIAL, PG11	30/500	5 litres	30 kg	1 litre	20 kg	LQ6/2	333	163, 650, 640 C & D
1263	PAINT OR PAINT RELATED MATERIAL, PG111	30/1000	5 litres	30 kg	5 litres	20 kg	LQ7/3	1000	163, 650, 640 E, F, G, H
1264	PARALDEHYDE	30/1000	5 litres	30 kg	5 litres	20 kg	LQ7/3	1000	

UN	Substance	Excepted Quantities	LQ Packages Receptacle Size	LQ Packages Package Gross	LQ Shrink Wrapped Trays Receptacle Size	LQ Shrink Wrapped Trays Package Gross	Limited Quantity Value/Transport Category	Max Load	Special Provisions
1265	PENTANES, LIQUID, PG1	30/300	500 ml	1 litre	Not	Allowed	LQ3/1	20	
1265	PENTANES, LIQUID, PG11	30/500	3 litres	30 kg	1 litre	20 kg	LQ4/2	333	
1266	PERFUMERY PRODUCTS, PG1	30/300	500 ml	1 litre	Not	Allowed	LQ3/1	20	640A & B
1266	PERFUMERY PRODUCTS, PG11	30/500	5 litres	30 kg	1 litre	20 kg	LQ6/2	333	640C & D
1266	PERFUMERY PRODUCTS, PG111	30/1000	5 litres	30 kg	5 litres	20 kg	LQ7/3	1000	640E, F, G, H
1267	PETROLEUM CRUDE OIL, PG1	30/300	500 ml	1 litre	Not	Allowed	LQ3/1	20	649
1267	PETROLEUM CRUDE OIL, PG11	30/500	3 litres	30 kg	1 litre	20 kg	LQ4/2	333	649, 640C, D
1267	PETROLEUM CRUDE OIL, PG111	30/1000	5 litres	30 kg	5 litres	20 kg	LQ7/3	1000	
1268	PETROLEUM DISTILLATES N.O.S. OR PETROLEUM PRODUCTS, N.O.S., PG1	30/300	500 ml	1 litre	Not	Allowed	LQ3/1	20	649
1268	PETROLEUM DISTILLATES N.O.S. OR PETROLEUM PRODUCTS, N.O.S., PG11	30/500	3 litres	30 kg	1 litre	20 kg	LQ4/2	222	649, 640C & D
1268	PETROLEUM DISTILLATES N.O.S. OR PETROLEUM PRODUCTS, N.O.S., PG111	30/1000	5 litres	30 kg	5 litres	20 kg	LQ7/3	1000	
1272	PINE OIL	30/1000	5 litres	30 kg	5 litres	20 kg	LQ7/3	1000	
1274	N-PROPANOL (PROPYL ALCOHOL, NORMAL), PG11	30/500	3 litres	30 kg	1 litre	20 kg	LQ4/2	333	

1274	N-PROPANOL (PROPYL ALCOHOL, NORMAL), PG111	30/1000	5 litres	30 kg	5 litres	20 kg	LQ7/3	1000	
1275	PROPIONALDEHYDE	30/500	3 litres	30 kg	1 litre	20 kg	LQ4/2	333	
1276	N-PROPYL ACETATE	30/500	3 litres	30 kg	1 litre	20 kg	LQ4/2	333	
1277	PROPYLAMINE	30/500	3 litres	30 kg	1 litre	20 kg	LQ4/2	333	
1278	1-CHLOROPROPANE	30/500	3 litres	30 kg	1 litre	20 kg	LQ4/2	333	
1279	1,2-DICHLOROPROPANE	30/500	3 litres	30 kg	1 litre	20 kg	LQ4/2	333	
1280	PROPYLENE OXIDE	30/300	500 ml	1 litre	Not	Allowed	Q3/1	20	
1281	PROPYL FORMATES	30/500	3 litres	30 kg	1 litre	20 kg	LQ4/2	333	
1282	PYRIDINE	30/500	3 litres	30 kg	1 litre	20 kg	LQ4/2	333	
1286	ROSIN OIL, PG1	30/300	500 ml	1 litre	Not	Allowed	LQ3/1	20	
1286	ROSIN OIL, PG11	30/500	5 litres	30 kg	1 litre	20 kg	LQ6/2	333	640C-D
1286	ROSIN OIL, PG111	30/1000	5 litres	30 kg	5 litres	20 kg	LQ7/3	1000	640E,F,G,H
1287	RUBBER SOLUTION, PG1	30/300	500 ml	1 litre	Not	Allowed	LQ3/1	20	
1287	RUBBER SOLUTION, PG11	30/500	5 litres	30 kg	1 litre	20 kg	LQ6/2	333	640C-D
1287	RUBBER SOLUTION, PG111	30/1000	5 litres	30 kg	5 litres	20 kg	LQ7/3	1000	640E,F,G,H
1288	SHALE OIL, PG11	30/500	3 litres	30 kg	1 litre	20 kg	LQ4/2	333	
1288	SHALE OIL, PG111	30/1000	5 litres	30 kg	5 litres	20 kg	LQ7/3	1000	
1289	SODIUM METHYLATE SOLUTION IN ALCOHOL, PG11	30/500	3 litres	30 kg	1 litre	20 kg	LQ4/2	333	

UN	Substance	Excepted Quantities	LQ Packages		LQ Shrink Wrapped Trays		Limited Quantity Value/Transport Category	Max Load	Special Provisions
			Receptacle Size	Gross Package	Receptacle Size	Gross Package			
1289	SODIUM METHYLATE SOLUTION IN ALCOHOL, PG111	30/1000	5 litres	30 kg	5 litres	20 kg	LQ7/3	1000	
1292	TETRAETHYL SILICATE	30/1000	5 litres	30 kg	5 litres	20 kg	LQ7/3	1000	
1293	TINCTURES, MEDICINAL, PG11	30/500	3 litres	30 kg	1 litre	20 kg	LQ4/2	333	601
1293	TINCTURES MEDICINAL, PG111	30/1000	5 litres	30 kg	5 litres	20 kg	LQ7/3	1000	601
1294	TOLUENE	30/500	3 litres	30 kg	1 litre	20 kg	LQ4/2	333	
1295	TRICHLOROSILANE	Nil	Nil	Nil	Nil	Nil	LQ0/0	Nil	
1296	TRIETHYLAMINE	30/500	3 litres	30 kg	1 litre	20 kg	LQ4/2	333	
1297	TRIMETHYLAMINE, AQUEOUS SOLUTION, PG1	Nil	500 ml	1 litre	Not	Allowed	LQ3/1	20	
1297	TRIMETHYLAMINE, AQUEOUS SOLUTION, PG11	30/500	3 litres	30 kg	1 litre	20 kg	LQ4/2	333	
1297	TRIMETHYLAMINE, AQUEOUS SOLUTION, PG111	30/1000	5 litres	30 kg	5 litres	20 kg	LQ7/3	1000	
1298	TRIMETHYLCHLOROSILANE	30/500	3 litres	30 kg	1 litre	20 kg	LQ4/2	333	
1299	TURPENTINE	30/1000	5 litres	30 kg	5 litres	20 kg	LQ7/3	1000	
1300	TURPENTINE SUBSTITUTE, PG11	30/500	3 litres	30 kg	1 litre	20 kg	LQ4/2	333	
1300	TURPENTINE SUBSTITUTE, PG111	30/1000	5 litres	30 kg	5 litres	20 kg	LQ7/3	1000	

1301	VINYL ACETATE, STABILISED	30/500	3 litres	30 kg	1 litre	20 kg	LQ4/2	333	
1302	VINYL ETHYL ETHER, STABILISED	30/300	500 ml	1 litre	Not	Allowed	LQ3/1	20	
1303	VINYLIDENE CHLORIDE, STABILISED	30/300	500 ml	1 litre	Not	Allowed	LQ3/1	20	
1304	VINYL ISOBUTYL ETHER, STABILISED	30/500	3 litres	30 kg	1 litre	20 kg	LQ4/2	333	
1305	VINYLTRICHLOROSILANE, STABILISED	30/500	3 litres	30 kg	1 litre	20 kg	LQ4/2	333	
1306	WOOD PRESERVATIVES, LIQUID, PG11	30/500	5 litres	30 kg	1 litre	20 kg	LQ6/2	333	640C-D
1306	WOOD PRESERVATIVES, LIQUID, PG111	30/1000	5 litres	30 kg	5 litres	20 kg	LQ7/3	1000	640E,F,G,H
1307	XYLENES, PG11	30/500	3 litres	30 kg	1 litre	20 kg	LQ4/2	222	
1307	XYLENES, PG111	30/1000	5 litres	30 kg	5 litres	20 kg	LQ7/3	1000	
1308	ZIRCONIUM SUSPENDED IN A FLAMMABLE LIQUID, PG1	30/300	500 ml	1 litre	Not	Allowed	LQ3/1	20	640A-B
1308	ZIRCONIUM SUSPENDED IN A FLAMMABLE LIQUID, PG11	30/500	3 litres	30 kg	1 litre	20 kg	LQ4/2	333	640C & D
1308	ZIRCONIUM SUSPENDED IN A FLAMMABLE LIQUID, PG111	30/1000	5 litres	30 kg	5 litres	20 kg	LQ7/3	1000	
1309	ALUMINIUM POWDER, COATED, PG11	30/500	3 kg	30 kg	500 kg	20 kg	LQ8/2	333	
1309	ALUMINIUM POWDER, COATED, PG111	30/1000	6 kg	30 kg	3 kg	20 kg	LQ9/3	1000	
1310	AMMONIUM PICRATE, WETTED WITH NOT LESS THAN 10% WATER, BY MASS	Nil	Nil	Nil	Nil	Nil	LQ0/1	20	
1312	BORNEOL	30/1000	6 kg	30 kg	3 kg	20 kg	LQ9/3	1000	
1313	CALCIUM RESINATE	30/1000	6 kg	30 kg	3 kg	20 kg	LQ9/3	1000	
1314	CALCIUM RESINATE, FUSED	30/1000	6 kg	30 kg	3 kg	20 kg	LQ9/3	1000	

UN	Substance	Excepted Quantities	LQ Packages		LQ Shrink Wrapped Trays		Limited Quantity Value/Transport Category	Max Load	Special Provisions
			Receptacle Size	Package Gross	Receptacle Size	Package Gross			
1318	COBALT RESINATE, PRECIPITATED	30/1000	6 kg	30 kg	3 kg	20 kg	LQ9/3	1000	
1320	DINITROPHENOL, WETTED WITH NOT LESS THAN 15% WATER, BY MASS	Nil	Nil	Nil	Nil	Nil	LQ0/1	20	
1321	DINITROPHENOLATES, WETTED WITH NOT LESS THAN 15% WATER, BY MASS	Nil	Nil	Nil	Nil	Nil	LQ0/1	20	
1322	DINITRORESORCINOL, WETTED WITH NOT LESS THAN 15% WATER, BY MASS	Nil	Nil	Nil	Nil	Nil	LQ0/1	20	
1323	FERROCERIUM	30/500	3 kg	30 kg	500 g	20 kg	LQ8/2	333	249
1324	FILMS, NITROCELLULOSE BASE, GELATIN COATED, EXCEPT SCRAP	30/1000	6 kg	30 kg	3 kg	20 kg	LQ9/3	1000	
1325	FLAMMABLE SOLID, ORGANIC, N.O.S., PG11	30/500	3 kg	30 kg	500 g	20 kg	LQ8/2	333	274
1325	FLAMMABLE SOLID ORGANIC N.O.S., PG111	30/1000	6 kg	30 kg	3 kg	20 kg	LQ9/3	1000	274
1326	HAFNIUM POWDER, WETTED WITH NOT LESS THAN 25% WATER	30/500	3 kg	30 kg	500 g	20 kg	LQ8/2	333	586
1327	HAY, STRAW OR BHUSA	Not Subject	Subject	To	ADR	–	Not Subject	To ADR	See IMDG Regs
1328	HEXAMETHYLENETETRAMINE	30/1000	6 kg	30 kg	3 kg	20 kg	LQ9/3	1000	
1330	MANGANESE RESINATE	30/1000	6 kg	30 kg	3 kg	20 kg	LQ9/3	1000	

UN No.	Name								
1331	MATCHES, 'STRIKE ANYWHERE'	30/1000	6 kg	30 kg	3 kg	20 kg	LQ9/4	Unlimited	293
1332	METALDEHYDE	30/1000	6 kg	30 kg	3 kg	20 kg	LQ9/3	1000	
1333	CERIUM, SLABS, INGOTS OR RODS	30/500	3 kg	30 kg	500 g	20 kg	LQ8/2	333	
1334	NAPHTHALENE, CRUDE OR NAPHTHALENE, REFINED	30/1000	6 kg	30 kg	3 kg	20 kg	LQ9/3	1000	
1336	NITROGUANIDINE (PICRITE), WETTED WITH NOT LESS THAN 20% WATER, BY MASS	Nil	Nil	Nil	Nil	Nil	LQ0/1	20	
1337	NITROSTARCH, WETTED WITH NOT LESS THAN 20% WATER, BY MASS	Nil	Nil	Nil	Nil	Nil	LQ0/1	20	
1338	PHOSPHORUS, AMORPHOUS	30/1000	6 kg	30 kg	3 kg	20 kg	LQ9/3	1000	
1339	PHOSPHORUS HEPTASULPHIDE, FREE FROM YELLOW AND WHITE PHOSPHORUS	30/500	3 kg	30 kg	500 g	20 kg	LQ8/2	333	602
1340	PHOSPHORUS PENTASULPHIDE, FREE FROM YELLOW AND WHITE PHOSPHORUS	30/500	500 g	30 kg	500 g	20 kg	LQ11/0	Nil	602
1341	PHOSPHORUS SESQUISULPHIDE, FREE FROM YELLOW AND WHITE PHOSPHORUS	30/500	3 kg	30 kg	500 g	20 kg	LQ8/2	333	602
1343	PHOSPHORUS TRISULPHIDE, FREE FROM YELLOW AND WHITE PHOSPHORUS	30/500	3 kg	30 kg	500 g	20 kg	LQ8/2	333	602
1344	TRINITROPHENOL, WETTED WITH NOT LESS THAN 30% WATER, BY MASS	Nil	Nil	Nil	Nil	Nil	LQ0/1	20	
1345	RUBBER SCRAP OR RUBBER SHODDY, POWDERED OR GRANULATED	30/500	3 kg	30 kg	500 g	20 kg	LQ8/4	Unlimited	
1346	SILICON POWDER, AMORPHOUS	30/1000	6 kg	30 kg	3 kg	20 kg	LQ9/3	1000	32
1347	SILVER PICRATE, WETTED, WITH NOT LESS THAN 30% WATER, BY MASS	Nil	Nil	Nil	Nil	Nil	LQ0/1	20	

UN	Substance	Excepted Quantities	LQ Packages		LQ Shrink Wrapped Trays		Limited Quantity Value/Transport Category	Max Load	Special Provisions
			Receptacle Size	Gross Package	Receptacle Size	Gross Package			
1348	SODIUM DINITRO-ORTHO-CRESOLATE, WETTED WITH NOT LESS THAN 15% WATER, BY MASS	Nil	Nil	Nil	Nil	Nil	LQ0/1	20	
1349	SODIUM PICRAMATE, WETTED WITH NOT LESS THAN 20% WATER, BY MASS	Nil	Nil	Nil	Nil	Nil	LQ0/1	20	
1350	SULPHUR	30/1000	6 kg	30 kg	3 kg	20 kg	LQ9/3	1000	242
1352	TITANIUM POWDER, WETTED WITH NOT LESS THAN 25% WATER	30/500	3 kg	30 kg	500 g	20 kg	LQ8/2	333	586
1353	FIBRES OR FABRICS IMPREGNATED WITH WEAKLY NITRATED NITROCELLULOSE, N.O.S.	30/1000	6 kg	30 kg	3 kg	20 kg	LQ9/3	1000	274, 502
1354	TRINITROBENZENE, WETTED WITH NOT LESS THAN 30% WATER, BY MASS	Nil	Nil	Nil	Nil	Nil	LQ0/1	20	
1355	TRINITROBENZOIC ACID, WETTED WITH NOT LESS THAN 30% WATER, BY MASS	Nil	Nil	Nil	Nil	Nil	LQ0/1	20	
1356	TRINITROTOLUENE (TNT), WETTED WITH NOT LESS THAN 30% WATER, BY MASS	Nil	Nil	Nil	Nil	Nil	LQ0/1	20	
1357	UREA NITRATE, WETTED WITH NOT LESS THAN 20% WATER, BY MASS	Nil	Nil	Nil	Nil	Nil	LQ0/1	20	227
1358	ZIRCONIUM POWDER, WETTED WITH NOT LESS THAN 25% WATER	30/500	3 kg	30 kg	500 g	20 kg	LQ8/2	333	586
1360	CALCIUM PHOSPHIDE	Nil	Nil	Nil	Nil	Nil	LQ0/1	20	

UN	Name							
1361	CARBON, ANIMAL OR VEGETABLE ORIGIN, PG11	30/500	Nil	Nil	Nil	LQ0/2	333	
1361	CARBON, ANIMAL OR VEGETABLE ORIGIN, PG111	30/1000	Nil	Nil	Nil	LQ0/4	Unlimited	
1362	CARBON, ACTIVATED	30/1000	Nil	Nil	Nil	LQ0/4	Unlimited	646
1364	COTTON WASTE, OILY	30/1000	Nil	Nil	Nil	LQ0/3	1000	
1365	COTTON , WET	30/1000	Nil	Nil	Nil	LQ0/3	1000	
1369	P-NITROSODIMETHYLANILINE	30/500	Nil	Nil	Nil	LQ0/2	333	
1372	FIBRES, ANIMAL OR FIBRES, VEGETABLE BURNT, WET OR DAMP	Not Subject	To	ADR	–	Not Subject	To	ADR
1373	FIBRES OR FABRICS, ANIMAL OR VEGETABLE OR SYNTHETIC, N.O.S. WITH OIL	30/1000	Nil	Nil	Nil	LQ0/3	1000	274
1374	FISH MEAL (FISH SCRAP), UNSTABILISED	30/500	Nil	Nil	Nil	LQ0/2	333	300
1376	IRON OXIDE, SPENT, OR IRON SPONGE, SPENT OBTAINED FROM COAL GAS PURIFICATION	30/1000	Nil	Nil	Nil	LQ0/3	1000	592
1378	METAL CATALYST, WETTED WITH A VISIBLE EXCESS OF LIQUID	30/500	Nil	Nil	Nil	LQ0/2	333	274
1379	PAPER, UNSATURATED OIL TREATED INCOMPLETELY DRIED (INCLUDES CARBON PAPER)	30/1000	Nil	Nil	Nil	LQ0/3	1000	
1380	PENTABORANE	Nil	Nil	Nil	Nil	LQ0/0	Nil	
1381	PHOSPHORUS, WHITE OR YELLOW, DRY OR UNDER WATER OR IN SOLUTION	Nil	Nil	Nil	Nil	LQ0/0	Nil	503

UN	Substance	Excepted Quantities	LQ Packages		LQ Shrink Wrapped Trays		Limited Quantity Value/Transport Category	Max Load	Special Provisions
			Receptacle Size	Package Gross	Receptacle Size	Package Gross			
1382	POTASSIUM SULPHIDE, ANHYDROUS OR POTASSIUM SULPHIDE WITH LESS THAN 30% WATER OF CRYSTALLISATION	30/500	Nil	Nil	Nil	Nil	LQ0/2	333	504
1383	PYROPHORIC METAL, N.O.S. OR PYROPHORIC ALLOY, N.O.S.	Nil	Nil	Nil	Nil	Nil	LQ0/0	Nil	274
1384	SODIUM DITHIONITE (SODIUM HYDROSULPHITE)	30/500	Nil	Nil	Nil	Nil	LQ0/2	333	
1385	SODIUM SULPHIDE ANHYDROUS OR SODIUM SULPHIDE WITH LESS THAN 30% WATER OF CRYSTALLISATION	30/500	Nil	Nil	Nil	Nil	LQ0/2	333	504
1386	SEED CAKE WITH MORE THAN 1.5% OIL AND NOT MORE THAN 11% MOISTURE	30/1000	Nil	Nil	Nil	Nil	LQ0/3	1000	
1387	WOOL WASTE, WET	Not	Subject	to	ADR	–	Not Subject	To	ADR
1389	ALKALI METAL AMALGAM	Nil	Nil	Nil	Nil	Nil	LQ0/1	20	182, 274
1390	ALKALI METAL AMIDES	30/500	500 g	30 kg	500 g	20 kg	LQ11/0	Nil	182, 274, 505
1391	ALKALI METAL DISPERSION OR ALKALINE EARTH METAL DISPERSION	Nil	Nil	Nil	Nil	Nil	LQ0/1	20	182, 183, 274, 506
1392	ALKALINE EARTH METAL AMALGAM	Nil	Nil	Nil	Nil	Nil	LQ0/1	20	183, 274, 506

UN No	Name								
1393	ALKALINE EARTH METAL ALLOY, N.O.S.	30/500	500 g	30 kg	500 g	20 kg	LQ11/2	333	183, 274, 506
1394	ALUMINIUM CARBIDE	30/500	500 g	30 kg	500 g	20 kg	LQ11/2	333	
1395	ALUMINIUM FERROSILICON POWDER	30/500	500 g	30 kg	500 g	20 kg	LQ11/2	333	
1396	ALUMINIUM POWDER, UNCOATED, PG11	30/500	1 kg	30 kg	1 kg	20 kg	LQ12/2	333	
1396	ALUMINIUM POWDER, UNCOATED, PG111	30/1000	1 kg	30 kg	1 kg	20 kg	LQ12/3	1000	
1397	ALUMINIUM PHOSPHIDE	Nil	Nil	Nil	Nil	Nil	LQ0/1	20	507
1398	ALUMINIUM SILICON POWDER, UNCOATED	30/1000	1 kg	30 kg	1 kg	20 kg	LQ12/3	1000	37
1400	BARIUM	30/500	500 g	30 kg	500 g	20 kg	LQ11/2	333	
1401	CALCIUM	30/500	500 g	30 kg	500 g	20 kg	LQ11/2	333	
1402	CALCIUM CARBIDE, PG1	Nil	Nil	Nil	Nil	Nil	LQ0/1	20	
1402	CALCIUM CARBIDE, PG11	30/500	500 g	30 kg	500 g	20 kg	LQ11/2	333	
1403	CALCIUM CYANAMIDE WITH MORE THAN 0.1% OF CALCIUM CARBIDE	30/1000	1 kg	30 kg	1 kg	20 kg	LQ12/0	Nil	38
1404	CALCIUM HYDRIDE	Nil	Nil	Nil	Nil	Nil	LQ0/1	20	
1405	CALCIUM SILICIDE, PG11	30/500	500 g	30 kg	500 g	20 kg	LQ11/2	333	
1405	CALCIUM SILICIDE, PG111	30/1000	1 kg	30 kg	1 kg	20 kg	LQ12/3	1000	
1407	CAESIUM	Nil	Nil	Nil	Nil	Nil	LQ0/1	20	
1408	FERROSILICON, WITH 30% OR MORE BUT LESS THAN 90% SILICON	30/1000	1 kg	30 kg	1 kg	20 kg	LQ12/3	1000	39
1409	METAL HYDRIDES, WATER-REACTIVE, N.O.S., PG1	Nil	Nil	Nil	Nil	Nil	LQ0/1	20	274, 508

UN	Substance	Excepted Quantities	LQ Packages		LQ Shrink Wrapped Trays		Limited Quantity Value/Transport Category	Max Load	Special Provisions
			Receptacle Size	Gross Package	Receptacle Size	Gross Package			
1409	METAL HYDRIDES, WATER-REACTIVE, N.O.S., PG11	30/500	500 g	30 kg	500 g	20 kg	LQ11/2	333	274, 508
1410	LITHIUM ALUMINIUM HYDRIDE	Nil	Nil	Nil	Nil	Nil	LQ0/1	20	
1411	LITHIUM ALUMINIUM HYDRIDE, ETHEREAL	Nil	Nil	Nil	Nil	Nil	LQ0/1	20	
1413	LITHIUM BOROHYDRIDE	Nil	Nil	Nil	Nil	Nil	LQ0/1	20	
1414	LITHIUM HYDRIDE	Nil	Nil	Nil	Nil	Nil	LQ0/1	20	
1415	LITHIUM	Nil	Nil	Nil	Nil	Nil	LQ0/1	20	
1417	LITHIUM SILICON	30/500	500 g	30 kg	500 g	20 kg	LQ11/2	333	
1418	MAGNESIUM POWDER OR MAGNESIUM ALLOYS POWDER, PG1	Nil	Nil	Nil	Nil	Nil	LQ0/1	20	
1418	MAGNESIUM POWDER OR MAGNESIUM ALLOYS POWDER, PG11	30/500	500 g	30 kg	500 g	20 kg	LQ11/2	333	
1418	MAGNESIUM POWDER OR MAGNESIUM ALLOYS POWDER, PG111	30/1000	1 kg	30 kg	1 kg	20 kg	LQ12/3	1000	
1419	MAGNESIUM ALUMINIUM PHOSPHIDE	Nil	Nil	Nil	Nil	Nil	LQ0/1	20	
1420	POTASSIUM METAL ALLOYS	Nil	Nil	Nil	Nil	Nil	LQ0/1	20	
1421	ALKALI METAL ALLOY, LIQUID, N.O.S.	Nil	Nil	Nil	Nil	Nil	LQ0/1	20	182, 274
1422	POTASSIUM SODIUM ALLOYS	Nil	Nil	Nil	Nil	Nil	LQ0/1	20	

1423	RUBIDIUM	Nil	Nil	Nil	Nil	Nil	LQ0/1	20	
1426	SODIUM BOROHYDRIDE	Nil	Nil	Nil	Nil	Nil	LQ0/1	20	
1427	SODIUM HYDRIDE	Nil	Nil	Nil	Nil	Nil	LQ0/1	20	
1428	SODIUM	Nil	Nil	Nil	Nil	Nil	LQ0/1	20	
1431	SODIUM METHYLATE	30/500	Nil	Nil	Nil	Nil	LQ0/2	333	
1432	SODIUM PHOSPHIDE	Nil	Nil	Nil	Nil	Nil	LQ0/1	20	
1433	STANNIC PHOSPHIDES	Nil	Nil	Nil	Nil	Nil	LQ0/1	20	
1435	ZINC ASHES	30/1000	1 kg	30 kg	1 kg	20 kg	LQ12/3	1000	
1436	ZINC POWDER OR ZINC DUST, PG1	Nil	Nil	Nil	Nil	Nil	LQ0/1	20	
1436	ZINC POWDER OR ZINC DUST, PG11	30/500	500 g	30 kg	500 g	20 kg	LQ11/2	333	
1436	ZINC POWDER OR ZINC DUST, PG111	30/1000	1 kg	30 kg	1 kg	20 kg	LQ12/3	1000	
1437	ZIRCONIUM HYDRIDE	30/500	3 kg	30 kg	500 g	20 kg	LQ8/2	333	
1438	ALUMINIUM NITRATE	30/1000	1 kg	30 kg	1 kg	20 kg	LQ12/3	1000	
1439	AMMONIUM DICHROMATE	30/500	500 g	30 kg	500 g	20 kg	LQ11/2	333	
1442	AMMONIUM PERCHLORATE	30/500	500 g	30 kg	500 g	20 kg	LQ11/2	333	152
1444	AMMONIUM PERSULPHATE	30/1000	1 kg	30 kg	1 kg	20 kg	LQ12/3	1000	
1445	BARIUM CHLORATE	30/500	500 g	30 kg	500 g	20 kg	LQ11/2	333	
1446	BARIUM NITRATE	30/500	500 g	30 kg	500 g	20 kg	LQ11/2	333	
1447	BARIUM PERCHLORATE	30/500	500 g	30 kg	500 g	20 kg	LQ11/2	333	
1448	BARIUM PERMANGANATE	30/500	500 g	30 kg	500 g	20 kg	LQ11/2	333	
1449	BARIUM PEROXIDE	30/500	500 g	30 kg	500 g	20 kg	LQ11/2	333	

UN	Substance	Excepted Quantities	LQ Packages		LQ Shrink Wrapped Trays		Limited Quantity Value/Transport Category	Max Load	Special Provisions
			Receptacle Size	Package Gross	Receptacle Size	Package Gross			
1450	BROMATES, INORGANIC, N.O.S.	30/500	500 g	30 kg	500 g	20 kg	LQ11/2	333	274, 604
1451	CAESIUM NITRATE	30/1000	1 kg	30 kg	1 kg	20 kg	LQ12/3	1000	
1452	CALCIUM CHLORATE	30/500	500 g	30 kg	500 g	20 kg	LQ11/2	333	
1453	CALCIUM CHLORITE	30/500	500 g	30 kg	500 g	20 kg	LQ11/2	333	
1454	CALCIUM NITRATE	30/1000	1 kg	30 kg	1 kg	20 kg	LQ12/3	1000	208
1455	CALCIUM PERCHLORATE	30/500	500 g	30 kg	500 g	20 kg	LQ11/2	333	
1456	CALCIUM PERMANGANATE	30/500	500 g	30 kg	500 g	20 kg	LQ11/2	333	
1457	CALCIUM PEROXIDE	30/500	500 g	30 kg	500 g	20 kg	LQ11/2	333	
1458	CHLORATE AND BORATE MIXTURE, PG11	30/500	500 g	30 kg	500 g	20 kg	LQ11/2	333	
1458	CHLORATE AND BORATE MIXTURE, PG111	30/1000	1 kg	30 kg	1 kg	20 kg	LQ12/3	1000	
1459	CHLORATE AND MAGNESIUM CHLORIDE MIXTURE, PG11	30/500	500 g	30 kg	500 g	20 kg	LQ11/2	333	
1459	CHLORATE AND MAGNESIUM CHLORIDE MIXTURE, PG111	30/1000	1 kg	30 kg	1 kg	20 kg	LQ12/3	1000	
1461	CHLORATES, INORGANIC, N.O.S.	30/500	500 g	30 kg	500 g	20 kg	LQ11/2	333	274, 605
1462	CHLORITES, INORGANIC, N.O.S.	30/500	500 g	30 kg	500 g	20 kg	LQ11/2	333	274, 509, 606
1463	CHROMIUM TRIOXIDE, ANHYDROUS	30/500	500 g	30 kg	500 g	20 kg	LQ11/2	333	510

1465	DIDYMIUM NITRATE	30/1000	1 kg	30 kg	1 kg	20 kg	LQ12/3	1000	
1466	FERRIC NITRATE	30/1000	1 kg	30 kg	1 kg	20 kg	LQ12/3	1000	
1467	GUANIDINE NITRATE	30/1000	1 kg	30 kg	1 kg	20 kg	LQ12/3	1000	
1469	LEAD NITRATE	30/500	500 g	30 kg	500 g	20 kg	LQ11/2	333	
1470	LEAD PERCHLORATE	30/500	500 g	30 kg	500 g	20 kg	LQ11/2	333	
1471	LITHIUM HYPOCHLORITE, DRY OR LITHIUM HYPOCHLORITE MIXTURE	30/500	500 g	30 kg	500 g	20 kg	LQ11/2	333	
1472	LITHIUM PEROXIDE	30/500	500 g	30 kg	500 g	20 kg	LQ11/2	333	
1473	MAGNESIUM BROMATE	30/500	500 g	30 kg	500 g	20 kg	LQ11/2	333	
1474	MAGNESIUM NITRATE	30/1000	1 kg	30 kg	1 kg	20 kg	LQ12/3	1000	332
1475	MAGNESIUM PERCHLORATE	30/500	500 g	30 kg	500 g	20 kg	LQ11/2	333	
1476	MAGNESIUM PEROXIDE	30/500	500 g	30 kg	500 g	20 kg	LQ11/2	333	
1477	NITRATES, INORGANIC, N.O.S., PG11	30/500	500 g	30 kg	500 g	20 kg	LQ11/2	333	274, 511
1477	NITRATES, INORGANIC, N.O.S., PG111	30/1000	1 kg	30 kg	1 kg	20 kg	LQ12/3	1000	274, 511
1479	OXIDISING SOLID, N.O.S., PG1	Nil	Nil	Nil	Nil	Nil	LQ0/1	20	274
1479	OXIDISING SOLID, N.O.S., PG11	30/500	500 g	30 kg	500 g	20 kg	LQ11/2	333	274
1479	OXIDISING SOLID, N.O.S., PG111	30/1000	1 kg	30 kg	1 kg	20 kg	LQ12/3	1000	274
1481	PERCHLORATES, INORGANIC, N.O.S., PG11	30/500	500 g	30 kg	500 g	20 kg	LQ11/2	333	274
1481	PERCHLORATES, INORGANIC, N.O.S., PG111	30/1000	1 kg	30 kg	1 kg	20 kg	LQ12/3	1000	274
1482	PERMANGANATES, INORGANIC, N.O.S., PG11	30/500	500 g	30 kg	500 g	20 kg	LQ11/2	333	274, 608

| UN | Substance | Excepted Quantities | LQ Packages | | LQ Shrink Wrapped Trays | | Limited Quantity Value/Transport Category | Max Load | Special Provisions |
			Receptacle Size	Package Gross	Receptacle Size	Package Gross			
1482	PERMANGANATES, INORGANIC, N.O.S., PG111	30/1000	1 kg	30 kg	1 kg	20 kg	LQ12/3	1000	274, 608
1483	PEROXIDES, INORGANIC, N.O.S., PG11	30/500	500 g	30 kg	500 g	20 kg	LQ11/2	333	274
1483	PEROXIDES, INORGANIC, N.O.S., PG111	30/1000	1 kg	30 kg	1 kg	20 kg	LQ12/3	1000	274
1484	POTASSIUM BROMATE	30/500	500 g	30 kg	500 g	20 kg	LQ11/2	333	
1485	POTASSIUM CHLORATE	30/500	500 g	30 kg	500 g	20 kg	LQ11/2	333	
1486	POTASSIUM NITRATE	30/1000	1 kg	30 kg	1 kg	20 kg	LQ12/3	1000	
1487	POTASSIUM NITRATE AND SODIUM NITRATE MIXTURE	30/500	500 g	30 kg	500 g	20 kg	LQ11/2	333	607
1488	POTASSIUM NITRITE	30/500	500 g	30 kg	500 g	20 kg	LQ11/2	333	
1489	POTASSIUM PERCHLORATE	30/500	500 g	30 kg	500 g	20 kg	LQ11/2	333	
1490	POTASSIUM PERMANGANATE	30/500	500 g	30 kg	500 g	20 kg	LQ11/2	333	
1491	POTASSIUM PEROXIDE	Nil	Nil	Nil	Nil	Nil	LQ0/1	20	
1492	POTASSIUM PERSULPHATE	30/1000	1 kg	30 kg	1 kg	20 kg	LQ12/3	1000	
1493	SILVER NITRATE	30/500	500 g	30 kg	500 g	20 kg	LQ11/2	333	
1494	SODIUM BROMATE	30/500	500 g	30 kg	500 g	20 kg	LQ11/2	333	
1495	SODIUM CHLORATE	30/500	500 g	30 kg	500 g	20 kg	LQ11/2	333	

1496	SODIUM CHLORITE	30/500	500 g	30 kg	500 g	20 kg	LQ11/2	333	
1498	SODIUM NITRATE	30/1000	1 kg	30 kg	1 kg	20 kg	LQ12/3	1000	
1499	SODIUM NITRATE AND POTASSIUM NITRATE MIXTURE	30/1000	1 kg	30 kg	1 kg	20 kg	LQ12/3	1000	
1500	SODIUM NITRITE	30/1000	1 kg	30 kg	1 kg	20 kg	LQ12/3	1000	
1502	SODIUM PERCHLORATE	30/500	500 g	30 kg	500 g	20 kg	LQ11/2	333	
1503	SODIUM PERMANGANATE	30/500	500 g	30 kg	500 g	20 kg	LQ11/2	333	
1504	SODIUM PEROXIDE	Nil	Nil	Nil	Nil	Nil	LQ0/1	20	
1505	SODIUM PERSULPHATE	30/1000	1 kg	30 kg	1 kg	20 kg	LQ12/3	1000	
1506	STRONTIUM CHLORATE	30/500	500 g	30 kg	500 g	20 kg	LQ11/2	333	
1507	STRONTIUM NITRATE	30/1000	1 kg	30 kg	1 kg	20 kg	LQ12/3	1000	
1508	STRONTIUM PERCHLORATE	30/500	500 g	30 kg	500 g	20 kg	LQ11/2	333	
1509	STRONTIUM PEROXIDE	30/500	500 g	30 kg	500 g	20 kg	LQ11/2	333	
1510	TETRANITROMETHANE	Nil	Nil	Nil	Nil	Nil	LQ0/1	20	609
1511	UREA HYDROGEN PEROXIDE	30/1000	1 kg	30 kg	1 kg	20 kg	LQ12/3	1000	
1512	ZINC AMMONIUM NITRITE	30/500	500 g	30 kg	500 g	20 kg	LQ11/2	333	
1513	ZINC CHLORATE	30/500	500 g	30 kg	500 g	20 kg	LQ11/2	333	
1514	ZINC NITRATE	30/500	500 g	30 kg	500 g	20 kg	LQ11/2	333	
1515	ZINC PERMANGANATE	30/500	500 g	30 kg	500 g	20 kg	LQ11/2	333	
1516	ZINC PEROXIDE	30/500	500 g	30 kg	500 g	20 kg	LQ11/2	333	

| UN | Substance | Excepted Quantities | LQ Packages | | LQ Shrink Wrapped Trays | | Limited Quantity Value/Transport Category | Max Load | Special Provisions |
			Receptacle Size	Package Gross	Receptacle Size	Package Gross			
1517	ZIRCONIUM PICRAMATE, WETTED WITH NOT LESS THAN 20% WATER, BY MASS	Nil	Nil	Nil	Nil	Nil	LQ0/1	20	
1541	ACETONE CYANOHYDRIN STABILISED	1/300	Nil	Nil	Nil	Nil	LQ0/1	20	
1544	ALKALOIDS, SOLID, N.O.S. OR ALKALOID SALTS, SOLID, N.O.S., PG1	1/300	Nil	Nil	Nil	Nil	LQ0/1	20	43, 274
1544	ALKALOIDS, SOLID, N.O.S. OR ALKALOID SALTS, SOLID, N.O.S., PG11	1/500	1 kg	4 kg	500 g	4 kg	LQ18/2	333	43, 274
1544	ALKALOIDS, SOLID, N.O.S. OR ALKALOID SALTS, SOLID, N.O.S., PG111	30/1000	6 kg	24 kg	3 kg	20 kg	LQ9/2	333	43, 274
1545	ALLYL ISOTHIOCYANATE, STABILISED	1/500	500 ml	2 litres	100 ml	2 litres	LQ17/2	333	
1546	AMMONIUM ARSENATE	1/500	1 kg	4 kg	500 g	4 kg	LQ18/2	333	
1547	ANILINE	1/500	500 ml	2 litres	100 ml	2 litres	LQ17/2	333	279
1548	ANILINE HYDROCHLORIDE	30/1000	6 kg	30 kg	3 kg	20 kg	LQ9/2	333	
1549	ANTIMONY COMPOUND, INORGANIC, SOLID, N.O.S.	30/1000	6 kg	30 kg	3 kg	20 kg	LQ9/2	333	45, 274, 512
1550	ANTIMONY LACTATE	30/1000	6 kg	30 kg	3 kg	20 kg	LQ9/2	333	
1551	ANTIMONY POTASSIUM TARTRATE	30/1000	6 kg	30 kg	3 kg	20 kg	LQ9/2	333	
1553	ARSENIC ACID, LIQUID	1/300	Nil	Nil	Nil	Nil	LQ0/1	20	

UN	Name								
1554	ARSENIC ACID, SOLID	1/500	1 kg	4 kg	500 g	4 kg	LQ18/2	333	
1555	ARSENIC BROMIDE	1/500	1 kg	4 kg	500 g	4 kg	LQ18/2	333	43, 274
1556	ARSENIC COMPOUND, LIQUID, N.O.S., INORGANIC, INCLUDING: ARSENATES, N.O.S., ARSENITES, N.O.S., ARSENIC SULPHIDES, N.O.S., PG1	1/300	Nil	Nil	Nil	Nil	LQ0/1	20	43, 274
1556	ARSENIC COMPOUND, LIQUID, N.O.S., INORGANIC, INCLUDING: ARSENATES, N.O.S., ARSENITES, N.O.S., ARSENIC SULPHIDES, N.O.S., PG11	1/500	500 ml	2 litres	100 ml	2 litres	LQ17/2	333	43, 274
1556	ARSENIC COMPOUND, LIQUID, N.O.S., INORGANIC, INCLUDING: ARSENATES, N.O.S., ARSENITES, N.O.S., ARSENIC SULPHIDES, N.O.S., PG111	30/1000	5 litres	30 kg	5 litres	20 kg	LQ7/2	333	43, 274
1557	ARSENIC COMPOUND, SOLID, N.O.S., INORGANIC, INCLUDING: ARSENATES, N.O.S., ARSENITES, N.O.S., ARSENIC SULPHIDES, N.O.S., PG1	1/300	Nil	Nil	Nil	Nil	LQ0/1	20	43, 274
1557	ARSENIC COMPOUND, SOLID, N.O.S., INORGANIC, INCLUDING: ARSENATES, N.O.S., ARSENITES, N.O.S., ARSENIC SULPHIDES, N.O.S., PG11	1/500	1 kg	4 kg	500 g	4 kg	LQ18/2	333	43, 274
1557	ARSENIC COMPOUND, SOLID, N.O.S., INORGANIC, INCLUDING: ARSENATES, N.O.S., ARSENITES, N.O.S., ARSENIC SULPHIDES, N.O.S., PG111	30/1000	6 kg	30 kg	3 kg	20 kg	LQ9/2	333	43, 274
1558	ARSENIC	1/500	1 kg	4 kg	500 g	4 kg	LQ18/2	333	
1559	ARSENIC PENTOXIDE	1/500	1 kg	4 kg	500 g	4 kg	LQ18/2	333	

UN	Substance	Excepted Quantities	LQ Packages Receptacle Size	LQ Packages Package Gross	LQ Shrink Wrapped Trays Receptacle Size	LQ Shrink Wrapped Trays Package Gross	Limited Quantity Value/Transport Category	Max Load	Special Provisions
1560	ARSENIC TRICHLORIDE	1/300	Nil	Nil	Nil	Nil	LQ0/1	20	
1561	ARSENIC TRIOXIDE	1/500	1 kg	4 kg	500 g	4 kg	LQ18/2	333	
1562	ARSENICAL DUST	1/500	1 kg	4 kg	500 g	4 kg	LQ18/2	333	
1564	BARIUM COMPOUND, N.O.S., PG11	1/500	1 kg	4 kg	500 g	4 kg	LQ18/2	333	177, 274, 513, 587
1564	BARIUM COMPOUND, N.O.S., PG111	30/1000	6 kg	30 kg	3 kg	20 kg	LQ9/2	333	177, 274, 513, 587
1565	BARIUM CYANIDE	1/300	Nil	Nil	Nil	Nil	LQ0/1	20	
1566	BERYLLIUM COMPOUND, N.O.S., PG11	1/500	1 kg	4 kg	500 g	4 kg	LQ18/2	333	274, 514
1566	BERYLLIUM COMPOUND, N.O.S., PG111	30/1000	6 kg	30 kg	3 kg	20 kg	LQ9/2	333	274, 514
1567	BERYLLIUM POWDER	1/500	1 kg	4 kg	500 g	4 kg	LQ18/2	333	
1569	BROMOACETONE	1/500	500 ml	2 litres	100 ml	2 litres	LQ17/2	333	
1570	BRUCINE	1/300	Nil	Nil	Nil	Nil	LQ0/1	20	43
1571	BARIUM AZIDE, WETTED WITH NOT LESS THAN 50% WATER, BY MASS	Nil	Nil	Nil	Nil	Nil	LQ0/1	20	568
1572	CACODYLIC ACID	1/500	1 kg	4 kg	500 g	4 kg	LQ18/2	333	
1573	CALCIUM ARSENATE	1/500	1 kg	4 kg	500 g	4 kg	LQ18/2	333	

UN No	Name						LQ		Remarks
1574	CALCIUM ARSENATE AND CALCIUM ARSENITE MIXTURE, SOLID	1/500	1 kg	4 kg	500 g	4 kg	LQ18/2	333	
1575	CALCIUM CYANIDE	1/300	Nil	Nil	Nil	Nil	LQ0/1	20	
1577	CHLORODINITROBENZENES, LIQUID	1/500	500 ml	2 litres	100 ml	2 litres	LQ17/2	333	279
1578	CHLORONITROBENZENES, SOLID	1/500	1 kg	4 kg	500 g	4 kg	LQ18/2	333	279
1579	4-CHLORO-O-TOLUIDINE HYDROCHLORIDE	30/1000	6 kg	30 kg	3 kg	20 kg	LQ9/2	333	
1580	CHLOROPICRIN	1/300	Nil	Nil	Nil	Nil	LQ0/1	20	
1581	CHLOROPICRIN AND METHYL BROMIDE MIXTURE, WITH MORE THAN 2% CHLOROPICRIN	Nil	Nil	Nil	Nil	Nil	LQ0/1	20	
1582	CHLOROPICRIN AND METHYL CHLORIDE MIXTURE	Nil	Nil	Nil	Nil	Nil	LQ0/1	20	
1583	CHLOROPICRIN MIXTURE, N.O.S., PG1	1/300	Nil	Nil	Nil	Nil	LQ0/1	20	274, 315, 515
1583	CHLOROPICRIN MIXTURE, N.O.S., PG11	1/500	500 ml	2 litres	100 ml	2 litres	LQ17/2	333	274, 515
1583	CHLOROPICRIN MIXTURE, N.O.S., PG111	30/1000	5 litres	30 kg	5 litres	20 kg	LQ7/2	333	274, 515
1585	COPPER ACETOARSENITE	1/500	1 kg	4 kg	500 g	4 kg	LQ18/2	333	
1586	COPPER ARSENITE	1/500	1 kg	4 kg	500 g	4 kg	LQ18/2	333	
1587	COPPER CYANIDE	1/500	1 kg	4 kg	500 g	4 kg	LQ18/2	333	
1588	CYANIDES, INORGANIC, SOLID, N.O.S., PG1	1/300	Nil	Nil	Nil	Nil	LQ0/1	20	47, 274
1588	CYANIDES, INORGANIC, SOLID, N.O.S., PG11	1/500	1 kg	4 kg	500 g	4 kg	LQ18/2	333	47, 274

UN	Substance	Excepted Quantities	LQ Packages		LQ Shrink Wrapped Trays		Limited Quantity Value/Transport Category	Max Load	Special Provisions
			Receptacle Size	Package Gross	Receptacle Size	Package Gross			
1588	CYANIDES, INORGANIC, SOLID, N.O.S., PG111	30/1000	6 kg	24 kg	3 kg	20 kg	LQ9/2	333	47, 274
1589	CYANOGEN CHLORIDE, STABILISED	Nil	Nil	Nil	Nil	Nil	LQ0/1	20	
1590	DICHLOROANILINES, LIQUID	1/500	500 ml	2 litres	100 ml	12 litres	LQ17/2	333	279
1591	O-DICHLOROBENZENE	30/1000	5 litres	30 kg	5 litres	20 kg	LQ7/2	333	279
1593	DICHLOROMETHANE	30/1000	5 litres	30 kg	5 litres	20 kg	LQ7/2	333	516
1594	DIETHYL SULPHATE	1/500	500 ml	2 litres	100 ml	2 litres	LQ17/2	333	
1595	DIMETHYL SULPHATE	1/300	Nil	Nil	Nil	Nil	LQ0/1	20	
1596	DINITROANILINES	1/500	1 kg	4 kg	500 g	4 kg	LQ18/2	333	
1597	DINITROBENZENES, LIQUID	1/500	500 ml	2 litres	100 ml	2 litres	LQ17/2	333	
1597	DINITROBENZENES, SOLID	30/1000	5 litres	30 kg	5 litres	20 kg	LQ7/2	333	
1598	DINITRO-O-CRESOL	1/500	1 kg	4 kg	500 g	4 kg	LQ18/2	333	43
1599	DINITROPHENOL SOLUTION, PG11	1/500	500 ml	2 litres	100 ml	2 litres	LQ17/2	333	
1599	DINITROPHENOL SOLUTION, PG111	30/1000	5 litres	30 kg	5 litres	20 kg	LQ7/2	333	
1600	DINITROTOLUENES, MOLTEN	Nil	Nil	Nil	Nil	Nil	LQ0/0	Nil	
1601	DISINFECTANT, SOLID, TOXIC, N.O.S., PG1	1/300	Nil	Nil	Nil	Nil	LQ0/1	20	274
1601	DISINFECTANT, SOLID, TOXIC, N.O.S., PG11	1/500	1 kg	4 kg	500 g	4 kg	LQ18/2	333	274

UN	Name								
1601	DISINFECTANT, SOLID, TOXIC, N.O.S., PG111	30/1000	6 kg	24 kg	3 kg	20 kg	LQ9/2	333	274
1602	DYE, LIQUID, TOXIC, N.O.S., OR DYE, INTERMEDIATE, LIQUID, TOXIC, N.O.S., PG1	1/300	Nil	Nil	Nil	Nil	LQ0/1	20	274
1602	DYE, LIQUID, TOXIC, N.O.S., OR DYE, INTERMEDIATE, LIQUID, TOXIC, N.O.S., PG11	1/500	500 ml	2 litres	100 ml	2 litres	LQ17/2	333	274
1602	DYE, LIQUID, TOXIC, N.O.S., OR DYE, INTERMEDIATE, LIQUID, TOXIC, N.O.S., PG111	30/1000	5 litres	30 kg	5 litres	20 kg	LQ7/2	333	274
1603	ETHYL BROMOACETATE	1/500	500 ml	2 litres	100 ml	2 litres	LQ17/2	333	
1604	ETHYLENEDIAMINE	30/500	1 litre	30 kg	500 ml	20 kg	LQ22/2	333	
1605	ETHYLENE DIBROMIDE	1/300	Nil	Nil	Nil	Nil	LQ0/1	20	
1606	FERRIC ARSENATE	1/500	1 kg	4 kg	500 g	4 kg	LQ18/2	333	
1607	FERRIC ARSENITE	1/500	1 kg	4 kg	500 g	4 kg	LQ18/2	333	
1608	FERROUS ARSENATE	1/500	1 kg	4 kg	500 g	4 kg	LQ18/2	333	
1611	HEXAETHYL TETRAPHOSPHATE	1/500	500 ml	2 litres	100 ml	2 litres	LQ17/2	333	
1612	HEXAETHYL TETRAPHOSPHATE AND COMPRESSED GAS MIXTURE	Nil	Nil	Nil	Nil	Nil	LQ0/1	20	
1613	HYDROCYANIC ACID, AQUEOUS SOLUTION (HYDROGEN CYANIDE, AQUEOUS SOLUTION) WITH NOT MORE THAN 20% HYDROGEN CYANIDE	1/300	Nil	Nil	Nil	Nil	LQ0/0	Nil	48
1614	HYDROGEN CYANIDE, STABILISED, CONTAINING LESS THEN 3% WATER AND ABSORBED IN A POROUS INERT MATERIAL	1/300	Nil	Nil	Nil	Nil	LQ0/0	Nil	603

UN	Substance	Excepted Quantities	LQ Packages		LQ Shrink Wrapped Trays		Limited Quantity Value/Transport Category	Max Load	Special Provisions
			Receptacle Size	Gross Package	Receptacle Size	Gross Package			
1616	LEAD ACETATE	30/1000	6 kg	30 kg	3 kg	20 kg	LQ9/2	333	
1617	LEAD ARSENATES	1/500	1 kg	4 kg	500 g	4 kg	LQ18/2	333	
1618	LEAD ARSENITES	1/500	1 kg	4 kg	500 g	4 kg	LQ18/2	333	
1620	LEAD CYANIDE	1/500	1 kg	4 kg	500 g	4 kg	LQ18/2	333	
1621	LONDON PURPLE	1/500	1 kg	4 kg	500 g	4 kg	LQ18/2	333	43
1622	MAGNESIUM ARSENATE	1/500	1 kg	4 kg	500 g	4 kg	LQ18/2	333	
1623	MERCURIC ARSENATE	1/500	1 kg	4 kg	500 g	4 kg	LQ18/2	333	
1624	MERCURIC CHLORIDE	1/500	1 kg	4 kg	500 g	4 kg	LQ18/2	333	
1625	MERCURIC NITRATE	1/500	1 kg	4 kg	500 g	4 kg	LQ18/2	333	
1626	MERCURIC POTASSIUM CYANIDE	1/300	Nil	Nil	Nil	Nil	LQ0/1	20	
1627	MERCUROUS NITRATE	1/500	1 kg	4 kg	500 g	4 kg	LQ18/2	333	
1629	MERCURY ACETATE	1/500	1 kg	4 kg	500 g	4 kg	LQ18/2	333	
1630	MERCURY AMMONIUM CHLORIDE	1/500	1 kg	4 kg	500 g	4 kg	LQ18/2	333	
1631	MERCURY BENZOATE	1/500	1 kg	4 kg	500 g	4 kg	LQ18/2	333	
1634	MERCURY BROMIDES	1/500	1 kg	4 kg	500 g	4 kg	LQ18/2	333	
1636	MERCURY CYANIDE	1/500	1 kg	4 kg	500 g	4 kg	LQ18/2	333	

1637	MERCURY GLUCONATE	1/500	1 kg	4 kg	500 g	4 kg	LQ18/2	333	
1638	MERCURY IODIDE	1/500	1 kg	4 kg	500 g	4 kg	LQ18/2	333	
1639	MERCURY NUCLEATE	1/500	1 kg	4 kg	500 g	4 kg	LQ18/2	333	
1640	MERCURY OLEATE	1/500	1 kg	4 kg	500 g	4 kg	LQ18/2	333	
1641	MERCURY OXIDE	1/500	1 kg	4 kg	500 g	4 kg	LQ18/2	333	
1642	MERCURY OXYCYANIDE, DESENSITISED	1/500	1 kg	4 kg	500 g	4 kg	LQ18/2	333	
1643	MERCURY POTASSIUM IODIDE	1/500	1 kg	4 kg	500 g	4 kg	LQ18/2	333	
1644	MERCURY SALICYLATE	1/500	1 kg	4 kg	500 g	4 kg	LQ18/2	333	
1645	MERCURY SULPHATE	1/500	1 kg	4 kg	500 g	4 kg	LQ18/2	333	
1646	MERCURY THIOCYANATE	1/500	1 kg	4 kg	500 g	4 kg	LQ18/2	333	
1647	METHYL BROMIDE AND ETHYLENE DIBROMIDE MIXTURE, LIQUID	1/300	Nil	Nil	Nil	Nil	LQ0/1	20	
1648	ACETONITRILE	30/500	3 litres	30 kg	1 litre	20 kg	LQ4/2	333	
1649	MOTOR FUEL ANTI-KNOCK MIXTURE	1/300	Nil	Nil	Nil	Nil	LQ0/1	20	
1650	BETA-NAPHTHYLAMINE	1/500	1 kg	4 kg	500 g	4 kg	LQ18/2	333	
1651	NAPHTHYLTHIOUREA	1/500	1 kg	4 kg	500 g	4 kg	LQ18/2	333	43
1652	NAPHTHYLUREA	1/500	1 kg	4 kg	500 g	4 kg	LQ18/2	333	
1653	NICKEL CYANIDE	1/500	1 kg	4 kg	500 g	4 kg	LQ18/2	333	
1654	NICOTINE	1/500	500 ml	2 litres	100 ml	2 litres	LQ17/2	333	
1655	NICOTINE COMPOUND, SOLID, N.O.S. OR NICOTINE PREPARATION, SOLID, N.O.S., PG1	1/300	Nil	Nil	Nil	Nil	LQ0/1	20	43, 274

UN	Substance	Excepted Quantities	LQ Packages		LQ Shrink Wrapped Trays		Limited Quantity Value/Transport Category	Max Load	Special Provisions
			Receptacle Size	Package Gross	Receptacle Size	Package Gross			
1655	NICOTINE COMPOUND, SOLID, N.O.S. OR NICOTINE PREPARATION, SOLID, N.O.S., PG11	1/500	1 kg	4 kg	500 g	4 kg	LQ18/2	333	43, 274
1655	NICOTINE COMPOUND, SOLID, N.O.S. OR NICOTINE PREPARATION, SOLID, N.O.S., PG111	30/1000	6 kg	30 kg	3 kg	20 kg	LQ9/2	333	43, 274
1656	NICOTINE HYDROCHLORIDE, LIQUID OR NICOTINE HYDROCHLORIDE, SOLUTION	1/500	500 ml	2 litres	100 ml	2 litres	LQ17/2	333	43
1656	NICOTINE HYDROCHLORIDE, SOLID	30/1000	5 litres	30 kg	5 litres	20 kg	LQ7/2	333	43
1657	NICOTINE SALICYLATE	1/500	1 kg	4 kg	500 g	4 kg	LQ18/2	333	
1658	NICOTINE SULPHATE, SOLUTION, PG11	1/500	500 ml	2 litres	100 ml	2 litres	LQ17/2	333	
1658	NICOTINE SULPHATE, SOLUTION, PG111	30/1000	5 litres	30 kg	5 litres	20 kg	LQ7/2	333	
1659	NICOTINE TARTRATE	1/500	1 kg	4 kg	500 g	4 kg	LQ18/2	333	
1660	NITRIC OXIDE, COMPRESSED	Nil	Nil	Nil	Nil	Nil	LQ0/1	20	
1661	NITROANILINES (O-,M-,P-)	1/500	1 kg	4 kg	500 g	4 kg	LQ18/2	333	279
1662	NITROBENZENE	1/500	500 ml	2 litres	100 ml	2 litres	LQ17/2	333	279
1663	NITROPHENOLS (O-,M-,P-)	30/1000	6 kg	30 kg	3 kg	20 kg	LQ9/2	333	279
1664	NITROTOLUENES, LIQUID	1/500	500 ml	2 litres	100 ml	2 litres	LQ17/2	333	
1665	NITROXYLENES, LIQUID	1/500	500 ml	2 litres	100 ml	2 litres	LQ17/2	333	

1669	PENTACHLOROETHANE	1/500	500 ml	2 litres	100 ml	2 litres	LQ17/2	333	
1670	PERCHLOROMETHYL MERCAPTAN	1/300	Nil	Nil	Nil	Nil	LQ0/1	20	
1671	PHENOL, SOLID	1/500	1 kg	4 kg	500 g	4 kg	LQ18/2	333	279
1672	PHENYLCARBYLAMINE CHLORIDE	1/300	Nil	Nil	Nil	Nil	LQ0/1	20	
1673	PHENYLENEDIAMINES (O-,M-,P-)	30/1000	6 kg	30 kg	3 kg	20 kg	LQ9/2	333	279
1674	PHENYLMERCURIC ACETATE	1/500	1 kg	4 kg	500 g	4 kg	LQ18/2	333	43
1677	POTASSIUM ARSENATE	1/500	1 kg	4 kg	500 g	4 kg	LQ18/2	333	
1678	POTASSIUM ARSENITE	1/500	1 kg	4 kg	500 g	4 kg	LQ18/2	333	
1679	POTASSIUM CUPROCYANIDE	1/500	1 kg	4 kg	500 g	4 kg	LQ18/2	333	
1680	POTASSIUM CYANIDE	1/300	Nil	Nil	Nil	Nil	LQ0/1	20	
1683	SILVER ARSENITE	1/500	1 kg	4 kg	500 g	4 kg	LQ18/2	333	
1684	SILVER CYANIDE	1/500	1 kg	4 kg	500 g	4 kg	LQ18/2	333	
1685	SODIUM ARSENATE	1/500	1 kg	4 kg	500 g	4 kg	LQ18/2	333	
1686	SODIUM ARSENITE, AQUEOUS SOLUTION, PG11	1/500	500 ml	2 litres	100 ml	2 litres	LQ17/2	333	43
1686	SODIUM ARSENITE, AQUEOUS SOLUTION, PG111	30/1000	5 litres	30 kg	5 litres	20 kg	LQ7/2	333	43
1687	SODIUM AZIDE	1/500	1 kg	4 kg	500 g	4 kg	LQ18/2	333	
1688	SODIUM CACODYLATE	1/500	1 kg	4 kg	500 g	4 kg	LQ18/2	333	
1689	SODIUM CYANIDE	1/300	Nil	Nil	Nil	Nil	LQ0/1	20	
1690	SODIUM FLUORIDE	30/1000	6 kg	30 kg	3 kg	20 kg	LQ9/2	333	

UN	Substance	Excepted Quantities	LQ Packages		LQ Shrink Wrapped Trays		Limited Quantity Value/Transport Category	Max Load	Special Provisions
			Receptacle Size	Package Gross	Receptacle Size	Package Gross			
1691	STRONTIUM ARSENITE	1/500	1 kg	4 kg	500 g	4 kg	LQ18/2	333	
1692	STRYCHNINE OR STRYCHNINE SALTS	1/300	Nil	Nil	Nil	Nil	LQ0/1	20	
1693	TEAR GAS SUBSTANCE, LIQUID, N.O.S., PG1	1/300	Nil	Nil	Nil	Nil	LQ0/1	20	274
1694	BROMOBENZYL CYANIDES, LIQUID	1/300	Nil	Nil	Nil	Nil	LQ0/1	20	138
1695	CHLOROACETONE, STABILISED	1/300	Nil	Nil	Nil	Nil	LQ0/1	20	
1697	CHLOROACETOPHENONE	1/500	1 kg	4 kg	500 g	4 kg	LQ18/2	333	
1698	DIPHENYLAMINE CHLOROARSINE	1/300	Nil	Nil	Nil	Nil	LQ0/1	20	
1699	DIPHENYLCHLOROARSINE, LIQUID	1/300	Nil	Nil	Nil	Nil	LQ0/1	20	
1700	TEAR GAS CANDLES	Nil	1 kg	4 kg	500 g	4 kg	LQ18/2	333	
1701	XYLYL BROMIDE	1/500	500 ml	2 litres	100 ml	2 litres	LQ17/2	333	
1702	1,1,2,2-TETRACHLOROETHANE	1/500	500 ml	2 litres	100 ml	2 litres	LQ17/2	333	
1704	TETRAETHYL DITHIOPYROPHOSPHATE	1/500	1 kg	4 kg	500 g	4 kg	LQ18/2	333	43
1707	THALLIUM COMPOUND, N.O.S.	1/500	1 kg	4 kg	500 g	4 kg	LQ18/2	333	43, 274
1708	TOLUIDINES, LIQUIDS	1/500	500 ml	2 litres	100 ml	2 litres	LQ17/2	333	279
1709	2,4-TOLUYLENEDIAMINE	30/1000	6 kg	30 kg	3 kg	20 kg	LQ9/2	333	
1710	TRICHLOROETHYLENE	30/1000	5 litres	30 kg	5 litres	20 kg	LQ7/2	333	

	Name								
1711	XYLIDINES, LIQUID	1/500	500 ml	2 litres	100 ml	2 litres	LQ17/2	333	
1712	ZINC ARSENATE, ZINC ARSENITE OR ZINC ARSENATE AND ZINC ARSENITE MIXTURE	1/500	1 kg	4 kg	500 g	4 kg	LQ18/2	333	
1713	ZINC CYANIDE	1/300	Nil	Nil	Nil	Nil	LQ0/1	20	
1714	ZINC PHOSPHIDE	Nil	Nil	Nil	Nil	Nil	LQ0/1	20	
1715	ACETIC ANHYDRIDE	30/500	1 litre	30 kg	500 ml	30 kg	LQ22/2	333	
1716	ACETYL BROMIDE	30/500	1 litre	30 kg	500 ml	30 kg	LQ22/2	333	
1717	ACETYL CHLORIDE	30/500	3 litres	30 kg	1 litre	30 kg	LQ4/2	333	
1718	BUTYL ACID PHOSPHATE	30/1000	5 litres	30 kg	5 litres	30 kg	LQ7/3	1000	
1719	CAUSTIC ALKALI LIQUID N.O.S., PG11	30/500	1 litre	30 kg	500 ml	30 kg	LQ22/2	333	274
1719	CAUSTIC ALKALI LIQUID N.O.S., PG111	30/1000	5 litres	30 kg	5 litres	30 kg	LQ7/3	1000	274
1722	ALLYL CHLOROFORMATE	1/300	Nil	Nil	Nil	Nil	LQ0/1	20	
1723	ALLYL IODIDE	30/500	3 litres	30 kg	1 litre	30 kg	LQ4/2	333	
1724	ALLYLTRICHLOROSILANE, STABILISED	30/500	1 litre	30 kg	500 ml	30 kg	LQ22/2	333	
1725	ALUMINIUM BROMIDE, ANHYDROUS	30/500	3 kg	30 kg	1 kg	30 kg	LQ23/2	333	588
1726	ALUMINIUM CHLORIDE, ANHYDROUS	30/500	3 kg	30 kg	1 kg	30 kg	LQ23/2	333	588
1727	AMMONIUM HYDROGENDIFLUORIDE, SOLID	30/500	3 kg	30 kg	1 kg	30 kg	LQ23/2	333	
1728	AMYLTRICHLOROSILANE	30/500	1 litre	30 kg	500 ml	30 kg	LQ22/2	333	
1729	ANISOYL CHLORIDE	30/500	3 kg	30 kg	1 kg	30 kg	LQ23/2	333	
1730	ANTIMONY PENTACHLORIDE, LIQUID	30/500	1 litre	30 kg	500 ml	30 kg	LQ22/2	333	

UN	Substance	Excepted Quantities	LQ Packages		LQ Shrink Wrapped Trays		Limited Quantity Value/Transport Category	Max Load	Special Provisions
			Receptacle Size	Gross Package	Receptacle Size	Package Gross			
1731	ANTIMONY PENTACHLORIDE, SOLUTION, PG11	30/500	1 litre	30 kg	500 ml	20 kg	LQ22//2	333	
1731	ANTIMONY PENTACHLORIDE, SOLUTION, PG111	30/1000	5 litres	30 kg	5 litres	20 kg	LQ7/3	1000	
1732	ANTIMONY PENTAFLUORIDE	30/500	1 litre	30 kg	500 ml	20 kg	LQ22/2	333	
1733	ANTIMONY TRICHLORIDE	30/500	3 kg	30 kg	1 kg	20 kg	LQ23/2	333	
1736	BENZOYL CHLORIDE	30/500	1 litre	30 kg	500 ml	20 kg	LQ22/2	333	
1737	BENZYL BROMIDE	1/500	500 ml	2 litres	100 ml	2 litres	LQ17/2	333	
1738	BENZYL CHLORIDE	1/500	500 ml	2 litres	100 ml	2 litres	LQ17/2	333	
1739	BENZYL CHLOROFORMATE	Nil	Nil	Nil	Nil	Nil	LQ0/1	20	
1740	HYDROGENDIFLUORIDES, N.O.S., PG11	30/500	3 kg	30 kg	1 kg	20 kg	LQ23/2	333	274, 517
1740	HYDROGENDIFLUORIDES, N.O.S., PG111	30/1000	6 kg	30 kg	2 kg	20 kg	LQ24/3	1000	274, 517
1741	BORON TRICHLORIDE	Nil	Nil	Nil	Nil	Nil	LQ0/1	20	
1742	BORON TRIFLUORIDE ACETIC ACID COMPLEX	30/500	1 litre	30 kg	500 ml	20 kg	LQ22/2	333	
1743	BORON TRIFLUORIDE PROPIONIC ACID COMPLEX	30/500	1 litre	30 kg	500 ml	20 kg	LQ22/2	333	
1744	BROMINE OR BROMINE SOLUTION	Nil	Nil	Nil	Nil	Nil	LQ0/1	20	

UN No.	Name						LQ		
1745	BROMINE PENTAFLUORIDE	Nil	Nil	Nil	Nil	Nil	LQ0/1	20	
1746	BROMINE TRIFLUORIDE	Nil	Nil	Nil	Nil	Nil	LQ0/1	20	
1747	BUTYLTRICHLOROSILANE	30/500	1 litre	30 kg	500 ml	20 kg	LQ22/2	333	
1748	CALCIUM HYPOCHLORITE, DRY OR CALCIUM HYPOCHLORITE MIXTURE, DRY WITH MORE THAN 39% AVAILABLE CHLORINE (8.8% AVAILABLE OXYGEN), PG11	30/500	500 g	30 kg	500 g	20 kg	LQ11/2	333	313, 314, 589
1748	CALCIUM HYPOCHLORITE, DRY OR CALCIUM HYPOCHLORITE MIXTURE, DRY WITH MORE THAN 39% AVAILABLE CHLORINE (8.8% AVAILABLE OXYGEN), PG111	30/1000	1 kg	30 kg	1 kg	20 kg	LQ12/3	1000	316, 589
1749	CHLORINE TRIFLUORIDE	Nil	Nil	Nil	Nil	Nil	LQ0/1	20	
1750	CHLOROACETIC ACID, SOLUTION	1/500	500 ml	2 litres	100 ml	2 litres	LQ17/2	333	
1751	CHLOROACETIC ACID, SOLID	1/500	1 kg	4 kg	500 g	4 kg	LQ18/2	333	
1752	CHLOROACETYL CHLORIDE	1/300	Nil	Nil	Nil	Nil	LQ0/1	20	
1753	CHLOROPHENYLTRICHLOROSILANE	30/500	1 litre	30 kg	500 ml	20 kg	LQ22/2	333	
1754	CHLOROSULPHONIC ACID (WITH OR WITHOUT SULPHUR TRIOXIDE)	Nil	Nil	Nil	Nil	Nil	LQ0/1	20	
1755	CHROMIC ACID, SOLUTION, PG11	30/500	1 litre	30 kg	500 ml	20 kg	LQ22/2	333	518
1756	CHROMIC FLUORIDE, SOLID	30/500	3 kg	30 kg	1 kg	20 kg	LQ23/2	333	
1757	CHROMIC FLUORIDE, SOLUTION, PG11	30/500	1 litre	30 kg	500 ml	20 kg	LQ22/2	333	
1757	CHROMIC FLUORIDE, SOLUTION, PG111	30/1000	5 litres	30 kg	5 litres	20 kg	LQ7/3	1000	
1758	CHROMIUM OXYCHLORIDE	Nil	Nil	Nil	Nil	Nil	LQ0/1	20	

UN	Substance	Excepted Quantities	LQ Packages		LQ Shrink Wrapped Trays		Limited Quantity Value/Transport Category	Max Load	Special Provisions
			Receptacle Size	Package Gross	Receptacle Size	Package Gross			
1759	CORROSIVE SOLID, N.O.S., PG1	Nil	Nil	Nil	Nil	Nil	LQ0/1	20	274
1759	CORROSIVE SOLID, N.O.S., PG11	30/500	3 kg	30 kg	1 kg	20 kg	LQ23/2	333	274
1759	CORROSIVE SOLID, N.O.S., PG111	30/1000	6 kg	30 kg	2 kg	20 kg	LQ24/3	1000	274
1760	CORROSIVE LIQUID, N.O.S., PG1	Nil	Nil	Nil	Nil	Nil	LQ0/1	20	274
1760	CORROSIVE LIQUID, N.O.S., PG11	30/500	1 litre	30 kg	500 ml	20 kg	LQ22/2	333	274
1760	CORROSIVE LIQUID, N.O.S., PG111	30/1000	5 litres	30 kg	5 litres	20 kg	LQ7/3	1000	274
1761	CUPRIETHYLENEDIAMINE SOLUTION, PG11	30/500	1 litre	30 kg	500 ml	20 kg	LQ22/2	333	
1761	CUPRIETHYLENEDIAMINE SOLUTION, PG111	30/1000	5 litres	30 kg	5 litres	20 kg	LQ7/3	1000	
1762	CYCLOHEXENYLTRICHLOROSILANE	30/500	1 litre	30 kg	500 ml	20 kg	LQ22/2	333	
1763	CYCLOHEXYLTRICHLOROSILANE	30/500	1 litre	30 kg	500 ml	20 kg	LQ22/2	333	
1764	DICHLOROACETIC ACID	30/500	1 litre	30 kg	500 ml	20 kg	LQ22/2	333	
1765	DICHLOROACETYL CHLORIDE	30/500	1 litre	30 kg	500 ml	20 kg	LQ22/2	333	
1766	DICHLOROPHENYLTRICHLOROSILANE	30/500	1 litre	30 kg	500 ml	20 kg	LQ22/2	333	
1767	DIETHYLDICHLOROSILANE	30/500	1 litre	30 kg	500 ml	20 kg	LQ22/2	333	
1768	DIFLUOROPHOSPHORIC ACID, ANHYDROUS	30/500	1 litre	30 kg	500 ml	20 kg	LQ22/2	333	

1769	DIPHENYLDICHLOROSILANE	30/500	1 litre	30 kg	500 ml	20 kg	LQ22/2	333	
1770	DIPHENYLMETHYL BROMIDE	30/500	3 kg	30 kg	1 kg	20 kg	LQ23/2	333	
1771	DODECYLTRICHLOROSILANE	30/500	1 litre	30 kg	500 ml	20 kg	LQ22/2	333	
1773	FERRIC CHLORIDE, ANHYDROUS	30/1000	6 kg	30 kg	2 kg	20 kg	LQ24/3	1000	590
1774	FIRE EXTINGUISHER CHARGES, CORROSIVE LIQUID	Nil	1 litre	30 kg	500 ml	20 kg	LQ22/2	333	
1775	FLUOROBORIC ACID	30/500	1 litre	30 kg	500 ml	20 kg	LQ22/2	333	
1776	FLUOROPHOSPHORIC ACID, ANHYDROUS	30/500	1 litre	30 kg	500 ml	20 kg	LQ22/2	333	
1777	FLUOROSULPHONIC ACID	Nil	Nil	Nil	Nil	Nil	LQ0/1	20	
1778	FLUOROSILICIC ACID	30/500	1 litre	30 kg	500 ml	20 kg	LQ22/2	333	
1779	FORMIC ACID	30/500	1 litre	30 kg	500 ml	20 kg	LQ22/2	333	
1780	FUMARYL CHLORIDE	30/500	1 litre	30 kg	500 ml	20 kg	LQ22/2	333	
1781	HEXADECYLTRICHLOROSILANE	30/500	1 litre	30 kg	500 ml	20 kg	LQ22/2	333	
1782	HEXAFLUOROPHOSPHORIC ACID	30/500	1 litre	30 kg	500 ml	20 kg	LQ22/2	333	
1783	HEXAMETHYLENEDIAMINE SOLUTION, PG11	30/500	1 litre	30 kg	500 ml	20 kg	LQ22/2	333	
1783	HEXAMETHYLENEDIAMINE SOLUTION, PG111	30/1000	5 litres	30 kg	5 litres	20 kg	LQ7/3	1000	
1784	HEXYLTRICHLOROSILANE	30/500	1 litre	30 kg	500 ml	20 kg	LQ22/2	333	
1786	HYDROFLUORIC ACID AND SULPHURIC ACID MIXTURE	Nil	Nil	Nil	Nil	Nil	LQ0/1	20	
1787	HYDRIODIC ACID, PG11	30/500	1 litre	30 kg	500 ml	20 kg	LQ22/2	333	

UN	Substance	Excepted Quantities	LQ Packages		LQ Shrink Wrapped Trays		Limited Quantity Value/Transport Category	Max Load	Special Provisions
			Receptacle Size	Package Gross	Receptacle Size	Package Gross			
1787	HYDRIODIC ACID, PG111	30/1000	5 litres	30 kg	5 litres	20 kg	LQ7/3	1000	
1788	HYDROBROMIC ACID, PG11	30/500	1 litre	30 kg	500 ml	20 kg	LQ22/2	333	519
1788	HYDROBROMIC ACID, PG111	30/1000	5 litres	30 kg	5 litres	20 kg	LQ7/3	1000	519
1789	HYDROCHLORIC ACID, PG11	30/500	1 litre	30 kg	500 ml	20 kg	LQ22/2	333	520
1789	HYDROCHLORIC ACID, PG111	30/1000	5 litres	30 kg	5 litres	20 kg	LQ7/3	1000	520
1790	HYDROFLUORIC ACID, WITH MORE THAN 85% HYDROFLUORIC ACID, PG1	Nil	Nil	Nil	Nil	Nil	LQ0/1	20	640I
1790	HYDROFLUORIC ACID, WITH MORE THAN 60% BUT NOT MORE THAN 85% HYDROFLUORIC ACID, PG1	Nil	Nil	Nil	Nil	Nil	LQ0/1	20	640J
1790	HYDROFLUORIC ACID, WITH NOT MORE THAN 60% HYDROFLUORIC ACID, PG11	30/500	1 litre	30 kg	500 ml	20 kg	LQ22/2	333	
1791	HYPOCHLORITE SOLUTION, PG11	30/500	1 litre	30 kg	500 ml	20 kg	LQ22/2	333	521
1791	HYPOCHLORITE SOLUTION, PG111	30/1000	5 litres	30 kg	5 litres	20 kg	LQ7/3	1000	521
1792	IODINE MONOCHLORIDE	30/500	1 litre	30 kg	500 ml	20 kg	LQ22/2	333	
1793	ISOPROPYL ACID PHOSPHATE	30/1000	5 litres	30 kg	5 litres	20 kg	LQ7/3	1000	
1794	LEAD SULPHATE WITH MORE THAN 3% FREE ACID	30/500	3 kg	30 kg	1 kg	20 kg	LQ23/2	333	591

1796	NITRATING ACID, MIXTURE, WITH MORE THAN 50% NITRIC ACID, PG1	Nil	Nil	Nil	Nil	Nil	LQ0/1	20	
1796	NITRATING ACID, MIXTURE, WITH NOT MORE THAN 50% NITRIC ACID, PG11	30/500	1 litre	30 kg	500 ml	20 kg	LQ22/2	333	
1798	NITROHYDROCHLORIC ACID	Carriage	Prohibited		-	-	Carriage	Prohibited	
1799	NONYLTRICHLOROSILANE	30/500	1 litre	30 kg	500 ml	20 kg	LQ22/2	333	
1800	OCTADECYLTRICHLOROSILANE	30/500	1 litre	30 kg	500 ml	20 kg	LQ22/2	333	
1801	OCTYLTRICHLOROSILANE	30/500	1 litre	30 kg	500 ml	20 kg	LQ22/2	333	
1802	PERCHLORIC ACID, WITH NOT MORE THAN 50% ACID, BY MASS	30/500	1 litre	30 kg	500 ml	20 kg	LQ22/2	333	522
1803	PHENOLSULPHONIC ACID, LIQUID	30/500	1 litre	30 kg	500 ml	20 kg	LQ22/2	333	
1804	PHENYLTRICHLOROSILANE	30/500	1 litre	30 kg	500 ml	20 kg	LQ22/2	333	
1805	PHOSPHORIC ACID, LIQUID	30/1000	5 litres	30 kg	5 litres	20 kg	LQ7/3	1000	
1806	PHOSPHORUS PENTACHLORIDE	30/500	3 kg	30 kg	1 kg	20 kg	LQ23/2	333	
1807	PHOSPHORUS PENTOXIDE	30/500	3 kg	30 kg	1 kg	20 kg	LQ23/2	333	
1808	PHOSPHORUS TRIBROMIDE	30/500	1 litre	30 kg	500 ml	20 kg	LQ22/2	333	
1809	PHOSPHORUS TRICHLORIDE	1/300	Nil	Nil	Nil	Nil	LQ0/1	20	
1810	PHOSPHORUS OXYCHLORIDE	30/500	1 litre	30 kg	500 ml	20 kg	LQ22/2	333	
1811	POTASSIUM HYDROGENDIFLUORIDE	30/500	3 kg	30 kg	1 kg	20 kg	LQ23/2	333	
1812	POTASSIUM FLUORIDE	30/1000	6 kg	30 kg	3 kg	20 kg	LQ9/2	333	
1813	POTASSIUM HYDROXIDE, SOLID	30/500	3 kg	30 kg	1 kg	20 kg	LQ23/2	333	

UN	Substance	Excepted Quantities	LQ Packages Receptacle Size	LQ Packages Gross Package	LQ Shrink Wrapped Trays Receptacle Size	LQ Shrink Wrapped Trays Gross Package	Limited Quantity Value/Transport Category	Max Load	Special Provisions
1814	POTASSIUM HYDROXIDE SOLUTION, PG11	30/500	1 litre	30 kg	500 ml	20 kg	LQ22/2	333	
1814	POTASSIUM HYDROXIDE SOLUTION, PG111	30/1000	5 litres	30 kg	5 litres	20 kg	LQ7/3	1000	
1815	PROPIONYL CHLORIDE	30/500	3 litres	30 kg	1 litre	20 kg	LQ4/2	333	
1816	PROPYLTRICHLOROSILANE	30/500	1 litre	30 kg	500 ml	20 kg	LQ22/2	333	
1817	PYROSULPHURYL CHLORIDE	30/500	1 litre	30 kg	500 ml	20 kg	LQ22/2	333	
1818	SILICON TETRACHLORIDE	30/500	Nil	Nil	Nil	Nil	LQ0/2	333	
1819	SODIUM ALUMINATE SOLUTION, PG11	30/500	1 litre	30 kg	500 ml	20 kg	LQ22/2	333	
1819	SODIUM ALUMINATE SOLUTION, PG111	30/1000	5 litres	30 kg	5 litres	20 kg	LQ7/3	1000	
1823	SODIUM HYDROXIDE, SOLID	30/500	3 kg	30 kg	1 kg	20 kg	LQ23/2	333	
1824	SODIUM HYDROXIDE SOLUTION, PG11	30/500	1 litre	30 kg	500 ml	20 kg	LQ22/2	333	
1824	SODIUM HYDROXIDE SOLUTION, PG111	30/1000	5 litres	30 kg	5 litres	20 kg	LQ7/3	1000	
1825	SODIUM MONOXIDE	30/500	3 kg	30 kg	1 kg	20 kg	LQ23/2	333	
1826	NITRATING ACID MIXTURE, SPENT, WITH MORE THAN 50% NITRIC ACID	Nil	Nil	Nil	Nil	Nil	LQ0/1	20	113
1826	NITRATING ACID MIXTURE, SPENT, WITH NOT MORE THAN 50% NITRIC ACID	30/500	1 litre	30 kg	500 ml	20 kg	LQ22/2	333	113
1827	STANNIC CHLORIDE, ANHYDROUS	30/500	1 litre	30 kg	500 ml	20 kg	LQ22/2	333	

1828	SULPHUR CHLORIDES	Nil	Nil	Nil	Nil	Nil	LQ0/1	20	
1829	SULPHUR TRIOXIDE, STABILISED	Nil	Nil	Nil	Nil	Nil	LQ0/1	20	623
1830	SULPHURIC ACID WITH MORE THAN 51% ACID	30/500	1 litre	30 kg	500 ml	20 kg	LQ22/2	333	
1831	SULPHURIC ACID, FUMING	Nil	Nil	Nil	Nil	Nil	LQ0/1	20	
1832	SULPHURIC ACID, SPENT	30/500	1 litre	30 kg	500 ml	20 kg	LQ22/2	333	113
1833	SULPHUROUS ACID	30/500	1 litre	30 kg	500 ml	20 kg	LQ22/2	333	
1834	SULPHURYL CHLORIDE	Nil	Nil	Nil	Nil	Nil	LQ0/1	20	
1835	TETRAMETHYLAMMONIUM HYDROXIDE, PG11	30/500	1 litre	30 kg	500 ml	20 kg	LQ22/2	333	
1835	TETRAMETHYLAMMONIUM HYDROXIDE, PG111	30/1000	5 litres	30 kg	5 litres	20 kg	LQ7/3	1000	
1836	THIONYL CHLORIDE	Nil	Nil	Nil	Nil	Nil	LQ0/1	20	
1837	THIOPHOSPHORYL CHLORIDE	30/500	1 litre	30 kg	500 ml	20 kg	LQ22/2	333	
1838	TITANIUM TETRACHLORIDE	30/500	1 litre	30 kg	500 ml	20 kg	LQ22/2	333	
1839	TRICHLOROACETIC ACID	30/500	3 kg	30 kg	1 kg	20 kg	LQ23/2	333	
1840	ZINC CHLORIDE SOLUTION	30/1000	5 litres	30 kg	5 litres	20 kg	LQ7/3	1000	
1841	ACETALDEHYDE AMMONIA	30/1000	6 kg	30 kg	6 kg	20 kg	LQ27/3	1000	
1843	AMMONIUM DINITRO-O-CRESOLATE	1/500	1 kg	4 kg	500 g	4 kg	LQ18/2	333	
1845	CARBON DIOXIDE, SOLID (DRY ICE)	Not	Subject	To ADR	-	-	Not subject	to	ADR
1846	CARBON TETRACHLORIDE	1/500	500 ml	2 litres	100 ml	2 litres	LQ17/2	333	

UN	Substance	Excepted Quantities	LQ Packages		LQ Shrink Wrapped Trays		Limited Quantity Value/Transport Category	Max Load	Special Provisions
			Receptacle Size	Gross Package	Receptacle Size	Gross Package			
1847	POTASSIUM SULPHIDE, HYDRATED WITH NOT LESS THAN 30% WATER OF CRYSTALLISATION	30/500	3 kg	30 kg	1 kg	20 kg	LQ23/2	333	
1848	PROPIONIC ACID	30/1000	5 litres	30 kg	5 litres	20 kg	LQ7/3	1000	
1849	SODIUM SULPHIDE, HYDRATED WITH NOT LESS THAN 30% WATER	30/500	3 kg	30 kg	1 kg	20 kg	LQ23/2	333	
1851	MEDICINE, LIQUID, TOXIC, N.O.S., PG11	1/500	500 ml	2 litres	100 ml	2 litres	LQ17/2	333	221, 274, 601
1851	MEDICINE, LIQUID, TOXIC, N.O.S., PG111	30/1000	5 litres	30 kg	5 litres	20 kg	LQ7/2	333	221, 274, 601
1854	BARIUM ALLOYS, PYROPHOBIC	Nil	Nil	Nil	Nil	Nil	LQ0/0	Nil	
1858	HEXAFLUOROPROPYLENE (REFRIGERANT GAS R1216)	30/1000	120 ml	30 kg	120 ml	20 kg	LQ1/3	1000	
1855	CALCIUM, PYROPHORIC OR CALCIUM ALLOYS, PYROPHORIC	Nil	Nil	Nil	Nil	Nil	LQ0/0	Nil	
1856	RAGS, OILY	Not	Subject	To	ADR	–	Not Subject	To	ADR
1857	TEXTILE WASTE, WET	Not	Subject	To	ADR	–	Not Subject	To	ADR
1859	SILICON TETRAFLUORIDE	Nil	Nil	Nil	Nil	Nil	LQ0/1	20	

1860	VINYL FLUORIDE, STABILISED	Nil	Nil	Nil	Nil	Nil	LQ0/2	333	
1862	ETHYL CROTONATE	30/500	3 litres	30 kg	1 litre	20 kg	LQ4/2	333	
1863	FUEL, AVIATION, TURBINE ENGINE, PG1	30/300	500 ml	1 litre	Not	Allowed	LQ3/1	20	
1863	FUEL, AVIATION, TURBINE ENGINE, PG11	30/500	3 litres	30 kg	1 litre	20 kg	LQ4/2	333	640 C or D
1863	FUEL, AVIATION, TURBINE ENGINE, PG111	30/1000	5 litres	30 kg	5 litres	20 kg	LQ7/3	1000	
1865	N-PROPYL NITRATE	30/500	3 litres	30 kg	1 litre	20 kg	LQ4/2	333	
1866	RESIN SOLUTION, FLAMMABLE, PG1	30/300	500 ml	1 litre	Not	Allowed	LQ3/1	20	
1866	RESIN SOLUTION, FLAMMABLE, PG11	30/500	5 litres	30 kg	1 litre	20 kg	LQ6/2	333	640 C or D
1866	RESIN SOLUTION, FLAMMABLE, PG111	30/1000	5 litres	30 kg	5 litres	20 kg	LQ7/3	1000	640 E-H
1868	DECABORANE	30/500	Nil	Nil	Nil	Nil	LQ0/2	333	
1869	MAGNESIUM OR MAGNESIUM ALLOYS, WITH MORE THAN 50% MAGNESIUM IN PELLETS, TURNING OR RIBBONS	30/1000	6 kg	30 kg	3 kg	20 kg	LQ9/3	1000	59
1870	POTASSIUM BOROHYDRIDE	Nil	Nil	Nil	Nil	Nil	LQ0/1	20	
1871	TITANIUM HYDRIDE	30/500	3 kg	30 kg	500 g	20 kg	LQ8/2	333	
1872	LEAD DIOXIDE	30/1000	1 kg	30 kg	1 kg	20 kg	LQ12/3	1000	
1873	PERCHLORIC ACID, WITH MORE THAN 50% BUT NOT MORE THAN 72% ACID, BY MASS	Nil	Nil	Nil	Nil	Nil	LQ0/1	20	60
1884	BARIUM OXIDE	30/1000	6 kg	24 kg	3 kg	20 kg	LQ9/2	333	
1885	BENZIDINE	1/500	1 kg	4 kg	500 g	4 kg	LQ18/2	333	
1886	BENZYLIDINE CHLORIDE	1/500	500 ml	2 litres	100 ml	2 litres	LQ17/2	333	

UN	Substance	Excepted Quantities	LQ Packages Receptacle Size	LQ Packages Package Gross	LQ Shrink Wrapped Trays Receptacle Size	LQ Shrink Wrapped Trays Package Gross	Limited Quantity Value/Transport Category	Max Load	Special Provisions
1887	BROMOCHLOROMETHANE	30/1000	5 litres	30 kg	5 litres	20 kg	LQ7/2	333	
1888	CHLOROFORM	30/1000	5 litres	30 kg	5 litres	20 kg	LQ7/2	333	
1889	CYANOGEN BROMIDE	1/300	Nil	Nil	Nil	Nil	LQ0/1	20	
1891	ETHYL BROMIDE	1/500	500 ml	2 litres	100 ml	2 litres	LQ17/2	333	
1892	ETHYLDICHLOROARSINE	1/300	Nil	Nil	Nil	Nil	LQ0/1	20	
1894	PHENYLMERCURIC HYDROXIDE	1/500	1 kg	4 kg	500 g	4 kg	LQ18/2	333	
1895	PHENYLMERCURIC NITRATE	1/500	1 kg	4 kg	500 g	4 kg	LQ18/2	333	
1897	TETRACHLOROETHYLENE	30/1000	5 litres	30 kg	5 litres	20 kg	LQ7/2	333	
1898	ACETYL IODIDE	30/500	1 litre	30 kg	500 ml	20 kg	LQ22/2	333	
1902	DIISOOCTYL ACID PHOSPHATE	30/1000	5 litres	30 kg	5 litres	20 kg	LQ7/3	1000	
1903	DISINFECTANT, LIQUID, CORROSIVE, N.O.S., PG1	Nil	Nil	Nil	Nil	Nil	LQ0/1	20	274
1903	DISINFECTANT, LIQUID, CORROSIVE, N.O.S., PG11	30/500	1 litre	30 kg	500 ml	20 kg	LQ22/2	333	274
1903	DISINFECTANT, LIQUID, CORROSIVE, N.O.S., PG111	30/1000	5 litres	30 kg	5 litres	20 kg	LQ7/3	1000	274
1905	SELENIC ACID	Nil	Nil	Nil	Nil	Nil	LQ0/1	20	
1906	SLUDGE ACID	30/500	1 litre	30 kg	500 ml	20 kg	LQ22/2	333	

		30/1000	6 kg	30 kg	2 kg	20 kg	LQ24/3	1000	62
1907	SODA LIME, WITH MORE THAN 4% SODIUM HYDROXIDE	30/1000	6 kg	30 kg	2 kg	20 kg	LQ24/3	1000	62
1908	CHLORITE SOLUTION, PG11	30/500	1 litre	30 kg	500 ml	20 kg	LQ22/2	333	521
1910	CALCIUM OXIDE	Not	Subject	To	ADR	–	Not Subject	to	ADR
1911	DIBORANE	Nil	Nil	Nil	Nil	Nil	LQ0/1	20	
1912	METHYL CHLORIDE AND METHYLENE CHLORIDE MIXTURE	Nil	Nil	Nil	Nil	Nil	LQ0/2	333	228
1913	NEON, REFRIGERATED, LIQUID	30/1000	120 ml	30 kg	120 ml	20 kg	LQ1/3	1000	593
1914	BUTYL PROPIONATES	30/1000	5 litres	30 kg	5 litres	20 kg	LQ7/3	1000	
1915	CYCLOHEXANONE	30/1000	5 litres	30 kg	5 litres	20 kg	LQ7/3	1000	
1916	2,2-DICHLORODIETHYL ETHER	1/500	500 ml	2 litres	100 ml	2 litres	LQ17/2	333	
1917	ETHYL ACRYLATE, STABILISED	30/500	3 litres	30 kg	1 litre	20 kg	LQ4/2	333	
1918	ISOPROPYLBENZENE	30/1000	5 litres	30 kg	5 litres	20 kg	LQ7/3	1000	
1919	METHYL ACRYLATE, STABILISED	30/500	3 litres	30 kg	1 litre	20 kg	LQ4/2	333	
1920	NONANES	30/1000	5 litres	30 kg	5 litres	20 kg	LQ7/3	1000	
1921	PROPYLENEIMINE, STABILISED	Nil	Nil	Nil	Nil	Nil	LQ0/1	20	
1922	PYRROLIDINE	30/500	3 litres	30 kg	1 litre	20 kg	LQ4/2	333	
1923	CALCIUM DITHIONITE (CALCIUM HYDROSULPHITE)	30/500	Nil	Nil	Nil	Nil	LQ0/2	333	
1928	METHYL MAGNESIUM BROMIDE IN ETHYL ETHER	Nil	Nil	Nil	Nil	Nil	LQ0/0	Nil	
1929	POTASSIUM DITHIONITE (POTASSIUM HYDROSULPHITE)	30/500	Nil	Nil	Nil	Nil	LQ0/2	333	

UN	Substance	Excepted Quantities	LQ Packages		LQ Shrink Wrapped Trays		Limited Quantity Value/Transport Category	Max Load	Special Provisions
			Receptacle Size	Package Gross	Receptacle Size	Package Gross			
1931	ZINC DITHIONITE (ZINC HYDROSULPHITE)	30/1000	6 kg	30 kg	6 kg	20 kg	LQ27/3	1000	
1932	ZIRCONIUM SCRAP	30/1000	Nil	Nil	Nil	Nil	LQ0/3	1000	524, 592
1935	CYANIDE SOLUTION, N.O.S., PG1	1/300	Nil	Nil	Nil	Nil	LQ0/1	20	274, 525
1935	CYANIDE SOLUTION, N.O.S., PG11	1/500	500 ml	2 litres	100 ml	2 litres	LQ17/2	333	274, 525
1935	CYANIDE SOLUTION, N.O.S., PG111	30/1000	5 litres	30 kg	5 litres	20 kg	LQ7/2	333	274, 525
1938	BROMOACETIC ACID, PG11	30/500	1 litre	30 kg	500 ml	20 kg	LQ22/2	333	
1938	BROMOACETIC ACID, PG111	30/1000	5 litres	30 kg	5 litres	20 kg	LQ7/3	1000	
1939	PHOSPHORUS OXYBROMIDE	30/500	3 kg	30 kg	1 kg	20 kg	LQ23/2	333	
1940	THIOGLYCOLIC ACID	30/500	1 litre	30 kg	500 ml	20 kg	LQ22/2	333	
1941	DIBROMODIFLUOROMETHANE	30/1000	3 litres	30 kg	3 litres	20 kg	LQ28/3	1000	
1942	AMMONIUM NITRATE	30/1000	1 kg	30 kg	1 kg	20 kg	LQ12/3	1000	306, 611
1945	MATCHES, WAX 'VESTA'	30/1000	6 kg	30 kg	3 kg	20 kg	LQ9/4	Unlimited	
1950	AEROSOLS 5A, 5C, 5CO, 5F, 5 FC, 5O (REFER TO CLASSIFICATION CODE)	Nil	1 litre	30 kg	1 litre	20 kg	LQ2/ 5A&5O = 3 5F =2 5C,5CO, 5FC, = 1	1000 33 20	All = 190, 327, 625
1950	AEROSOLS 5T, 5TC, 5TFC, 5TO, 5TOC	Nil	120 ml	30 kg	120 ml	20 kg	LQ1/1	20	190, 327, 625

UN No.	Name								
1951	ARGON, REFRIGERATED, LIQUID	30/1000	120 ml	30 kg	120 ml	20 kg	LQ1/3	1000	593
1952	ETHYLENE OXIDE AND CARBON DIOXIDE MIXTURE WITH NOT MORE THAN 9% ETHYLENE OXIDE	30/1000	120 ml	30 kg	120 ml	20 kg	LQ1/3	1000	
1953	COMPRESSED GAS, TOXIC, FLAMMABLE, N.O.S.	Nil	Nil	Nil	Nil	Nil	LQ0/1	20	274
1954	COMPRESSED GAS, FLAMMABLE, N.O.S.	Nil	Nil	Nil	Nil	Nil	LQ0/2	333	274
1955	COMPRESSED GAS, TOXIC, N.O.S.	Nil	Nil	Nil	Nil	Nil	LQ0/1	20	274
1956	COMPRESSED GAS, N.O.S.	30/1000	120 ml	30 kg	120 ml	20 kg	LQ1/3	1000	274, 292 567
1957	DEUTERIUM, COMPRESSED	Nil	Nil	Nil	Nil	Nil	LQ0/2	333	
1958	1,2-DICHLORO-1,1,2,2-TETRAFLUOROETHANE (REFRIGERANT GAS R114)	30/1000	120 ml	30 kg	120 ml	20 kg	LQ1/3	1000	
1959	1,1-DIFLUOROETHYLENE (REFRIGERANT GAS R1132A)	Nil	Nil	Nil	Nil	Nil	LQ0/2	333	
1961	ETHANE, REFRIGERATED LIQUID	Nil	Nil	Nil	Nil	Nil	LQ0/2	333	
1962	ETHYLENE	Nil	Nil	Nil	Nil	Nil	LQ0/2	333	
1963	HELIUM, REFRIGERATED LIQUID	30/1000	120 ml	30 kg	120 ml	20 kg	LQ1/3	1000	593
1964	HYDROCARBON GAS MIXTURE, COMPRESSED, N.O.S.	Nil	Nil	Nil	Nil	Nil	LQ0/2	333	274
1965	HYDROCARBON GAS MIXTURE, LIQUEFIED, N.O.S.	Nil	Nil	Nil	Nil	Nil	LQ0/2	333	274, 583, 652
1966	HYDROGEN, REFRIGERATED LIQUID	Nil	Nil	Nil	Nil	Nil	LQ0/2	333	
1967	INSECTICIDE GAS, TOXIC, N.O.S.	Nil	Nil	Nil	Nil	Nil	LQ0/1	20	274

UN	Substance	Excepted Quantities	LQ Packages		LQ Shrink Wrapped Trays		Limited Quantity Value/Transport Category	Max Load	Special Provisions
			Receptacle Size	Package Gross	Receptacle Size	Package Gross			
1968	INSECTICIDE GAS, N.O.S.	30/1000	120 ml	30 kg	120 ml	20 kg	LQ1/3	1000	274
1969	ISOBUTANE	Nil	Nil	Nil	Nil	Nil	LQ0/2	333	
1970	KRYPTON, REFRIGERATED LIQUID	30/1000	120 ml	30 kg	120 ml	20 kg	LQ1/3	1000	593
1971	METHANE, COMPRESSED OR NATURAL GAS, COMPRESSED (WITH HIGH METHANE CONTENT)	Nil	Nil	Nil	Nil	Nil	LQ0/2	333	
1972	METHANE, REFRIGERATED LIQUID OR NATURAL GAS, REFRIGERATED LIQUID (WITH HIGH METHANE CONTENT)	Nil	Nil	Nil	Nil	Nil	LQ0/2	333	
1973	CHLORODIFLUOROMETHANE AND CHLOROPENTAFLUOROETHANE MIXTURE, WITH FIXED BOILING POINT WITH APPROXIMATELY 49% OF CHLORODIFLUOROMETHANE (REFRIGERANT GAS R502)	30/1000	120 ml	30 kg	120 ml	20 kg	LQ1/3	1000	
1974	CHLORODIFLUOROBROMOMETHANE (REFRIGERANT GAS R12B1)	30/1000	120 ml	30 kg	120 ml	20 kg	LQ1/3	1000	
1975	NITRIC OXIDE AND DINITROGEN TETROXIDE MIXTURE (NITRIC OXIDE AND NITROGEN DIOXIDE MIXTURE)	Nil	Nil	Nil	Nil	Nil	LQ0/1	20	
1976	OCTAFLUOROCYCLOBUTANE (REFRIGERANT GAS RC318)	30/1000	120 ml	30 kg	120 ml	20 kg	LQ1/3	1000	

1977	NITROGEN, REFRIGERATED LIQUID	30/1000	120 ml	30 kg	120 ml	20 kg	LQ1/3	1000	593
1978	PROPANE	Nil	Nil	Nil	Nil	Nil	LQ0/2	333	652
1982	TETRAFLUOROMETHANE (REFRIGERANT GAS R14)	30/1000	120 ml	30 kg	120 ml	20 kg	LQ1/3	1000	
1983	1-CHLORO-2,2,2-TRIFLUOROETHANE (REFRIGERANT GAS R133A)	30/1000	120 ml	30 kg	120 ml	20 kg	LQ1/3	1000	
1984	TRIFLUOROMETHANE (REFRIGERANT GAS R23)	30/1000	120 ml	30 kg	120 ml	20 kg	LQ1/3	1000	
1986	ALCOHOLS, FLAMMABLE, TOXIC, N.O.S., PG1	Nil	Nil	Nil	Nil	Nil	LQ0/1	20	274
1986	ALCOHOLS, FLAMMABLE, TOXIC, N.O.S., PG11	30/500	Nil	Nil	Nil	Nil	LQ0/2	333	274
1986	ALCOHOLS, FLAMMABLE, TOXIC, N.O.S., PG111	30/1000	5 litres	30 kg	5 litres	20 kg	LQ7/3	1000	274
1987	ALCOHOLS, N.O.S., PG11	30/500	3 litres	30 kg	1 litre	20 kg	LQ4/2	333	274, 330, 601, 640 C& D
1987	ALCOHOLS, N.O.S., PG111	30/1000	5 litres	30 kg	5 litres	20 kg	LQ7/3	1000	274, 601
1988	ALDEHYDES, FLAMMABLE, TOXIC, N.O.S., PG1	Nil	Nil	Nil	Nil	Nil	LQ0/1	20	274
1988	ALDEHYDES, FLAMMABLE, TOXIC, N.O.S., PG11	30/500	Nil	Nil	Nil	Nil	LQ0/2	333	274
1988	ALDEHYDES, FLAMMABLE, TOXIC, N.O.S., PG111	30/1000	5 litres	30 kg	5 litres	20 kg	LQ7/3	1000	274
1989	ALDEHYDES, N.O.S., PG1	30/300	500 ml	1 litre	Not	Allowed	LQ3/1	20	274, 640A-B
1989	ALDEHYDES, N.O.S., PG11	30/500	3 litres	30 kg	1 litre	20 kg	LQ4/2	333	274, 640C-D

UN	Substance	Excepted Quantities	LQ Packages		LQ Shrink Wrapped Trays		Limited Quantity Value/Transport Category	Max Load	Special Provisions
			Receptacle Size	Package Gross	Receptacle Size	Package Gross			
1989	ALDEHYDES, N.O.S., PG111	30/1000	5 litres	30 kg	5 litres	20 kg	LQ7/3	1000	274
1990	BENZALDEHYDE	30/1000	3 litres	30 kg	3 litres	20 kg	LQ28/3	1000	
1991	CHLOROPRENE, STABILISED	Nil	Nil	Nil	Nil	Nil	LQ0/1	20	
1992	FLAMMABLE LIQUID, TOXIC, N.O.S., PG1	Nil	Nil	Nil	Nil	Nil	LQ0/1	20	274
1992	FLAMMABLE LIQUID, TOXIC, N.O.S., PG11	30/500	Nil	Nil	Nil	Nil	LQ0/2	333	274
1992	FLAMMABLE LIQUID, TOXIC, N.O.S., PG111	30/1000	5 litres	30 kg	5 litres	20 kg	LQ7/3	1000	274
1993	FLAMMABLE LIQUID, N.O.S., PG1	30/300	500 ml	1 litre	Not	Allowed	LQ3/1	20	274
1993	FLAMMABLE LIQUID, N.O.S., PG11	30/500	3 litres	30 kg	1 litre	20 kg	LQ4/2	333	274, 601, 640C-D
1993	FLAMMABLE LIQUID, N.O.S., PG111	30/1000	5 litres	30 kg	5 litres	20 kg	LQ7/3	1000	274, 601, 640E-H
1994	IRON PENTACARBONYL	1/300	Nil	Nil	Nil	Nil	LQ0/1	20	
1999	TARS. LIQUID, INCLUDING ROAD ASPHALT AND OILS, BITUMEN AND CUT BACKS, PG11	30/500	5 litres	30 kg	1 litre	20 kg	LQ6/2	333	640C-D
1999	TARS. LIQUID, INCLUDING ROAD ASPHALT AND OILS, BITUMEN AND CUT BACKS, PG111	30/1000	5 litres	30 kg	5 litres	20 kg	LQ7/3	1000	640E-H
2000	CELLULOID, IN BLOCKS, RODS, ROLLS, SHEETS, TUBES, ETC, EXCEPT SCRAP	30/1000	6 kg	30 kg	3 kg	20 kg	LQ9/3	1000	502

UN No.	Name								
2001	COBALT NAPTHENATES, POWDER	30/1000	6 kg	30 kg	3 kg	20 kg	LQ9/3	1000	
2002	CELLULOID, SCRAP	30/1000	Nil	Nil	Nil	Nil	LQ0/3	1000	526, 592
2004	MAGNESIUM DIAMIDE	30/500	Nil	Nil	Nil	Nil	LQ0/2	333	
2006	PLASTICS, NITROCELLULOSE-BASED, SELF-HEATING, N.O.S.	30/1000	Nil	Nil	Nil	Nil	LQ0/3	1000	274, 528
2008	ZIRCONIUM, POWDER, DRY, PG1	Nil	Nil	Nil	Nil	Nil	LQ0/0	Nil	524, 540
2008	ZIRCONIUM, POWDER, DRY, PG11	30/500	Nil	Nil	Nil	Nil	LQ0/2	333	524, 540
2008	ZIRCONIUM, POWDER, DRY, PG111	30/1000	Nil	Nil	Nil	Nil	LQ0/3	1000	524, 540
2009	ZIRCONIUM, DRY, FINISHED SHEETS, STRIP OR COILED WIRE	30/1000	Nil	Nil	Nil	Nil	LQ0/3	1000	524, 592
2010	MAGNESIUM HYDRIDE	Nil	Nil	Nil	Nil	Nil	LQ0/1	20	
2011	MAGNESIUM PHOSPHIDE	Nil	Nil	Nil	Nil	Nil	LQ0/1	20	
2012	POTASSIUM PHOSPHIDE	Nil	Nil	Nil	Nil	Nil	LQ0/1	20	
2013	STRONTIUM PHOSPHIDE	Nil	Nil	Nil	Nil	Nil	LQ0/1	20	
2014	HYDROGEN PEROXIDE, AQUEOUS SOLUTION WITH NOT LESS THAN 20% BUT NOT MORE THAN 60% HYDROGEN PEROXIDE (STABILISED AS NECESSARY)	30/500	500 ml	30 kg	500 ml	20 kg	LQ10/2	333	
2015	HYDROGEN PEROXIDE, AQUEOUS SOLUTION, STABILISED WITH MORE THAN 60% HYDROGEN PEROXIDE AND NOT MORE THAN 70% HYDROGEN PEROXIDE	Nil	Nil	Nil	Nil	Nil	LQ0/1	20	640N-O
2016	AMMUNITION, TOXIC, NON-EXPLOSIVE	Nil	Nil	Nil	Nil	Nil	LQ0/2	333	
2017	AMMUNITION, TEAR-PRODUCING, NON-EXPLOSIVE	Nil	Nil	Nil	Nil	Nil	LQ0/2	333	

UN	Substance	Excepted Quantities	LQ Packages		LQ Shrink Wrapped Trays		Limited Quantity Value/Transport Category	Max Load	Special Provisions
			Receptacle Size	Package Gross	Receptacle Size	Package Gross			
2018	CHLOROANILINES, SOLID	1/500	1 kg	4 kg	500 g	4 kg	LQ18/2	333	
2019	CHLOROANILINES, LIQUID	1/500	500 ml	2 litres	100 ml	2 litres	LQ17/2	333	
2020	CHLOROPHENOLS, SOLID	30/1000	6 kg	30 kg	3 kg	20 kg	LQ9/2	333	205
2021	CHLOROPHENOLS, LIQUID	30/1000	5 litres	30 kg	5 litres	20 kg	LQ7/2	333	
2022	CRESYLIC ACID	1/500	500 ml	2 litres	100 ml	2 litres	LQ17/2	333	
2023	EPICHLOROHYDRIN	1/500	500 ml	2 litres	100 ml	2 litres	LQ17/2	333	279
2024	MERCURY COMPOUND, LIQUID, N.O.S., PG1	1/300	Nil	Nil	Nil	Nil	LQ0/1	20	43, 274
2024	MERCURY COMPOUND, LIQUID, N.O.S., PG11	1/500	500 ml	2 litres	100 ml	2 litres	LQ17/2	333	43, 274
2024	MERCURY COMPOUND, LIQUID, N.O.S., PG111	30/1000	5 litres	30 kg	5 litres	20 kg	LQ7/2	333	43, 274
2025	MERCURY COMPOUND , SOLID, N.O.S., PG1	1/300	Nil	Nil	Nil	Nil	LQ0/1	20	43, 274, 529, 585
2025	MERCURY COMPOUND , SOLID, N.O.S., PG11	1/500	1 kg	4 kg	500 g	4 kg	LQ18/2	333	43, 274, 529, 585
2025	MERCURY COMPOUND , SOLID, N.O.S., PG111	30/1000	6 kg	30 kg	3 kg	20 kg	LQ9/2	333	43, 274, 529, 585
2026	PHENYLMERCURIC COMPOUND, N.O.S., PG1	1/300	Nil	Nil	Nil	Nil	LQ0/1	20	43, 274

UN	Name								
2026	PHENYLMERCURIC COMPOUND, N.O.S., PG11	1/500	1 kg	4 kg	500 g	4 kg	LQ18/2	333	43, 274
2026	PHENYLMERCURIC COMPOUND, N.O.S., PG111	30/1000	6 kg	30 kg	3 kg	20 kg	LQ9/2	333	43, 274
2027	SODIUM ARSENITE, SOLID	1/500	1 kg	4 kg	500 g	4 kg	LQ18/2	333	43
2028	BOMBS, SMOKE, NON-EXPLOSIVES WITH CORROSIVE LIQUID	Nil	Nil	Nil	Nil	Nil	LQ0/2	333	
2029	HYDRAZINE, ANHYDROUS	Nil	Nil	Nil	Nil	Nil	LQ0/1	20	
2030	HYDRAZINE, AQUEOUS SOLUTION WITH MORE THAN 37% HYDRAZINE BY MASS, PACKING GROUP I	Nil	Nil	Nil	Nil	Nil	LQ0/1	20	530
2030	HYDRAZINE AQUEOUS SOLUTION WITH MORE THAN 37% HYDRAZINE BY MASS, PACKING GROUP II	30/500	1 litre	30 kg	500 ml	20 kg	LQ22/2	333	530
2030	HYDRAZINE AQUEOUS SOLUTION WITH MORE THAN 37% HYDRAZINE BY MASS, PACKING GROUP III	30/1000	5 litres	30 kg	5 litres	20 kg	LQ7/3	1000	530
2031	NITRIC ACID, OTHER THAN RED FUMING, WITH MORE THAN 70% NITRIC ACID, PG1	Nil	Nil	Nil	Nil	Nil	LQ0/1	20	
2031	NITRIC ACID, OTHER THAN RED FUMING, WITH NOT MORE THAN 70% NITRIC ACID, PG11	30/500	1 litre	30 kg	500 ml	20 kg	LQ22/2	333	
2032	NITRIC ACID, RED FUMING	Nil	Nil	Nil	Nil	Nil	LQ0/1	20	
2033	POTASSIUM MONOXIDE	30/500	3 kg	30 kg	1 kg	20 kg	LQ23/2	333	
2034	HYDROGEN AND METHANE MIXTURE, COMPRESSED	Nil	Nil	Nil	Nil	Nil	LQ0/2	333	

UN	Substance	Excepted Quantities	LQ Packages		LQ Shrink Wrapped Trays		Limited Quantity Value/Transport Category	Max Load	Special Provisions
			Receptacle Size	Gross Package	Receptacle Size	Gross Package			
2035	1,1,1-TRIFLUOROETHANE (REFRIGERANT GAS R143A)	Nil	Nil	Nil	Nil	Nil	LQ0/2	333	
2036	XENON	30/1000	120 ml	30 kg	120 ml	20 kg	LQ1/3	1000	
2037	RECEPTACLES, SMALL, CONTAINING GAS (GAS CARTRIDGES) CLASS 5A, 5O	Nil	1 litre	30 kg	1 litre	20 kg	LQ2/3	1000	191, 303
2037	RECEPTACLES, SMALL, CONTAINING GAS (GAS CARTRIDGES) CLASS 5F	Nil	1 litre	30 kg	1 litre	20 kg	LQ2/2	333	191, 303
2037	RECEPTACLES, SMALL, CONTAINING GAS (GAS CARTRIDGES) CLASS 5T, 5TC, 5TF, 5TFC, 5TO, 5TOC	Nil	120 ml	30 kg	120 ml	20 kg	LQ1/1	20	303
2038	DINITROTOLUENES, LIQUID	1/500	500 ml	2 litres	100 ml	2 litres	LQ17/2	333	
2044	2,2-DIMETHYLPROPANE	Nil	Nil	Nil	Nil	Nil	LQ0/2	333	
2045	ISOBUTYRALDEHYDE (ISOBUTYL ALDEHYDE)	30/500	3 litres	30 kg	1 litre	20 kg	LQ4/2	333	
2046	CYMENES	30/1000	5 litres	30 kg	5 litres	20 kg	LQ7/3	1000	
2047	DICHLOROPROPENES, PG11	30/500	3 litres	30 kg	1 litre	20 kg	LQ4/2	333	
2047	DICHLOROPROPENES, PG111	30/1000	5 litres	30 kg	5 litres	20 kg	LQ7/3	1000	
2048	DICYCLOPENTADIENE	30/1000	5 litres	30 kg	5 litres	20 kg	LQ7/3	1000	
2049	DIETHYLBENZENE	30/1000	5 litres	30 kg	5 litres	20 kg	LQ7/3	1000	

2050	DIISOBUTYLENE, ISOMERIC COMPOUNDS	30/500	3 litres	30 kg	1 litre	20 kg	LQ4/2	333	
2051	2-DIMETHYLAMINOETHANOL	30/500	1 litre	30 kg	500 ml	20 kg	LQ22/2	333	
2052	DIPENTENE	30/1000	5 litres	30 kg	5 litres	20 kg	LQ7/3	1000	
2053	METHYL ISOBUTYL CARBINOL	30/1000	5 litres	30 kg	5 litres	20 kg	LQ7/3	1000	
2054	MORPHOLINE	Nil	Nil	Nil	Nil	Nil	LQ0/1	20	
2055	STYRENE MONOMER, STABILISED	30/1000	5 litres	30 kg	5 litres	20 kg	LQ7/3	1000	
2056	TETRAHYDROFURAN	30/500	3 litres	30 kg	1 litre	20 kg	LQ4/2	333	
2057	TRIPROPYLENE, PG11	30/500	3 litres	30 kg	1 litre	20 kg	LQ4/2	333	
2057	TRIPROPYLENE, PG111	30/1000	5 litres	30 kg	5 litres	20 kg	LQ7/3	1000	
2058	VALERALDEHYDE	30/500	3 litres	30 kg	1 litre	20 kg	LQ4/2	333	
2059	NITROCELLULOSE SOLUTION, FLAMMABLE, PG1	Nil	500 ml	1 litre	Not	Allowed	LQ3/1	20	198, 531
2059	NITROCELLULOSE SOLUTION, FLAMMABLE, PG11	Nil	3 litres	30 kg	1 litre	20 kg	LQ4/2	333	198, 531, 640C-D
2059	NITROCELLULOSE SOLUTION, FLAMMABLE, PG111	Nil	5 litres	30 kg	5 litres	20 kg	LQ7/3	1000	198, 531
2067	AMMONIUM NITRATE BASED FERTILIZERS	30/1000	1 kg	30 kg	1 kg	20 kg	LQ12/3	1000	186, 306, 307
2071	AMMONIUM NITRATE BASED FERTILIZERS	Not	Subject	To	ADR	-	Not Subject	to	ADR
2073	AMMONIA SOLUTION, RELATIVE DENSITY LESS THAN 0.880 AT 15 °C IN WATER, WITH MORE THAN 35% AND NOT MORE THAN 50% AMMONIA	30/1000	120 ml	30 kg	120 ml	20 kg	LQ1/3	1000	532

UN	Substance	Excepted Quantities	LQ Packages		LQ Shrink Wrapped Trays		Limited Quantity Value/Transport Category	Max Load	Special Provisions
			Receptacle Size	Package Gross	Receptacle Size	Package Gross			
2074	ACRYLAMIDE	30/1000	6 kg	30 kg	3 kg	20 kg	LQ9/2	333	
2075	CHLORAL, ANHYDROUS, STABILISED	1/500	500 ml	2 litres	100 ml	2 litres	LQ17/2	333	
2076	CRESOLS, LIQUID	1/500	500 ml	2 litres	100 ml	2 litres	LQ17/2	333	
2077	ALPHA-NAPHTHYLAMINE	30/1000	6 kg	30 kg	3 kg	20 kg	LQ9/2	333	
2078	TOLUENE DIISOCYANATE	1/500	500 ml	2 litres	100 ml	2 litres	LQ17/2	333	279
2079	DIETHYLENETRIAMINE	30/500	1 litre	30 kg	500 ml	20 kg	LQ22/2	333	
2186	HYDROGEN CHLORIDE, REFRIGERATED LIQUID	Carriage Prohibited	Prohibited	–	–	Carriage	Prohibited		
2187	CARBON DIOXIDE, REFRIGERATED LIQUID	30/1000	120 ml	30 kg	120 ml	20 kg	LQ1/3	1000	593
2188	ARSINE	Nil	Nil	Nil	Nil	Nil	LQ0/1	20	
2189	DICHLOROSILANE	Nil	Nil	Nil	Nil	Nil	LQ0/1	20	
2190	OXYGEN DIFLUORIDE, COMPRESSED	Nil	Nil	Nil	Nil	Nil	LQ0/1	20	
2191	SULPHURYL FLUORIDE	Nil	Nil	Nil	Nil	Nil	LQ0/1	20	
2192	GERMANE	Nil	Nil	Nil	Nil	Nil	LQ0/1	20	632
2193	HEXAFLUOROETHANE (REFRIGERANT GAS R116)	30/1000	120 ml	30 kg	120 ml	20 kg	LQ1/3	1000	

UN	Name						LQ		
2194	SELENIUM HEXAFLUORIDE	Nil	Nil	Nil	Nil	Nil	LQ0/1	20	
2195	TELLURIUM HEXAFLUORIDE	Nil	Nil	Nil	Nil	Nil	LQ0/1	20	
2196	TUNGSTEN HEXAFLUORIDE	Nil	Nil	Nil	Nil	Nil	LQ0/1	20	
2197	HYDROGEN IODIDE, ANHYDROUS	Nil	Nil	Nil	Nil	Nil	LQ0/1	20	
2198	PHOSPHORUS PENTAFLUORIDE	Nil	Nil	Nil	Nil	Nil	LQ0/1	20	
2199	PHOSPHINE	Nil	Nil	Nil	Nil	Nil	LQ0/1	20	632
2200	PROPADIENE, STABILISED	Nil	Nil	Nil	Nil	Nil	LQ0/2	333	
2201	NITROUS OXIDE, REFRIGERATED LIQUID	Nil	Nil	Nil	Nil	Nil	LQ0/3	1000	
2202	HYDROGEN SELENIDE, ANHYDROUS	Nil	Nil	Nil	Nil	Nil	LQ0/1	20	
2203	SILANE	Nil	Nil	Nil	Nil	Nil	LQ0/2	333	632
2204	CARBONYL SULPHIDE	Nil	Nil	Nil	Nil	Nil	LQ0/1	20	
2205	ADIPONITRILE	30/1000	5 litres	30 kg	5 litres	20 kg	LQ7/2	333	
2206	ISOCYANATES, TOXIC, N.O.S., OR ISOCYANATE SOLUTION, TOXIC, N.O.S., PG11	1/500	500 ml	2 litres	100 ml	2 litres	LQ17/2	333	274, 551
2206	ISOCYANATES, TOXIC, N.O.S., OR ISOCYANATE SOLUTION, TOXIC, N.O.S., PG111	30/1000	5 litres	30 kg	5 litres	20 kg	LQ7/2	333	274, 551
2208	CALCIUM HYPOCHLORITE MIXTURE, DRY WITH MORE THAN 10% BUT NOT MORE THAN 39% AVAILABLE CHLORINE	30/1000	1 kg	30 kg	1 kg	20 kg	LQ12/3	1000	313, 314
2209	FORMALDEHYDE SOLUTION WITH NOT LESS THAN 25% FORMALDEHYDE	30/1000	5 litres	30 kg	5 litres	20 kg	LQ7/3	1000	533

UN	Substance	Excepted Quantities	LQ Packages		LQ Shrink Wrapped Trays		Limited Quantity Value/Transport Category	Max Load	Special Provisions
			Receptacle Size	Package Gross	Receptacle Size	Package Gross			
2210	MANEB OR MANEB PREPARATIONS, WITH NOT LESS THAN 60% MANEB	30/1000	Nil	Nil	Nil	Nil	LQ0/3	1000	273
2211	POLYMERIC BEADS, EXPANDABLE, EVOLVING FLAMMABLE VAPOUR	30/1000	6 kg	30 kg	6 kg	20 kg	LQ27/3	1000	207, 633
2212	BLUE ASBESTOS (CROCIDOLITE) OR BROWN ASBESTOS (AMOSITE, MYSORITE)	30/500	1 kg	30 kg	1 kg	20 kg	LQ25/2	333	168
2213	PARAFORMALDEHYDE	30/1000	6 kg	30 kg	3 kg	20 kg	LQ9/3	1000	
2214	PHTHALIC ANHYDRIDE WITH MORE THAN 0.05% MALEIC ANHYDRIDE	30/1000	6 kg	30 kg	2 kg	20 kg	LQ24/3	1000	169
2215	MALEIC ANHYDRIDE MOLTEN	Nil	Nil	Nil	Nil	Nil	LQ0/0	Nil	
2215	MALEIC ANHYDRIDE	30/1000	6 kg	30 kg	2 kg	20 kg	LQ24/3	1000	
2216	FISH MEAL, (FISH SCRAP), STABILISED	Not	Subject	To ADR	–	–	Not Subject	to	ADR
2217	SEED CAKE WITH NOT MORE THAN 1.5% OIL AND NOT MORE THAN 11% MOISTURE	30/1000	Nil	Nil	Nil	Nil	LQ0/3	1000	142
2218	ACRYLIC ACID, STABILISED	30/500	1 litre	30 kg	500 ml	20 kg	LQ22/2	333	
2219	ALLYL GLYCIDYL ETHER	30/1000	5 litres	30 kg	5 litres	20 kg	LQ7/3	1000	
2222	ANISOLE	30/1000	5 litres	30 kg	5 litres	20 kg	LQ7/3	1000	
2224	BENZONITRILE	1/500	500 ml	2 litres	100 ml	2 litres	LQ17/2	333	

2225	BENZENESULPHONYL CHLORIDE	30/1000	5 litres	30 kg	5 litres	20 kg	LQ7/3	1000
2226	BENZOTRICHLORIDE	30/500	1 litre	30 kg	500 ml	20 kg	LQ22/2	333
2227	N-BUTYL METHACRYLATE, STABILISED	30/1000	5 litres	30 kg	5 litres	20 kg	LQ7/3	1000
2232	2-CHLOROETHANAL	1/300	Nil	Nil	Nil	Nil	LQ0/1	20
2233	CHLOROANISIDINES	30/1000	6 kg	30 kg	3 kg	20 kg	LQ9/2	333
2234	CHLOROBENZOTRIFLUORIDES	30/1000	5 litres	30 kg	5 litres	20 kg	LQ7/3	1000
2235	CHLOROBENZYL CHLORIDES	30/1000	5 litres	30 kg	5 litres	20 kg	LQ7/2	333
2236	3-CHLORO-4-METHYLPHENYL ISOCYANATE	1/500	500 ml	2 litres	100 ml	2 litres	LQ17/2	333
2237	CHLORONITROANILINES	30/1000	6 kg	30 kg	3 kg	20 kg	LQ9/2	333
2238	CHLOROTOLUENES	30/1000	5 litres	30 kg	5 litres	20 kg	LQ7/3	1000
2239	CHLOROTOLUIDINES, SOLID	30/1000	6 kg	30 kg	3 kg	20 kg	LQ9/2	333
2240	CHROMOSULPHURIC ACID	Nil	Nil	Nil	Nil	Nil	LQ0/1	20
2241	CYCLOHEPTANE	30/500	3 litres	30 kg	1 litre	20 kg	LQ4/2	333
2242	CYCLOHEPTENE	30/500	3 litres	30 kg	1 litre	20 kg	LQ4/2	333
2243	CYCLOHEXYL ACETATE	30/1000	5 litres	30 kg	5 litres	20 kg	LQ7/3	1000
2244	CYCLOPENTANOL	30/1000	5 litres	30 kg	5 litres	20 kg	LQ7/3	1000
2245	CYCLOPENTANONE	30/1000	5 litres	30 kg	5 litres	20 kg	LQ7/3	1000
2246	CYCLOPENTENE	30/500	3 litres	30 kg	1 litre	20 kg	LQ4/2	333
2247	N-DECANE	30/1000	5 litres	30 kg	5 litres	20 kg	LQ7/3	1000
2248	DI-N-BUTYLAMINE	30/500	1 litre	30 kg	500 ml	20 kg	LQ22/2	333

UN	Substance	Excepted Quantities	LQ Packages		LQ Shrink Wrapped Trays		Limited Quantity Value/Transport Category	Max Load	Special Provisions
			Receptacle Size	Gross Package	Receptacle Size	Gross Package			
2249	DICHLORODIMETHYL ETHER, SYMMETRICAL	Carriage	Prohibited	–	–	Carriage			
2250	DICHLOROPHENYL ISOCYANATES	1/500	1 kg	4 kg	500 g	4 kg	LQ18/2	333	
2251	BICYCLO[2,2,1] HEPTA-2, 5-DIENE, STABILISED (2,5-NORBORNADIENE, STABILISED)	30/500	3 litres	30 kg	1 litre	20 kg	LQ4/2	333	
2252	1,2-DIMETHOXYETHANE	30/500	3 litres	30 kg	1 litre	20 kg	LQ4/2	333	
2253	N,N-DIMETHYLANILINE	1/500	500 ml	2 litres	100 ml	2 litres	LQ17/2	333	
2254	MATCHES, FUSE	30/1000	6 kg	30 kg	3 kg	20 kg	LQ9/4	Unlimited	293
2256	CYCLOHEXENE	30/500	3 litres	30 kg	1 litre	20 kg	LQ4/2	333	
2257	POTASSIUM	Nil	Nil	Nil	Nil	Nil	LQ0/1	20	
2258	1,2-PROPYLENEDIAMINE	30/500	1 litre	30 kg	500 ml	20 kg	LQ22/2	333	
2259	TRIETHYLENETETRAMINE	30/500	1 litre	30 kg	500 ml	20 kg	LQ22/2	333	
2260	TRIPROPYLAMINE	30/1000	5 litres	30 kg	5 litres	20 kg	LQ7/3	1000	
2261	XYLENOLS, LIQUID	1/500	1 kg	4 kg	500 gm	4 kg	LQ18/2	333	
2262	DIMETHYLCARBAMOYL CHLORIDE	30/500	1 litre	30 kg	500 ml	20 kg	LQ22/2	333	
2263	DIMETHYLCYCLOHEXANES	30/500	3 litres	30 kg	1 litre	20 kg	LQ4/2	333	

2264	N,N-DIMETHYLCYCLOHEXYLAMINE	30/500	1 litre	30 kg	500 ml	20 kg	LQ22/2	333	
2265	N,N-DIMETHYLFORMAMIDE	30/1000	5 litres	30 kg	5 litres	20 kg	LQ7/3	1000	
2266	DIMETHYL-N-PROPYLAMINE	30/500	3 litres	30 kg	1 litre	20 kg	LQ4/2	333	
2267	DIMETHYL THIOPHOSPHORYL CHLORIDE	1/500	500 ml	2 litres	100 ml	2 litres	LQ17/2	333	
2269	3,3-IMINODIPROPYLAMINE	30/1000	5 litres	30 kg	5 litres	20 kg	LQ7/3	1000	
2270	ETHYLAMINE, AQUEOUS SOLUTION WITH NOT LESS THAN 50% BUT NOT MORE THAN 70% ETHYLAMINE	30/500	3 litres	30 kg	1 litre	20 kg	LQ4/2	333	
2271	ETHYL AMYL KETONE	30/1000	5 litres	30 kg	5 litres	20 kg	LQ7/3	1000	
2272	N-ETHYLANILINE	30/1000	5 litres	30 kg	5 litres	20 kg	LQ7/2	333	
2273	2-ETHYLANILINE	30/1000	5 litres	30 kg	5 litres	20 kg	LQ7/2	333	
2274	N-ETHYL-N-BENZYLANILINE	30/1000	5 litres	30 kg	5 litres	20 kg	LQ7/2	333	
2275	2-ETHYLBUTANOL	30/1000	5 litres	30 kg	5 litres	20 kg	LQ7/3	1000	
2276	2-ETHYLHEXYLAMINE	30/1000	5 litres	30 kg	5 litres	20 kg	LQ7/3	1000	
2277	ETHYL METHACRYLATE, STABILISED	30/500	3 litres	30 kg	1 litre	20 kg	LQ4/2	333	
2278	N-HEPTENE	30/500	3 litres	30 kg	1 litre	20 kg	LQ4/2	333	
2279	HEXACHLOROBUTADIENE	30/1000	5 litres	30 kg	5 litres	20 kg	LQ7/2	333	
2280	HEXAMETHYLENEDIAMINE, SOLID	30/1000	6 kg	30 kg	2 kg	20 kg	LQ24/3	1000	
2281	HEXAMETHYLENE DIISOCYANATE	1/500	500 ml	2 litres	100 ml	2 litres	LQ17/2	333	
2282	HEXANOLS	30/1000	5 litres	30 kg	5 litres	20 kg	LQ7/3	1000	
2283	ISOBUTYL METHACRYLATE, STABILISED	30/1000	5 litres	30 kg	5 litres	20 kg	LQ7/3	1000	

| UN | Substance | Excepted Quantities | LQ Packages | | LQ Shrink Wrapped Trays | | Limited Quantity Value/Transport Category | Max Load | Special Provisions |
			Receptacle Size	Gross Package	Receptacle Size	Gross Package			
2284	ISOBUTYRONITRILE	30/500	Nil	Nil	Nil	Nil	LQ0/2	333	
2285	ISOCYANATOBENZOTRIFLUORIDES	1/500	500 ml	2 litres	100 ml	2 litres	LQ17/2	333	
2286	PENTAMETHYLHEPTANE	30/1000	5 litres	30 kg	5 litres	20 kg	LQ7/3	1000	
2287	ISOHEPTENE	30/500	3 litres	30 kg	1 litre	20 kg	LQ4/2	333	
2288	ISOHEXENE	30/500	3 litres	30 kg	1 litre	20 kg	LQ4/2	333	
2289	ISOPHORONEDIAMINE	30/1000	5 litres	30 kg	5 litres	20 kg	LQ7/3	1000	
2290	ISOPHORONE DIISOCYANATE	30/1000	5 litres	30 kg	5 litres	20 kg	LQ7/2	333	
2291	LEAD COMPOUND, SOLUBLE, N.O.S.	30/1000	6 kg	30 kg	3 kg	20 kg	LQ9/2	333	199, 274, 535
2293	4-METHOXY-4-METHYLPENTAN-2-ONE	30/1000	5 litres	30 kg	5 litres	20 kg	LQ7/3	1000	
2294	N-METHYLANILINE	30/1000	5 litres	30 kg	5 litres	20 kg	LQ7/2	333	
2295	METHYL CHLOROACETATE	1/300	Nil	Nil	Nil	Nil	LQ0/1	20	
2296	METHYLCYCLOHEXANE	30/500	3 litres	30 kg	1 litre	20 kg	LQ4/2	333	
2297	METHYLCYCLOHEXANONE	30/1000	5 litres	30 kg	5 litres	20 kg	LQ7/3	1000	
2298	METHYLCYCLOPENTANE	30/500	3 litres	30 kg	1 litre	20 kg	LQ4/2	333	
2299	METHYL DICHLOROACETATE	30/1000	5 litres	30 kg	5 litres	20 kg	LQ7/2	333	

2300	2-METHYL-5-ETHYLPYRIDINE	30/1000	5 litres	30 kg	5 litres	20 kg	LQ7/2	333	
2301	2-METHYLFURAN	30/500	3 litres	30 kg	1 litre	20 kg	LQ4/2	333	
2302	5-METHYLHEXAN-2-ONE	30/1000	5 litres	30 kg	5 litres	20 kg	LQ7/3	1000	
2303	ISOPROPENYLBENZENE	30/1000	5 litres	30 kg	5 litres	20 kg	LQ7/3	1000	
2304	NAPHTHALENE, MOLTEN	Nil	Nil	Nil	Nil	Nil	LQ0/3	1000	536
2305	NITROBENZENESULPHONIC ACID	30/500	3 kg	30 kg	1 kg	20 kg	LQ23/2	333	
2306	NITROBENZOTRIFLUORIDES, LIQUID	1/500	500 ml	2 litres	100 ml	2 litres	LQ17/2	333	
2307	3-NITRO-4-CHLOROBENZOTRIFLUORIDE	1/500	500 ml	2 litres	100 ml	2 litres	LQ17/2	333	
2308	NITROSYLSULPHURIC ACID, LIQUID	30/500	1 litre	30 kg	500 ml	20 kg	LQ22/2	333	
2309	OCTADIENE	30/500	3 litres	30 kg	1 litre	20 kg	LQ4/2	333	
2310	PENTANE-2, 4-DIONE	30/1000	5 litres	30 kg	5 litres	20 kg	LQ7/3	1000	
2311	PHENETIDINES	30/1000	5 litres	30 kg	5 litres	20 kg	LQ7/2	333	279
2312	PHENOL, MOLTEN	Nil	Nil	Nil	Nil	Nil	LQ0/0	Nil	
2313	PICOLINES	30/1000	5 litres	30 kg	5 litres	20 kg	LQ7/3	1000	
2315	POLYCHLORINATED BIPHENYLS	30/500	500 ml	2 litres	500 ml	2 litres	LQ26/0	Nil	305
2316	SODIUM CUPROCYANIDE, SOLID	1/300	Nil	Nil	Nil	Nil	LQ0/1	20	
2317	SODIUM CUPROCYANIDE SOLUTION	1/300	Nil	Nil	Nil	Nil	LQ0/1	20	
2318	SODIUM HYDROSULPHIDE WITH LESS THAN 25% WATER OF CRYSTALLISATION	30/500	Nil	Nil	Nil	Nil	LQ0/2	333	504
2319	TERPENE HYDROCARBONS, N.O.S.	30/1000	5 litres	30 kg	5 litres	20 kg	LQ7/3	1000	

UN	Substance	Excepted Quantities	LQ Packages		LQ Shrink Wrapped Trays		Limited Quantity Value/Transport Category	Max Load	Special Provisions
			Receptacle Size	Package Gross	Receptacle Size	Package Gross			
2320	TETRAETHYLENEPENTAMINE	30/1000	5 litres	30 kg	5 litres	20 kg	LQ7/3	1000	
2321	TRICHLOROBENZENES, LIQUID	30/1000	5 litres	30 kg	5 litres	20 kg	LQ7/2	333	
2322	TRICHLOROBUTENE	1/500	500 ml	2 litres	100 ml	2 litres	LQ17/2	333	
2323	TRIETHYL PHOSPHITE	30/1000	5 litres	30 kg	5 litres	20 kg	LQ7/3	1000	
2324	TRIISOBUTYLENE	30/1000	5 litres	30 kg	5 litres	20 kg	LQ7/3	1000	
2325	1,3,5-TRIMETHYLBENZENE	30/1000	5 litres	30 kg	5 litres	20 kg	LQ7/3	1000	
2326	TRIMETHYLCYCLOHEXYLAMINE	30/1000	5 litres	30 kg	5 litres	20 kg	LQ7/3	1000	
2327	TRIMETHYLHEXAMETHYLENEDIAMINES	30/1000	5 litres	30 kg	5 litres	20 kg	LQ7/3	1000	
2328	TRIMETHYLHEXAMETHYLENE DIISOCYANATE	30/1000	5 litres	30 kg	5 litres	20 kg	LQ7/2	333	
2329	TRIMETHYL PHOSPHITE	30/1000	5 litres	30 kg	5 litres	20 kg	LQ7/3	1000	
2330	UNDECANE	30/1000	5 litres	30 kg	5 litres	20 kg	LQ7/3	1000	
2331	ZINC CHLORIDE, ANHYDROUS	30/1000	6 kg	30 kg	2 kg	20 kg	LQ24/3	1000	
2332	ACETALDEHYDE OXIME	30/1000	5 litres	30 kg	5 litres	20 kg	LQ7/3	1000	
2333	ALLYL ACETATE	30/500	Nil	Nil	Nil	Nil	LQ0/2	333	
2334	ALLYLAMINE	1/300	Nil	Nil	Nil	Nil	LQ0/1	20	
2335	ALLYL ETHYL ETHER	30/500	Nil	Nil	Nil	Nil	LQ0/2	333	

UN No.	Name							
2336	ALLYL FORMATE	Nil	Nil	Nil	Nil	Nil	LQ0/1	20
2337	PHENYL MERCAPTAN	1/300	Nil	Nil	Nil	Nil	LQ0/1	20
2338	BENZOTRIFLUORIDE	30/500	3 litres	30 kg	1 litre	20 kg	LQ4/2	333
2339	2-BROMOBUTANE	30/500	3 litres	30 kg	1 litre	20 kg	LQ4/2	333
2340	2-BROMOETHYL ETHYL ETHER	30/500	3 litres	30 kg	1 litre	20 kg	LQ4/2	333
2341	1-BROMO-3-METHYLBUTANE	30/1000	5 litres	30 kg	5 litres	20 kg	LQ7/3	1000
2342	BROMOMETHYLPROPANES	30/500	3 litres	30 kg	1 litre	20 kg	LQ4/2	333
2343	2-BROMOPENTANE	30/500	3 litres	30 kg	1 litre	20 kg	LQ4/2	333
2344	BROMOPROPANES, PG11	30/500	3 litres	30 kg	1 litre	20 kg	LQ4/2	333
2344	BROMOPROPANES, PG111	30/1000	5 litres	30 kg	5 litres	20 kg	LQ7/3	1000
2345	3-BROMOPROPYNE	30/500	3 litres	30 kg	1 litre	20 kg	LQ4/2	333
2346	BUTANEDIONE	30/500	3 litres	30 kg	1 litre	20 kg	LQ4/2	333
2347	BUTYL MERCAPTAN	30/500	3 litres	30 kg	1 litre	20 kg	LQ4/2	333
2348	BUTYL ACRYLATES, STABILISED	30/1000	5 litres	30 kg	5 litres	20 kg	LQ7/3	1000
2350	BUTYL METHYL ETHER	30/500	3 litres	30 kg	1 litre	20 kg	LQ4/2	333
2351	BUTYL NITRITES, PG11	30/500	3 litres	30 kg	1 litre	20 kg	LQ4/2	333
2351	BUTYL NITRITES, PG111	30/1000	5 litres	30 kg	5 litres	20 kg	LQ7/3	1000
2352	BUTYL VINYL ETHER, STABILISED	30/500	3 litres	30 kg	1 litre	20 kg	LQ4/2	333
2353	BUTYRYL CHLORIDE	30/500	3 litres	30 kg	1 litre	20 kg	LQ4/2	333
2354	CHLOROMETHYL ETHYL ETHER	30/500	Nil	Nil	Nil	Nil	LQ0/2	333

UN	Substance	Excepted Quantities	LQ Packages		LQ Shrink Wrapped Trays		Limited Quantity Value/Transport Category	Max Load	Special Provisions
			Receptacle Size	Gross Package	Receptacle Size	Gross Package			
2356	2-CHLOROPROPANE	30/300	500 ml	1 litre	Not	Allowed	LQ3/1	20	
2357	CYCLOHEXYLAMINE	30/500	1 litre	30 kg	500 ml	20 kg	LQ22/2	333	
2358	CYCLOOCTATETRAENE	30/500	3 litres	30 kg	1 litre	20 kg	LQ4/2	333	
2359	DIALLYLAMINE	30/500	Nil	Nil	Nil	Nil	LQ0/2	333	
2360	DIALLYL ETHER	30/500	Nil	Nil	Nil	Nil	LQ0/2	333	
2361	DIISOBUTYLAMINE	30/1000	5 litres	30 kg	5 litres	20 kg	LQ7/3	1000	
2362	1,1-DICHLOROETHANE	30/500	3 litres	30 kg	1 litre	20 kg	LQ4/2	333	
2363	ETHYL MERCAPTAN	30/300	500 ml	1 litre	Not	Allowed	LQ3/1	20	
2364	N-PROPYLBENZENE	30/1000	5 litres	30 kg	5 litres	20 kg	LQ7/3	1000	
2366	DIETHYL CARBONATE	30/1000	5 litres	30 kg	5 litres	20 kg	LQ7/3	1000	
2367	ALPHA-METHYLVALERALDEHYDE	30/500	3 litres	30 kg	1 litre	20 kg	LQ4/2	333	
2368	ALPHA-PINENE	30/1000	5 litres	30 kg	5 litres	20 kg	LQ7/3	1000	
2370	1-HEXENE	30/500	3 litres	30 kg	1 litre	20 kg	LQ4/2	333	
2371	ISOPENTENES	30/300	500 ml	1 litre	Not	Allowed	LQ3/1	20	
2372	1,2-DI-(DIMETHYLAMINO) ETHANE	30/500	3 litres	30 kg	1 litre	20 kg	LQ4/2	333	
2373	DIETHOXYMETHANE	30/500	3 litres	30 kg	1 litre	20 kg	LQ4/2	333	

2374	3,3-DIETHOXYPROPENE	30/500	3 litres	30 kg	1 litre	20 kg	LQ4/2	333
2375	DIETHYL SULPHIDE	30/500	3 litres	30 kg	1 litre	20 kg	LQ4/2	333
2376	2,3-DIHYDROPYRAN	30/500	3 litres	30 kg	1 litre	20 kg	LQ4/2	333
2377	1,1-DIMETHOXYETHANE	30/500	3 litres	30 kg	1 litre	20 kg	LQ4/2	333
2378	2-DIMETHYLAMINOACETONITRILE	30/500	Nil	Nil	Nil	Nil	LQ0/2	333
2379	1,3-DIMETHYLBUTYLAMINE	30/500	3 litres	30 kg	1 litre	20 kg	LQ4/2	333
2380	DIMETHYLDIETHOXYSILANE	30/500	3 litres	30 kg	1 litre	20 kg	LQ4/2	333
2381	DIMETHYL DISULPHIDE	30/500	3 litres	30 kg	1 litre	20 kg	LQ4/2	333
2382	DIMETHYLHYDRAZINE, SYMMETRICAL	1/300	Nil	Nil	Nil	Nil	LQ0/1	20
2383	DIPROPYLAMINE	30/500	3 litres	30 kg	1 litre	20 kg	LQ4/2	333
2384	DI-N-PROPYL ETHER	30/500	3 litres	30 kg	1 litre	20 kg	LQ4/2	333
2385	ETHYL ISOBUTYRATE	30/500	3 litres	30 kg	1 litre	20 kg	LQ4/2	333
2386	1-ETHYLPIPERIDINE	30/500	3 litres	30 kg	1 litre	20 kg	LQ4/2	333
2387	FLUOROBENZENE	30/500	3 litres	30 kg	1 litre	20 kg	LQ4/2	333
2388	FLUOROTOLUENES	30/500	3 litres	30 kg	1 litre	20 kg	LQ4/2	333
2389	FURAN	30/300	500 ml	1 litre	Not	Allowed	LQ3/1	20
2390	2-IODOBUTANE	30/500	3 litres	30 kg	1 litre	20 kg	LQ4/2	333
2391	IODOMETHYLPROPANES	30/500	3 litres	30 kg	1 litre	20 kg	LQ4/2	333
2392	IODOPROPANES	30/1000	5 litres	30 kg	5 litres	20 kg	LQ7/3	1000
2393	ISOBUTYL FORMATE	30/500	3 litres	30 kg	1 litre	20 kg	LQ4/2	333

UN	Substance	Excepted Quantities	LQ Packages		LQ Shrink Wrapped Trays			Limited Quantity Value/Transport Category	Max Load	Special Provisions
			Receptacle Size	Package Gross	Receptacle Size	Package Gross				
2394	ISOBUTYL PROPIONATE	30/1000	5 litres	30 kg	5 litres	20 kg		LQ7/3	1000	
2395	ISOBUTYRYL CHLORIDE	30/500	3 litres	30 kg	1 litre	20 kg		LQ4/2	333	
2396	METHACRYLALDEHYDE, STABILISED	30/500	Nil	Nil	Nil	Nil		LQ0/2	333	
2397	3-METHYLBUTAN-2-ONE	30/500	3 litres	30 kg	1 litre	20 kg		LQ4/2	333	
2398	METHYL TERT-BUTYL ETHER	30/500	3 litres	30 kg	1 litre	20 kg		LQ4/2	333	
2399	1-METHYLPIPERIDINE	30/500	3 litres	30 kg	1 litre	20 kg		LQ4/2	333	
2400	METHYL ISOVALERATE	30/500	3 litres	30 kg	1 litre	20 kg		LQ4/2	333	
2401	PIPERIDINE	Nil	Nil	Nil	Nil	Nil		LQ0/1	20	
2402	PROPANETHIOLS	30/500	3 litres	30 kg	1 litre	20 kg		LQ4/2	333	
2403	ISOPROPENYL ACETATE	30/500	3 litres	30 kg	1 litre	20 kg		LQ4/2	333	
2404	PROPIONITRILE	30/500	Nil	Nil	Nil	Nil		LQ0/2	333	
2405	ISOPROPYL BUTYRATE	30/1000	5 litres	30 kg	5 litres	20 kg		LQ7/3	1000	
2406	ISOPROPYL ISOBUTYRATE	30/500	3 litres	30 kg	1 litre	20 kg		LQ4/2	333	
2407	ISOPROPYL CHLOROFORMATE	1/300	Nil		Nil	Nil		LQ0/1	20	
2409	ISOPROPYL PROPIONATE	30/500	3 litres	30 kg	1 litre	20 kg		LQ4/2	333	
2410	1,2,3,6-TETRAHYDROPYRIDINE	30/500	3 litres	30 kg	1 litre	20 kg		LQ4/2	333	

No.	Name								
2411	BUTYRONITRILE	30/500	Nil	Nil	Nil	Nil	LQ0/2	333	
2412	TETRAHYDROTHIOPHENE	30/500	3 litres	30 kg	1 litre	20 kg	LQ4/2	333	
2413	TETRAPROPYL ORTHOTITANATE	30/1000	5 litres	30 kg	5 litres	20 kg	LQ7/3	1000	
2414	THIOPHENE	30/500	3 litres	30 kg	1 litre	20 kg	LQ4/2	333	
2416	TRIMETHYL BORATE	30/500	3 litres	30 kg	1 litre	20 kg	LQ4/2	333	
2417	CARBONYL FLUORIDE	Nil	Nil	Nil	Nil	Nil	LQ0/1	20	
2418	SULPHUR TETRAFLUORIDE	Nil	Nil	Nil	Nil	Nil	LQ0/1	20	
2419	BROMOTRIFLUOROETHYLENE	Nil	Nil	Nil	Nil	Nil	LQ0/2	333	
2420	HEXAFLUOROACETONE	Nil	Nil	Nil	Nil	Nil	LQ0/1	20	
2421	NITROGEN TRIOXIDE	Carriage	–	–	Prohibited				
2422	OCTAFLUOROBUT-2-ENE (REFRIGERANT GAS R1318)	30/1000	120 ml	30 kg	120 ml	20 kg	LQ1/3	1000	
2424	OCTAFLUOROPROPANE (REFRIGERANT GAS R218)	30/1000	120 ml	30 kg	120 ml	20 kg	LQ1/3	1000	
2426	AMMONIUM NITRATE, LIQUID (HOT CONCENTRATED SOLUTION)	Nil	Nil	Nil	Nil	Nil	LQ0/0	Nil	252, 644
2427	POTASSIUM CHLORATE, AQUEOUS SOLUTION, PG11	30/500	500 ml	30 kg	500 ml	20 kg	LQ10/2	333	
2427	POTASSIUM CHLORATE, AQUEOUS SOLUTION, PG111	30/1000	1 litre	30 kg	1 litre	20 kg	LQ13/3	1000	
2428	SODIUM CHLORATE, AQUEOUS SOLUTION, PG11	30/500	500 ml	30 kg	500 ml	20 kg	LQ10/2	333	

UN	Substance	Excepted Quantities	LQ Packages		LQ Shrink Wrapped Trays		Limited Quantity Value/Transport Category	Max Load	Special Provisions
			Receptacle Size	Package Gross	Receptacle Size	Package Gross			
2428	SODIUM CHLORATE, AQUEOUS SOLUTION, PG111	30/1000	1 litre	30 kg	1 litre	20 kg	LQ13/3	1000	
2429	CALCIUM CHLORATE, AQUEOUS SOLUTION, PG11	30/500	500 ml	30 kg	500 ml	20 kg	LQ10/2	333	
2429	CALCIUM CHLORATE, AQUEOUS SOLUTION, PG111	30/1000	1 litre	30 kg	1 litre	20 kg	LQ13/3	1000	
2430	ALKYL PHENOLS, SOLID, N.O.S. (INCLUDING C2-C12 HOMOLOGUES), PG1	Nil	Nil	Nil	Nil	Nil	LQ0/1	20	274
2430	ALKYL PHENOLS, SOLID, N.O.S. (INCLUDING C2-C12 HOMOLOGUES), PG11	30/500	3 kg	30 kg	1 kg	20 kg	LQ23/2	333	274
2430	ALKYL PHENOLS, SOLID, N.O.S. (INCLUDING C2-C12 HOMOLOGUES), PG111	30/1000	6 kg	30 kg	2 kg	20 kg	LQ24/3	1000	274
2431	ANISIDINES	30/1000	5 litres	30 kg	5 litres	20 kg	LQ7/2	333	
2432	N, N-DIETHYLANILINE	30/1000	5 litres	30 kg	5 litres	20 kg	LQ7/2	333	
2433	CHLORONITROTOLUENES, LIQUID	30/1000	5 litres	30 kg	5 litres	20 kg	LQ7/2	333	
2434	DIBENZYLDICHLOROSILANE	30/500	1 litre	30 kg	500 ml	20 kg	LQ22/2	333	
2435	ETHYLPHENYLDICHLOROSILANE	30/500	1 litre	30 kg	500 ml	20 kg	LQ22/2	333	
2436	THIOACETIC ACID	30/500	3 litres	30 kg	1 litre	20 kg	LQ4/2	333	
2437	METHYLPHENYLDICHLOROSILANE	30/500	1 litre	30 kg	500 ml	20 kg	LQ22/2	333	

UN No	Name							LQ		
2438	TRIMETHYLACETYL CHLORIDE	1/300	Nil	Nil	Nil	Nil	Nil	LQ0/1	20	
2439	SODIUM HYDROGENDIFLUORIDE	30/500	3 kg	30 kg	1 kg	20 kg	20 kg	LQ23/2	333	
2440	STANNIC CHLORIDE PENTAHYDRATE	30/1000	6 kg	30 kg	2 kg	20 kg	20 kg	LQ24/3	1000	
2441	TITANIUM TRICHLORIDE, PYROPHORIC OR TITANIUM TRICHLORIDE MIXTURE, PYROPHORIC	Nil	Nil	Nil	Nil	Nil	Nil	LQ0/0	Nil	537
2442	TRICHLOROACETYL CHLORIDE	30/500	1 litre	30 kg	500 ml	20 kg	20 kg	LQ22/2	333	
2443	VANADIUM OXYTRICHLORIDE	30/500	1 litre	30 kg	500 ml	20 kg	20 kg	LQ22/2	333	
2444	VANADIUM TETRACHLORIDE	Nil	Nil	Nil	Nil	Nil	Nil	LQ0/1	20	
2446	NITROCRESOLS, SOLID	30/1000	6 kg	30 kg	3 kg	20 kg	20 kg	LQ9/2	333	
2447	PHOSPHORUS WHITE, MOLTEN	Nil	Nil	Nil	Nil	Nil	Nil	LQ0/0	Nil	
2448	SULPHUR, MOLTEN	Nil	Nil	Nil	Nil	Nil	Nil	LQ0/3	1000	538
2451	NITROGEN TRIFLUORIDE	Nil	Nil	Nil	Nil	Nil	Nil	LQ0/3	1000	
2452	ETHYL ACETYLENE, STABILISED	Nil	Nil	Nil	Nil	Nil	Nil	LQ0/2	333	
2453	ETHYL FLUORIDE (REFRIGERANT GAS R161)	Nil	Nil	Nil	Nil	Nil	Nil	LQ0/2	333	
2454	METHYL FLUORIDE (REFRIGERANT GAS R41)	Nil	Nil	Nil	Nil	Nil	Nil	LQ0/2	333	
2455	METHYL NITRITE	Carriage	Prohibited		-	-	-	Carriage		Prohibited
2456	2-CHLOROPROPENE	30/300	500 ml	1 litre	Not	Not	Allowed	LQ3/1	20	
2457	2,3-DIMETHYLBUTANE	30/500	3 litres	30 kg	1 litre	20 kg	20 kg	LQ4/2	333	
2458	HEXADIENES	30/500	3 litres	30 kg	1 litre	20 kg	20 kg	LQ4/2	333	

UN	Substance	Excepted Quantities	LQ Packages Receptacle Size	LQ Packages Package Gross	LQ Shrink Wrapped Trays Receptacle Size	LQ Shrink Wrapped Trays Package Gross	Limited Quantity Value/Transport Category	Max Load	Special Provisions
2459	2-METHYL-1-BUTENE	30/300	500 ml	1 litre	Not	Allowed	LQ3/1	20	
2460	2-METHYL-2-BUTENE	30/500	3 litres	30 kg	1 litre	20 kg	LQ4/2	333	
2461	METHYLPENTADIENE	30/500	3 litres	30 kg	1 litre	20 kg	LQ4/2	333	
2463	ALUMINIUM HYDRIDE	Nil	Nil	Nil	Nil	Nil	LQ0/1	20	
2464	BERYLLIUM NITRATE	30/500	500 g	30 kg	500 g	20 kg	LQ11/2	333	
2465	DICHLOROISOCYANURIC ACID DRY OR DICHLOROISOCYANURIC ACID SALTS	30/500	500 g	30 kg	500 g	20 kg	LQ11/2	333	135
2466	POTASSIUM SUPEROXIDE	Nil	Nil	Nil	Nil	Nil	LQ0/1	20	
2468	TRICHLOROISOCYANURIC ACID, DRY	30/500	500 g	30 kg	500 g	20 kg	LQ11/2	333	
2469	ZINC BROMATE	30/1000	1 kg	30 kg	1 kg	20 kg	LQ12/3	1000	
2470	PHENYLACETONITRILE, LIQUID	30/1000	5 litres	30 kg	5 litres	20 kg	LQ7/2	333	
2471	OSMIUM TETROXIDE	1/300	Nil	Nil	Nil	Nil	LQ0/1	20	
2473	SODIUM ARSANILATE	30/1000	6 kg	30 kg	3 kg	20 kg	LQ9/2	333	
2474	THIOPHOSGENE	1/500	500 ml	2 litres	100 ml	2 litres	LQ17/2	333	279
2475	VANADIUM TRICHLORIDE	30/1000	6 kg	30 kg	2 kg	20 kg	LQ24/3	1000	
2477	METHYL ISOTHIOCYANATE	1/300	Nil	Nil	Nil	Nil	LQ0/1	20	

UN	Name						LQ		
2478	ISOCYANATES, FLAMMABLE, TOXIC, N.O.S. OR ISOCYANATE SOLUTION, FLAMMABLE, TOXIC, N.O.S., PG11	30/500	Nil	Nil	Nil	Nil	LQ0/2	333	274, 539
2478	ISOCYANATES, FLAMMABLE, TOXIC, N.O.S. OR ISOCYANATE SOLUTION, FLAMMABLE, TOXIC, N.O.S., PG111	30/1000	5 litres	30 kg	5 litres	20 kg	LQ7/3	1000	274
2480	METHYL ISOCYANATE	1/300	Nil	Nil	Nil	Nil	LQ0/1	20	
2481	ETHYL ISOCYANATE	Nil	Nil	Nil	Nil	Nil	LQ0/1	20	
2482	N-PROPYL ISOCYANATE	1/300	Nil	Nil	Nil	Nil	LQ0/1	20	
2483	ISOPROPYL ISOCYANATE	Nil	Nil	Nil	Nil	Nil	LQ0/1	20	
2484	TERT-BUTYL ISOCYANATE	1/300	Nil	Nil	Nil	Nil	LQ0/1	20	
2485	N-BUTYL ISOCYANATE	1/300	Nil	Nil	Nil	Nil	LQ0/1	20	
2486	ISOBUTYL ISOCYANATE	30/500	Nil	Nil	Nil	Nil	LQ0/2	333	
2487	PHENYL ISOCYANATE	1/300	Nil	Nil	Nil	Nil	LQ0/1	20	
2488	CYLOHEXYL ISOCYANATE	1/300	Nil	Nil	Nil	Nil	LQ0/1	20	
2490	DICHLOROISOPROPYL ETHER	1/500	500 ml	2 litres	100 ml	2 litres	LQ17/2	333	
2491	ETHANOLAMINE OR ETHANOLAMINE SOLUTION	30/1000	5 litres	30 kg	5 litres	20 kg	LQ7/3	1000	
2493	HEXAMETHYLENEIMINE	30/500	3 litres	30 kg	1 litre	20 kg	LQ4/2	333	
2495	IODINE PENTAFLUORIDE	Nil	Nil	Nil	Nil	Nil	LQ0/1	20	
2496	PROPIONIC ANHYDRIDE	30/1000	5 litres	30 kg	5 litres	20 kg	LQ7/3	1000	
2498	1,2,3,6-TETRAHYDROBENZALDEHYDE	30/1000	5 litres	30 kg	5 litres	20 kg	LQ7/3	1000	

UN	Substance	Excepted Quantities	LQ Packages		LQ Shrink Wrapped Trays		Limited Quantity Value/Transport Category	Max Load	Special Provisions
			Receptacle Size	Package Gross	Receptacle Size	Package Gross			
2501	TRIS(1-AZIRIDINYL) PHOSPHINE OXIDE SOLUTION, PG11	1/500	500 ml	2 litres	100 ml	2 litres	LQ17/2	333	
2501	TRIS(1-AZIRIDINYL) PHOSPHINE OXIDE SOLUTION, PG111	30/1000	5 litres	30 kg	5 litres	20 kg	LQ7/2	333	
2502	VALERYL CHLORIDE	30/500	1 litre	30 kg	500 ml	20 kg	LQ22/2	333	
2503	ZIRCONIUM TETRACHLORIDE	30/1000	6 kg	30 kg	2 kg	20 kg	LQ24/3	1000	
2504	TETRABROMOETHANE	30/1000	5 litres	30 kg	5 litres	20 kg	LQ7/2	333	
2505	AMMONIUM FLUORIDE	30/1000	6 kg	30 kg	3 kg	20 kg	LQ9/2	333	
2506	AMMONIUM HYDROGEN SULPHATE	30/500	3 kg	30 kg	1 kg	20 kg	LQ23/2	333	
2507	CHLOROPLATINIC ACID, SOLID	30/1000	6 kg	30 kg	2 kg	20 kg	LQ24/3	1000	
2508	MOLYBDENUM PENTACHLORIDE	30/1000	6 kg	30 kg	2 kg	20 kg	LQ24/3	1000	
2509	POTASSIUM HYDROGEN SULPHATE	30/500	3 kg	30 kg	1 kg	20 kg	LQ23/2	333	
2511	2-CHLOROPROPIONIC ACID	30/1000	5 litres	30 kg	5 litre	20 kg	LQ7/3	1000	
2512	AMINOPHENOLS (O-,M-,P-)	30/1000	6 kg	30 kg	3 kg	20 kg	LQ9/2	333	279
2513	BROMOACETYL BROMIDE	30/500	1 litre	30 kg	500 ml	20 kg	LQ22/2	333	
2514	BROMOBENZENE	30/1000	5 litres	30 kg	5 litres	20 kg	LQ7/3	1000	
2515	BROMOFORM	30/1000	5 litres	30 kg	1 litre	20 kg	LQ7/2	333	

		30/1000	6 kg	30 kg	3 kg	20 kg	LQ9/2	333
2516	CARBON TETRABROMIDE	30/1000	Nil	Nil	Nil	Nil	LQ9/2	333
2517	1-CHLORO-1, 1-DIFLUOROETHANE (REFRIGERANT GAS R142B)	Nil	Nil	Nil	Nil	Nil	LQ0/2	333
2518	1,5,9-CYCLODODECATRIENE	30/1000	5 litres	30 kg	5 litres	20 kg	LQ7/2	333
2520	CYCLOOCTADIENES	30/1000	5 litres	30 kg	5 litres	20 kg	LQ7/3	1000
2521	DIKETENE, STABILISED	1/300	Nil	Nil	Nil	Nil	LQ0/1	20
2522	2-DIMETHYLAMINOETHYL METHACRYLATE	1/500	500 ml	2 litres	100 ml	2 litres	LQ17/2	333
2524	ETHYL ORTHOFORMATE	30/1000	5 litres	30 kg	5 litres	20 kg	LQ7/3	1000
2525	ETHYL OXALATE	30/1000	5 litres	30 kg	5 litres	20 kg	LQ7/2	333
2526	FURFURYLAMINE	30/1000	5 litres	30 kg	5 litres	20 kg	LQ7/3	1000
2527	ISOBUTYL ACRYLATE, STABILISED	30/1000	5 litres	30 kg	5 litres	20 kg	LQ7/3	1000
2528	ISOBUTYL ISOBUTYRATE	30/1000	5 litres	30 kg	5 litres	20 kg	LQ7/3	1000
2529	ISOBUTYRIC ACID	30/1000	5 litres	30 kg	5 litres	20 kg	LQ7/3	1000
2531	METHACRYLIC ACID, STABILISED	30/500	1 litre	30 kg	500 ml	20 kg	LQ22/2	333
2533	METHYL TRICHLOROACETATE	30/1000	5 litres	30 kg	5 litres	20 kg	LQ7/2	333
2534	METHYLCHLOROSILANE	Nil	Nil	Nil	Nil	Nil	LQ0/1	20
2535	4-METHYLMORPHOLINE (N-METHYLMORPHOLINE)	30/500	3 litres	30 kg	1 litre	20 kg	LQ4/2	333
2536	METHYLTETRAHYDROFURAN	30/500	3 litres	30 kg	1 litre	20 kg	LQ4/2	333
2538	NITRONAPHTHALENE	30/1000	6 kg	30 kg	3 kg	20 kg	LQ9/3	1000
2541	TERPINOLENE	30/1000	5 litres	30 kg	5 litres	20 kg	LQ7/3	1000

UN	Substance	Excepted Quantities	LQ Packages Receptacle Size	LQ Packages Package Gross	LQ Shrink Wrapped Trays Receptacle Size	LQ Shrink Wrapped Trays Package Gross	Limited Quantity Value/Transport Category	Max Load	Special Provisions
2542	TRIBUTYLAMINE	1/500	500 ml	2 litres	100 ml	2 litres	LQ17/2	333	
2545	HAFNIUM POWDER, DRY, PG1	Nil	Nil	Nil	Nil	Nil	LQ0/0	Nil	540
2545	HAFNIUM POWDER, DRY, PG11	30/500	Nil	Nil	Nil	Nil	LQ0/2	333	540
2545	HAFNIUM POWDER, DRY, PG111	30/1000	Nil	Nil	Nil	Nil	LQ0/3	1000	540
2546	TITANIUM POWDER, DRY, PG1	Nil	Nil	Nil	Nil	Nil	LQ0/0	Nil	540
2546	TITANIUM POWDER, DRY, PG11	30/500	Nil	Nil	Nil	Nil	LQ0/2	333	540
2546	TITANIUM POWDER, DRY, PG111	30/1000	Nil	Nil	Nil	Nil	LQ0/3	1000	540
2547	SODIUM SUPEROXIDE	Nil	Nil	Nil	Nil	Nil	LQ0/1	20	
2548	CHLORINE PENTAFLUORIDE	Nil	Nil	Nil	Nil	Nil	LQ0/1	20	
2552	HEXAFLUOROACETONE HYDRATE	1/500	500 ml	2 litres	100 ml	2 litres	LQ17/2	333	
2554	METHYLALLYL CHLORIDE	30/500	3 litres	30 kg	1 litre	20 kg	LQ4/2	333	
2555	NITROCELLULOSE WITH WATER (NOT LESS THAN 25% WATER BY MASS)	Nil	Nil	Nil	Nil	Nil	LQ0/2	333	541
2556	NITROCELLULOSE WITH ALCOHOL (NOT LESS THAN 25% ALCOHOL BY MASS AND NOT MORE THAN 12.6% NITROGEN BY DRY MASS)	Nil	Nil	Nil	Nil	Nil	LQ0/2	333	541

UN No	Name								
2557	NITROCELLULOSE, WITH NOT MORE THAN 12.6% NITROGEN BY DRY MASS, MIXTURE, WITH OR WITHOUT PLASTICISER, WITH OR WITHOUT PIGMENT	Nil	Nil	Nil	Nil	Nil	LQ0/2	333	541, 241
2558	EPIBROMOHYDRIN	1/300	Nil	Nil	Nil	Nil	LQ0/1	20	
2560	2-METHYLPENTAN-2-OL	30/1000	5 litres	30 kg	5 litres	20 kg	LQ7/3	1000	
2561	3-METHYL-1-BUTENE	30/300	500 ml	1 litre	Not	Allowed	LQ3/1	20	
2564	TRICHLOROACETIC ACID SOLUTION, PG11	30/500	1 litre	30 kg	500 ml	20 kg	LQ22/2	333	274, 596
2564	TRICHLOROACETIC ACID SOLUTION, PG111	30/1000	5 litres	30 kg	5 litres	20 kg	LQ7/3	1000	274, 596
2565	DICYCLOHEXYLAMINE	30/1000	5 litres	30 kg	5 litres	20 kg	LQ7/3	1000	
2567	SODIUM PENTACHLOROPHENATE	1/500	1 kg	4 kg	500 g	4 kg	LQ18/2	333	
2570	CADMIUM COMPOUND, PG1	1/300	Nil	Nil	Nil	Nil	LQ0/1	20	274, 596
2570	CADMIUM COMPOUND, PG11	1/500	1 kg	4 kg	500 g	4 kg	LQ18/2	333	274, 596
2570	CADMIUM COMPOUND, PG111	30/1000	6 kg	30 kg	3 kg	20 kg	LQ9/2	333	274, 596
2571	ALKYLSULPHURIC ACIDS	30/500	1 litre	30 kg	500 ml	20 kg	LQ22/2	333	274, 596
2572	PHENYLHYDRAZINE	1/500	500 ml	2 litres	100 ml	2 litres	LQ17/2	333	
2573	THALLIUM CHLORATE	30/500	500 g	30 kg	500 g	20 kg	LQ11/2	333	
2574	TRICRESYL PHOSPHATE WITH MORE THAN 3% ORTHO ISOMER	1/500	500 ml	2 litres	100 ml	2 litres	LQ17/2	333	
2576	PHOSPHORUS OXYBROMIDE, MOLTEN	Nil	Nil	Nil	Nil	Nil	LQ0/2	333	
2577	PHENYLACETYL CHLORIDE	30/500	1 litre	30 kg	500 ml	20 kg	LQ22/2	333	

UN	Substance	Excepted Quantities	LQ Packages		LQ Shrink Wrapped Trays		Limited Quantity Value/Transport Category	Max Load	Special Provisions
			Receptacle Size	Package Gross	Receptacle Size	Package Gross			
2578	PHOSPHORUS TRIOXIDE	30/1000	6 kg	30 kg	2 kg	20 kg	LQ24/3	1000	
2579	PIPERAZINE	30/1000	6 kg	30 kg	2 kg	20 kg	LQ24/3	1000	
2580	ALUMINIUM BROMIDE SOLUTION	30/1000	5 litre	30 kg	5 litres	20 kg	LQ7/3	1000	
2581	ALUMINIUM CHLORIDE SOLUTION	30/1000	5 litres	30 kg	5 litres	20 kg	LQ7/3	1000	
2582	FERRIC CHLORIDE SOLUTION	30/1000	5 litres	30 kg	5 litres	20 kg	LQ7/3	1000	
2583	ALKYLSULPHONIC ACIDS, SOLID OR ARYLSULPHONIC ACIDS, SOLID WITH MORE THAN 5% FREE SULPHURIC ACID	30/500	3 kg	30 kg	1 kg	20 kg	LQ23/2	333	274
2584	ALKYLSULPHONIC ACIDS, LIQUID OR ARYLSULPHONIC ACIDS, LIQUID WITH MORE THAN 5% FREE SULPHURIC ACID	30/500	1 litre	30 kg	500 ml	20 kg	LQ22/2	333	274
2585	ALKYLSULPHONIC ACIDS, SOLID OR ARYLSULPHONIC ACIDS, SOLID WITH NOT MORE THAN 5% FREE SULPHURIC ACID	30/1000	6 kg	30 kg	2 kg	20 kg	LQ24/3	1000	274
2586	ALKYLSULPHONIC ACIDS, LIQUID OR ARYLSULPHONIC ACIDS, LIQUID WITH NOT MORE THAN 5% FREE SULPHURIC ACID	30/1000	5 litres	30 kg	5 litres	20 kg	LQ7/3	1000	274
2587	BENZOQUINONE	1/500	1 kg	4 kg	500 g	4 kg	LQ18/2	333	
2588	PESTICIDE, SOLID, TOXIC, N.O.S., PG1	1/300	Nil	Nil	Nil	Nil	LQ0/1	20	61, 274,648
2588	PESTICIDE, SOLID, TOXIC, N.O.S., PG11	1/500	1 kg	4 kg	500 g	4 kg	LQ18/2	333	61, 274, 648

	Name								
2588	PESTICIDE, SOLID, TOXIC, N.O.S., PG III	30/1000	6 kg	30 kg	3 kg	20 kg	LQ9/2	333	61, 274, 648
2589	VINYL CHLOROACETATE	1/500	500 ml	2 litres	100 ml	2 litres	LQ17/2	333	
2590	WHITE ASBESTOS (CHRYSOTILE, ACTINOLITE, ANTHOPHYLLITE, TREMOLITE)	30/1000	6 kg	30 kg	6 kg	20 kg	LQ27/3	1000	168, 542
2591	XENON, REFRIGERATED LIQUID	30/1000	120 ml	30 kg	120 ml	20 kg	LQ1/3	1000	593
2599	CHLOROTRIFLUOROMETHANE AND TRIFLUOROMETHANE AZEOTROPIC MIXTURE (REFRIGERANT GAS R503) WITH APPROXIMATELY 60% CHLOROTRIFLUOROMETHANE	30/1000	120 ml	30 kg	120 ml	20 kg	LQ1/3	1000	
2601	CYCLOBUTANE	Nil	Nil	Nil	Nil	Nil	LQ0/2	333	
2602	DICHLORODIFLUOROMETHANE AND DIFLUOROETHANE AZEOTROPIC MIXTURE (REFRIGERANT GAS R500) WITH APPROXIMATELY 74% DICHLORODIFLUOROMETHANE	30/1000	120 ml	30 kg	120 ml	20 kg	LQ1/3	1000	
2603	CYCLOHEPTATRIENE	30/500	Nil	Nil	Nil	Nil	LQ0/2	333	
2604	BORON TRIFLUORIDE DIETHYL ETHERATE	Nil	Nil	Nil	Nil	Nil	LQ0/1	20	
2605	METHOXYMETHYL ISOCYANATE	Nil	Nil	Nil	Nil	Nil	LQ0/1	20	
2606	METHYL ORTHOSILICATE	1/300	Nil	Nil	Nil	Nil	LQ0/1	20	
2607	ACROLEIN DIMER, STABILISED	30/1000	5 litres	30 kg	5 litres	20 kg	LQ7/3	1000	
2608	NITROPROPANES	30/1000	5 litres	30 kg	5 litres	20 kg	LQ7/3	1000	
2609	TRIALLYL BORATE	30/1000	5 litres	30 kg	5 litres	20 kg	LQ7/2	333	
2610	TRIALLYLAMINE	30/1000	5 litres	30 kg	5 litres	20 kg	LQ7/3	1000	

UN	Substance	Excepted Quantities	LQ Packages Receptacle Size	LQ Packages Package Gross	LQ Shrink Wrapped Trays Receptacle Size	LQ Shrink Wrapped Trays Package Gross	Limited Quantity Value/Transport Category	Max Load	Special Provisions
2611	PROPYLENE CHLOROHYDRIN	1/500	500 ml	2 litres	100 ml	2 litres	LQ17/2	333	
2612	METHYL PROPYL ETHER	30/500	3 litres	30 kg	1 litre	20 kg	LQ4/2	333	
2614	METHALLYL ALCOHOL	30/1000	5 litres	30 kg	5 litres	20 kg	LQ7/3	1000	
2615	ETHYL PROPYL ETHER	30/500	3 litres	30 kg	1 litre	20 kg	LQ4/2	333	
2616	TRIISOPROPYL BORATE, PG11	30/500	3 litres	30 kg	1 litre	20 kg	LQ4/2	333	
2616	TRIISOPROPYL BORATE, PG111	30/1000	5 litres	30 kg	5 litres	20 kg	LQ7/3	1000	
2617	METHYLCYCLOHEXANOLS, FLAMMABLE	30/1000	5 litres	30 kg	5 litres	20 kg	LQ7/3	1000	
2618	VINYLTOLUENES, STABILISED	30/1000	5 litres	30 kg	5 litres	20 kg	LQ7/3	1000	
2619	BENZYLDIMETHYLAMINE	30/500	1 litre	30 kg	500 ml	20 kg	LQ22/2	333	
2620	AMYL BUTYRATES	30/1000	5 litres	30 kg	5 litres	20 kg	LQ7/3	1000	
2621	ACETYL METHYL CARBINOL	30/1000	5 litres	30 kg	5 litres	20 kg	LQ7/3	1000	
2622	GLYCIDALDEHYDE	30/500	Nil	Nil	Nil	Nil	LQ0/2	333	
2623	FIRELIGHTERS, SOLID WITH FLAMMABLE LIQUID	30/1000	6 kg	30 kg	3 kg	20 kg	LQ9/4	Unlimited	
2624	MAGNESIUM SILICIDE	30/500	500 g	30 kg	500 g	20 kg	LQ11/2	333	
2626	CHLORIC ACID, AQUEOUS SOLUTION WITH NOT MORE THAN 10% CHLORIC ACID	30/500	500 ml	30 kg	500 ml	20 kg	LQ10/2	333	613

2627	NITRITES, INORGANIC, N.O.S.	30/500	500 g	30 kg	Nil	Nil	LQ11/2	333	103, 274
2628	POTASSIUM FLUOROACETATE	1/300	Nil	Nil	Nil	Nil	LQ0/1	20	
2629	SODIUM FLUOROACETATE	1/300	Nil	Nil	Nil	Nil	LQ0/1	20	
2630	SELENATES OR SELENITES	1/300	Nil	Nil	Nil	Nil	LQ0/1	20	274
2642	FLUOROACETIC ACID	1/300	Nil	Nil	Nil	Nil	LQ0/1	20	
2643	METHYL BROMOACETATE	1/500	500 ml	2 litres	100 ml	2 litres	LQ17/2	333	
2644	METHYL IODIDE	1/300	Nil	Nil	Nil	Nil	LQ0/1	20	
2645	PHENACYL BROMIDE	1/500	1 kg	4 kg	500 g	4 kg	LQ18/2	333	
2646	HEXACHLOROCYCLOPENTADIENE	1/300	Nil	Nil	Nil	Nil	LQ0/1	20	
2647	MALONONITRILE	1/500	1 kg	4 kg	500 g	4 kg	LQ18/2	333	
2648	1,2-DIBROMOBUTAN-3-ONE	1/500	500 ml	2 litres	100 ml	2 litres	LQ17/2	333	
2649	1,3-DICHLOROACETONE	1/500	1 kg	4 kg	500 g	4 kg	LQ18/2	333	
2650	1-1-DICHLORO-1-NITROETHANE	1/500	500 ml	2 litres	100 ml	2 litres	LQ17/2	333	
2651	4,4'-DIAMINODIPHENYLMETHANE	30/1000	6 kg	30 kg	3 kg	20 kg	LQ9/2	333	
2653	BENZYL IODIDE	1/500	500 ml	2 litres	100 ml	2 litres	LQ17/2	333	
2655	POTASSIUM FLUOROSILICATE	30/1000	6 kg	30 kg	3 kg	20 kg	LQ9/2	333	
2656	QUINOLINE	30/1000	5 kg	30 kg	5 kg	20 kg	LQ7/2	333	
2657	SELENIUM DISULPHIDE	1/500	1 kg	4 kg	500 g	4 kg	LQ18/2	333	
2659	SODIUM CHLOROACETATE	30/1000	6 kg	30 kg	3 kg	20 kg	LQ9/2	333	
2660	NITROTOLUIDINES (MONO)	30/1000	6 kg	30 kg	3 kg	20 kg	LQ9/2	333	
2661	HEXACHLOROACETONE	30/1000	5 kg	30 kg	5 kg	20 kg	LQ7/2	333	

UN	Substance	Excepted Quantities	LQ Packages		LQ Shrink Wrapped Trays		Limited Quantity Value/Transport Category	Max Load	Special Provisions
			Receptacle Size	Package Gross	Receptacle Size	Package Gross			
2664	DIBROMOMETHANE	30/1000	5 litres	30 kg	5 litres	20 kg	LQ7/2	333	
2667	BUTYLTOLUENES	30/1000	5 litres	30 kg	5 litres	20 kg	LQ7/2	333	
2668	CHLOROACETONITRILE	1/500	500 ml	2 litres	100 ml	2 litres	LQ17/2	333	
2669	CHLOROCRESOLS, SOLUTION, PG11	1/500	500 ml	2 litres	100 ml	2 litres	LQ17/2	333	
2669	CHLOROCRESOLS, SOLUTION, PG111	30/1000	5 litres	30 kg	5 litres	20 kg	LQ7/2	333	
2670	CYANURIC CHLORIDE	30/500	3 kg	30 kg	1 kg	20 kg	LQ23/2	333	
2671	AMINOPYRIDINES (O-,M-,P-)	1/500	1 kg	4 kg	500 g	4 kg	LQ18/2	333	
2672	AMMONIA SOLUTION, RELATIVE DENSITY BETWEEN 0.880 AND 0.957 AT 15 °C IN WATER WITH MORE THAN 10% BUT NOT MORE THAN 35% AMMONIA	30/1000	5 litres	30 kg	5 litres	20 kg	LQ7/3	1000	543
2673	2-AMINO-4-CHLOROPHENOL	1/500	1 kg	4 kg	500 g	4 kg	LQ18/2	333	
2674	SODIUM FLUOROSILICATE	30/1000	6 kg	30 kg	3 kg	20 kg	LQ9/2	333	
2676	STIBINE	Nil	Nil	Nil	Nil	Nil	LQ0/1	20	
2677	RUBIDIUM HYDROXIDE SOLUTION, PG11	30/500	1 litre	30 kg	500 ml	20 kg	LQ22/2	333	
2677	RUBIDIUM HYDROXIDE SOLUTION, PG111	30/1000	5 litres	30 kg	5 litres	20 kg	LQ7/3	1000	
2678	RUBIDIUM HYDROXIDE	30/500	3 kg	30 kg	1 kg	20 kg	LQ23/2	333	
2679	LITHIUM HYDROXIDE SOLUTION, PG11	30/500	1 litre	30 kg	500 ml	20 kg	LQ22/2	333	

2679	LITHIUM HYDROXIDE SOLUTION, PG111	30/1000	5 litres	30 kg	5 litres	20 kg	LQ7/3	1000	
2680	LITHIUM HYDROXIDE	30/500	3 kg	30 kg	1 kg	20 kg	LQ23/2	333	
2681	CAESIUM HYDROXIDE SOLUTION, PG11	30/500	1 litre	30 kg	500 ml	20 kg	LQ22/2	333	
2681	CAESIUM HYDROXIDE SOLUTION, PG111	30/1000	5 litres	30 kg	5 litres	20 kg	LQ7/3	1000	
2682	CAESIUM HYDROXIDE	30/500	3 kg	30 kg	1 kg	20 kg	LQ23/2	333	
2683	AMMONIUM SULPHIDE SOLUTION	30/500	1 litre	30 kg	500 ml	20 kg	LQ22/2	333	
2684	3-DIETHYLAMINOPROPYLAMINE	30/1000	5 litres	30 kg	5 litres	20 kg	LQ7/3	1000	
2685	N,N-DIETHYLETHYLENEDIAMINE	30/500	1 litre	30 kg	500 ml	20 kg	LQ22/2	333	
2686	2-DIETHYLAMINOETHANOL	30/500	1 litre	30 kg	500 ml	20 kg	LQ22/2	333	
2687	DICYCLOHEXYLAMMONIUM NITRITE	30/1000	6 kg	30 kg	3 kg	20 kg	LQ9/3	1000	
2688	1-BROMO-3-CHLOROPROPANE	30/1000	5 litres	30 kg	5 litres	20 kg	LQ7/2	333	
2689	GLYCEROL ALPHA-MONOCHLOROHYDRIN	30/1000	5 litres	30 kg	5 litres	20 kg	LQ7/2	333	
2690	N-N-BUTYLIMIDAZOLE	1/500	500 ml	2 litres	100 ml	2 litres	LQ17/2	333	
2691	PHOSPHORUS PENTABROMIDE	30/500	3 kg	30 kg	1 kg	20 kg	LQ23/2	333	
2692	BORON TRIBROMIDE	Nil	Nil	Nil	Nil	Nil	LQ0/1	20	
2693	BISULPHITES, AQUEOUS SOLUTION, N.O.S.	30/1000	5 litres	30 kg	5 litres	20 kg	LQ7/3	1000	274
2698	TETRAHYDROPHTHALIC ANHYDRIDES WITH MORE THAN 0.05% OF MALEIC ANHYDRIDE	30/1000	6 kg	30 kg	2 kg	20 kg	LQ24/3	1000	169
2699	TRIFLUOROACETIC ACID	Nil	Nil	Nil	Nil	Nil	LQ0/1	20	
2705	1-PENTOL	30/500	1 litre	30 kg	500 ml	20 kg	LQ22/2	333	

UN	Substance	Excepted Quantities	LQ Packages Receptacle Size	LQ Packages Package Gross	LQ Shrink Wrapped Trays Receptacle Size	LQ Shrink Wrapped Trays Package Gross	Limited Quantity Value/Transport Category	Max Load	Special Provisions
2707	DIMETHYLDIOXANES, PG11	30/500	3 litres	30 kg	1 litre	20 kg	LQ4/2	333	
2707	DIMETHYLDIOXANES, PG111	30/1000	5 litres	30 kg	5 litres	20 kg	LQ7/3	1000	
2709	BUTYLBENZENES	30/1000	5 litres	30 kg	5 litres	20 kg	LQ7/3	1000	
2710	DIPROPYL KETONE	30/1000	5 litres	30 kg	5 litres	20 kg	LQ7/3	1000	
2713	ACRIDINE	30/1000	6 kg	30 kg	3 kg	20 kg	LQ9/2	333	
2714	ZINC RESINATE	30/1000	6 kg	30 kg	3 kg	20 kg	LQ9/3	1000	
2715	ALUMINIUM RESINATE	30/1000	6 kg	30 kg	3 kg	20 kg	LQ9/3	1000	
2716	1,4-BUTYNEDIOL	30/1000	6 kg	30 kg	3 kg	20 kg	LQ9/2	333	
2717	CAMPHOR, SYNTHETIC	30/1000	6 kg	30 kg	3 kg	20 kg	LQ9/3	1000	
2719	BARIUM BROMATE	30/500	500 g	30 kg	500 g	20 kg	LQ11/2	333	
2720	CHROMIUM NITRATE	30/1000	1 kg	30 kg	1 kg	20 kg	LQ12/3	1000	
2721	COPPER CHLORATE	30/500	500 g	30 kg	500 g	20 kg	LQ11/2	333	
2722	LITHIUM NITRATE	30/1000	1 kg	30 kg	1 kg	20 kg	LQ12/3	1000	
2723	MAGNESIUM CHLORATE	30/500	500 g	30 kg	500 g	20 kg	LQ11/2	333	
2724	MANGANESE NITRATE	30/1000	1 kg	30 kg	1 kg	20 kg	LQ12/3	1000	
2725	NICKEL NITRATE	30/1000	1 kg	30 kg	1 kg	20 kg	LQ12/3	1000	

2726	NICKEL NITRITE	30/1000	1 kg	30 kg	1 kg	20 kg	LQ12/3	1000	
2727	THALLIUM NITRATE	1/500	1 kg	4 kg	500 g	4 kg	LQ18/2	333	
2728	ZIRCONIUM NITRATE	30/1000	1 kg	30 kg	1 kg	20 kg	LQ12/3	1000	
2729	HEXACHLOROBENZENE	30/1000	6 kg	30 kg	3 kg	20 kg	LQ9/2	333	
2730	NITROANISOLE, LIQUID	30/1000	5 litres	30 kg	5 litres	20 kg	LQ7/2	333	
2732	NITROBROMOBENZENES, LIQUID	30/1000	5 litres	30 kg	5 litres	20 kg	LQ7/2	333	
2733	AMINES, FLAMMABLE, CORROSIVE, N.O.S. OR POLYAMINES, FLAMMABLE CORROSIVE, N.O.S., PG1	Nil	500 ml	1 litre	Not	Allowed	LQ3/1	20	274, 544
2733	AMINES, FLAMMABLE, CORROSIVE, N.O.S. OR POLYAMINES, FLAMMABLE CORROSIVE, N.O.S., PG11	30/500	3 litres	30 kg	1 litre	20 kg	LQ4/2	333	274, 544
2733	AMINES, FLAMMABLE, CORROSIVE, N.O.S. OR POLYAMINES, FLAMMABLE CORROSIVE, N.O.S., PG111	30/1000	5 litres	30 kg	5 litres	20 kg	LQ7/3	1000	274, 544
2734	AMINES, LIQUID, CORROSIVE, FLAMMABLE, N.O.S. OR POLYAMINES, LIQUID, CORROSIVE, FLAMMABLE, N.O.S., PG1	Nil	Nil	Nil	Nil	Nil	LQ0/1	20	274
2734	AMINES, LIQUID, CORROSIVE, FLAMMABLE, N.O.S. OR POLYAMINES, LIQUID, CORROSIVE, FLAMMABLE, N.O.S., PG11	30/500	1 litre	30 kg	500 ml	20 kg	LQ22/2	333	274
2735	AMINES, LIQUID, CORROSIVE, N.O.S. OR POLYAMINES, LIQUID, CORROSIVE, N.O.S., PG1	Nil	Nil	Nil	Nil	Nil	LQ0/1	20	274

UN	Substance	Excepted Quantities	LQ Packages		LQ Shrink Wrapped Trays		Limited Quantity Value/Transport Category	Max Load	Special Provisions
			Receptacle Size	Package Gross	Receptacle Size	Package Gross			
2735	AMINES, LIQUID, CORROSIVE, N.O.S. OR POLYAMINES, LIQUID, CORROSIVE, N.O.S., PG11	30/500	1 litre	30 kg	500 ml	20 kg	LQ22/2	333	274
2735	AMINES, LIQUID, CORROSIVE, N.O.S. OR POLYAMINES, LIQUID, CORROSIVE, N.O.S., PG111	30/1000	5 litres	30 kg	5 litres	20 kg	LQ7/3	1000	274
2738	N-BUTYLANILINE	1/500	500 ml	2 litres	100 ml	2 litres	LQ17/2	333	
2739	BUTYRIC ANHYDRIDE	30/1000	5 litres	30 kg	5 litres	20 kg	LQ7/3	1000	
2740	N-PROPYL CHLOROFORMATE	1/300	Nil	Nil	Nil	Nil	LQ0/1	20	
2741	BARIUM HYPOCHLORITE WITH MORE THAN 22% AVAILABLE CHLORINE	30/500	500 g	30 kg	500 g	20 kg	LQ11/2	333	
2742	CHLOROFORMATES, TOXIC, CORROSIVE, FLAMMABLE, N.O.S.	1/500	500 ml	2 litres	100 ml	2 litres	LQ17/2	333	
2743	N-BUTYL CHLOROFORMATE	1/500	500 ml	2 litres	100 ml	2 litres	LQ17/2	333	
2744	CYCLOBUTYL CHLOROFORMATE	1/500	500 ml	2 litres	100 ml	2 litres	LQ17/2	333	
2745	CHLOROMETHYL CHLOROFORMATE	1/500	500 ml	2 litres	100 ml	2 litres	LQ17/2	333	
2746	PHENYL CHLOROFORMATE	1/500	500 ml	2 litres	100 ml	2 litres	LQ17/2	333	
2747	TERT-BUTYLCYCLOHEXYL CHLOROFORMATE	30/1000	5 litres	30 kg	5 litres	20 kg	LQ7/2	333	

UN	Name								
2748	2-ETHYLHEXYL CHLOROFORMATE	1/500	500 ml	2 litres	100 ml	2 litres	LQ17/2	333	
2749	TETRAMETHYSILANE	30/300	500 ml	1 litre	Not	Allowed	LQ3/1	20	
2750	1,3-DICHLOROPROPANOL-2	1/500	500 ml	2 litres	100 ml	2 litres	LQ17/2	333	
2751	DIETHYLTHIOPHOSPHORYL CHLORIDE	30/500	1 litre	30 kg	500 ml	20 kg	LQ22/2	333	
2752	1,2-EPOXY-3-ETHOXYPROPANE	30/1000	5 litres	30 kg	5 litres	20 kg	LQ7/3	1000	
2753	N-ETHYLBENZYLTOLUIDINES, LIQUID	30/1000	5 litres	30 kg	5 litres	20 kg	LQ7/2	333	
2754	N-ETHYLTOLUIDINES	1/500	500 ml	2 litres	100 ml	2 litres	LQ17/2	333	
2757	CARBAMATE PESTICIDE, SOLID, TOXIC, PG1	1/300	Nil	Nil	Nil	Nil	LQ0/1	20	61, 274, 648
2757	CARBAMATE PESTICIDE, SOLID, TOXIC, PG11	1/500	1 kg	4 kg	500 g	4 kg	LQ18/2	333	61, 274, 648
2757	CARBAMATE PESTICIDE, SOLID, TOXIC, PG111	30/1000	6 kg	30 kg	3 kg	20 kg	LQ9/2	333	61, 274, 648
2758	CARBAMATE PESTICIDE, LIQUID, FLAMMABLE, TOXIC, PG1	Nil	500 ml	1 litre	Not	Allowed	LQ3/1	20	61, 274
2758	CARBAMATE PESTICIDE, LIQUID, FLAMMABLE, TOXIC, PG11	30/500	3 litres	30 kg	1 litre	20 kg	LQ4/2	333	61, 274
2759	ARSENICAL PESTICIDE, SOLID, TOXIC, PG1	1/300	Nil	Nil	Nil	Nil	LQ0/1	20	61, 274, 648
2759	ARSENICAL PESTICIDE, SOLID, TOXIC, PG11	1/500	1 kg	4 kg	500 g	4 kg	LQ18/2	333	61, 274, 648
2759	ARSENICAL PESTICIDE, SOLID, TOXIC, PG111	30/1000	6 kg	30 kg	3 kg	20 kg	LQ9/2	333	61, 274, 648
2760	ARSENICAL PESTICIDE, LIQUID, FLAMMABLE, TOXIC, PG1	Nil	500 ml	1 litre	Not	Allowed	LQ3/1	20	61, 274

UN	Substance	Excepted Quantities	LQ Packages Receptacle Size	LQ Packages Package Gross	LQ Shrink Wrapped Trays Receptacle Size	LQ Shrink Wrapped Trays Package Gross	Limited Quantity Value/Transport Category	Max Load	Special Provisions
2760	ARSENICAL PESTICIDE, LIQUID, FLAMMABLE, TOXIC, PG11	30/500	3 litres	30 kg	1 litre	20 kg	LQ4/2	333	61, 274
2761	ORGANOCHLORINE PESTICIDE, SOLID, TOXIC, PG1	1/300	Nil	Nil	Nil	Nil	LQ0/1	20	61, 274, 648
2761	ORGANOCHLORINE PESTICIDE, SOLID, TOXIC, PG11	1/500	1 kg	4 kg	500 g	4 kg	LQ18/2	333	61, 274, 648
2761	ORGANOCHLORINE PESTICIDE, SOLID, TOXIC, PG111	30/1000	6 kg	30 kg	3 kg	20 kg	LQ9/2	333	61, 274, 648
2762	ORGANOCHLORINE PESTICIDE, LIQUID, FLAMMABLE, TOXIC, PG1	Nil	500 ml	1 litre	Not	Allowed	LQ3/1	20	61, 274
2762	ORGANOCHLORINE PESTICIDE, LIQUID, FLAMMABLE, TOXIC, PG11	30/500	3 litres	30 kg	1 litre	20 kg	LQ4/2	333	61, 274
2763	TRIAZINE PESTICIDE, SOLID, TOXIC, PG1	1/300	Nil	Nil	Nil	Nil	LQ0/1	20	61, 274, 648
2763	TRIAZINE PESTICIDE, SOLID, TOXIC, PG11	1/500	1 kg	4 kg	500 g	4 kg	LQ18/2	333	61, 274, 648
2763	TRIAZINE PESTICIDE, SOLID, TOXIC, PG111	30/1000	6 kg	30 kg	3 kg	20 kg	LQ9/2	333	61, 274, 648
2764	TRIAZINE PESTICIDE, LIQUID, FLAMMABLE, TOXIC, PG1	Nil	500 ml	1 litre	Not	Allowed	LQ3/1	20	61,274
2764	TRIAZINE PESTICIDE, LIQUID, FLAMMABLE, TOXIC, PG11	30/500	3 litres	30 kg	1 litre	20 kg	LQ4/2	333	61, 274

UN	Name and Description								
2771	THIOCARBAMATE PESTICIDE, SOLID, TOXIC, PG1	1/300	Nil	Nil	Nil	Nil	LQ0/1	20	61, 274, 648
2771	THIOCARBAMATE PESTICIDE, SOLID, TOXIC, PG11	1/500	1 kg	4 kg	500 g	4 kg	LQ18/2	333	61, 274, 648
2771	THIOCARBAMATE PESTICIDE, SOLID, TOXIC, PG111	30/1000	6 kg	30 kg	3 kg	20 kg	LQ9/2	333	61, 274, 648
2772	THIOCARBAMATE PESTICIDE, LIQUID, FLAMMABLE, TOXIC, PG1	Nil	500 ml	1 litre	Not	Allowed	LQ3/1	20	61, 274
2772	THIOCARBAMATE PESTICIDE, LIQUID, FLAMMABLE, TOXIC, PG11	30/500	3 litres	30 kg	1 litre	20 kg	LQ4/2	333	61, 274
2775	COPPER BASED PESTICIDE, SOLID, TOXIC, PG1	1/300	Nil	Nil	Nil	Nil	LQ0/1	20	61, 274, 648
2775	COPPER BASED PESTICIDE, SOLID, TOXIC, PG11	1/500	1 kg	4 kg	500 g	4 kg	LQ18/2	333	61, 274, 648
2775	COPPER BASED PESTICIDE, SOLID, TOXIC, PG111	30/1000	6 kg	30 kg	3 kg	20 kg	LQ9/2	333	61, 274, 648
2776	COPPER BASED PESTICIDE, LIQUID, FLAMMABLE, TOXIC, PG1	Nil	500 ml	1 litre	Not	Allowed	LQ3/1	20	61, 274
2776	COPPER BASED PESTICIDE, LIQUID, FLAMMABLE, TOXIC, PG11	30/500	3 litres	30 kg	1 litre	20 kg	LQ4/2	333	61, 274
2777	MERCURY BASED PESTICIDE, SOLID, TOXIC, PG1	1/300	Nil	Nil	Nil	Nil	LQ0/1	20	61, 274, 648
2777	MERCURY BASED PESTICIDE, SOLID, TOXIC, PG11	1/500	1 kg	4 kg	500 g	4 kg	LQ18/2	333	61, 274, 648
2777	MERCURY BASED PESTICIDE, SOLID, TOXIC, PG111	30/1000	6 kg	30 kg	3 kg	20 kg	LQ9/2	333	61, 274, 648

UN	Substance	Excepted Quantities	LQ Packages		LQ Shrink Wrapped Trays		Limited Quantity Value/Transport Category	Max Load	Special Provisions
			Receptacle Size	Package Gross	Receptacle Size	Package Gross			
2778	MERCURY BASED PESTICIDE, LIQUID, FLAMMABLE, TOXIC, PG1	Nil	500 ml	1 litre	Not	Allowed	LQ3/1	20	61, 274
2778	MERCURY BASED PESTICIDE, LIQUID, FLAMMABLE, TOXIC, PG11	30/500	3 litre	30 kg	1 litre	20 kg	LQ4/2	333	61, 274
2779	SUBSTITUTED NITROPHENOL PESTICIDE, SOLID, TOXIC, PG1	1/300	Nil	Nil	Nil	Nil	LQ0/1	20	61, 274, 648
2779	SUBSTITUTED NITROPHENOL PESTICIDE, SOLID, TOXIC, PG11	1/500	1 kg	4 kg	500 g	4 kg	LQ18/2	333	61, 274, 648
2779	SUBSTITUTED NITROPHENOL PESTICIDE, SOLID, TOXIC, PG111	30/1000	6 kg	30 kg	3 kg	20 kg	LQ9/2	333	61, 274, 648
2780	SUBSTITUTED NITROPHENOL PESTICIDE, LIQUID, FLAMMABLE, TOXIC, PG1	Nil	500 ml	1 litre	Not	Allowed	LQ3/1	20	61, 274
2780	SUBSTITUTED NITROPHENOL PESTICIDE, LIQUID, FLAMMABLE, TOXIC, PG11	30/500	3 litres	30 kg	1 litre	20 kg	LQ4/2	333	61, 274
2781	BIPYRIDILIUM PESTICIDE, SOLID, TOXIC, PG1	1/300	Nil	Nil	Nil	Nil	LQ0/1	20	61, 274, 648
2781	BIPYRIDILIUM PESTICIDE, SOLID, TOXIC, PG11	1/500	1 kg	4 kg	500 g	4 kg	LQ18/2	333	61, 274, 648
2781	BIPYRIDILIUM PESTICIDE, SOLID, TOXIC, PG111	30/1000	6 kg	30 kg	3 kg	20 kg	LQ9/2	333	61, 274

UN	Name								
2782	BIPYRIDILIUM PESTICIDE, LIQUID, FLAMMABLE, TOXIC, PG1	Nil	500 ml	1 litre	Not	Allowed	LQ3/1	20	61, 274
2782	BIPYRIDILIUM PESTICIDE, LIQUID, FLAMMABLE, TOXIC, PG11	30/500	3 litres	30 kg	1 litre	20 kg	LQ4/2	333	61, 274
2783	ORGANOPHOSPHORUS PESTICIDE, SOLID, TOXIC, PG1	1/300	Nil	Nil	Nil	Nil	LQ0/1	20	61, 274, 648
2783	ORGANOPHOSPHORUS PESTICIDE, SOLID, TOXIC, PG11	1/500	1 kg	4 kg	500 g	4 kg	LQ18/2	333	61, 274, 648
2783	ORGANOPHOSPHORUS PESTICIDE, SOLID, TOXIC, PG111	30/1000	6 kg	30 kg	3 kg	20 kg	LQ9/2	333	61, 274, 648
2784	ORGANOPHOSPHORUS PESTICIDE, LIQUID, FLAMMABLE, TOXIC, PG1	Nil	500 ml	1 litre	Not	Allowed	LQ3/1	20	61, 274
2784	ORGANOPHOSPHORUS PESTICIDE, LIQUID, FLAMMABLE, TOXIC, PG11	30/500	3 litres	30 kg	1 litre	20 kg	LQ4/2	333	61, 274
2785	4-THIAPENTANAL	30/100	5 litres	30 kg	5 litres	20 kg	LQ7/2	333	
2786	ORGANOTIN PESTICIDE, SOLID, TOXIC, PG11	1/300	1 kg	4 kg	500 g	4 kg	LQ18/2	333	61, 274, 648
2786	ORGANOTIN PESTICIDE, SOLID, TOXIC, PG111	30/1000	6 kg	30 kg	3 kg	20 kg	LQ9/2	333	61, 274, 648
2787	ORGANOTIN PESTICIDE, LIQUID, FLAMMABLE, TOXIC, PG1	Nil	500 ml	1 litre	Not	Allowed	LQ3/1	20	61, 274
2787	ORGANOTIN PESTICIDE, LIQUID, FLAMMABLE, TOXIC, PG11	30/500	3 litres	30 kg	1 litre	20 kg	LQ4/2	333	61, 274
2788	ORGANOTIN COMPOUND, LIQUID, N.O.S., PG1	1/300	Nil	Nil	Nil	Nil	LQ0/1	20	43, 274

UN	Substance	Excepted Quantities	LQ Packages Receptacle Size	LQ Packages Package Gross	LQ Shrink Wrapped Trays Receptacle Size	LQ Shrink Wrapped Trays Package Gross	Limited Quantity Value/Transport Category	Max Load	Special Provisions
2788	ORGANOTIN COMPOUND, LIQUID, N.O.S., PG11	1/500	500 ml	2 litres	100 ml	2 litres	LQ17/2	333	43, 274
2788	ORGANOTIN COMPOUND, LIQUID, N.O.S., PG111	30/1000	5 litres	30 kg	5 litres	20 kg	LQ7/2	333	43, 274
2789	ACETIC ACID, GLACIAL OR ACETIC ACID SOLUTION, MORE THAN 80% ACID, BY MASS	30/500	1 litre	30 kg	500 ml	20 kg	LQ22/2	333	
2790	ACETIC ACID SOLUTION, PG11	30/500	1 litre	30 kg	500 ml	20 kg	LQ22/2	333	
2790	ACETIC ACID SOLUTION, PG111	30/1000	5 litres	30 kg	5 litres	20 kg	LQ7/3	1000	597, 647
2793	FERROUS METAL BORINGS, SHAVINGS, TURNINGS OR CUTTINGS, IN A FORM LIABLE TO SELF-HEATING	30/1000	Nil	Nil	Nil	Nil	LQ0/3	1000	592
2794	BATTERIES, WET, FILLED WITH ACID, ELECTRIC, STORAGE	Nil	Nil	Nil	Nil	Nil	LQ0/3	1000	295, 598
2795	BATTERIES, WET, FILLED WITH ALKALI, ELECTRIC, STORAGE	Nil	Nil	Nil	Nil	Nil	LQ0/3	1000	295, 598
2796	SULPHURIC ACID, WITH NOT MORE THAN 51% ACID OR BATTERY FLUID, ACID	30/500	1 litre	30 kg	500 ml	20 kg	LQ22/2	333	
2797	BATTERY FLUID, ALKALI	30/500	1 litre	30 kg	500 ml	20 kg	LQ22/2	333	
2798	PHENYLPHOSPHORUS DICHLORIDE	30/500	1 litre	30 kg	500 ml	20 kg	LQ22/2	333	

UN No	Name								
2799	PHENYLPHOSPHORUS THIODICHLORIDE	30/500	1 litre	30 kg	500 ml	20 kg	LQ22/2	333	
2800	BATTERIES, WET, NON-SPILLABLE, ELECTRIC, STORAGE	Nil	Nil	Nil	Nil	Nil	LQ0/3	1000	238, 295, 598
2801	DYE, LIQUID, CORROSIVE, N.O.S., OR DYE INTERMEDIATE, LIQUID, CORROSIVE, N.O.S., PG1	Nil	Nil	Nil	Nil	Nil	LQ0/1	20	274
2801	DYE, LIQUID, CORROSIVE, N.O.S., OR DYE INTERMEDIATE, LIQUID, CORROSIVE, N.O.S., PG11	30/500	1 litre	30 kg	500 ml	20 kg	LQ22/2	333	274
2801	DYE, LIQUID, CORROSIVE, N.O.S., OR DYE INTERMEDIATE, LIQUID, CORROSIVE, N.O.S., PG111	30/1000	5 litres	30 kg	5 litres	20 kg	LQ7/3	1000	274
2802	COPPER CHLORIDE	30/1000	6 kg	30 kg	2 kg	20 kg	LQ24/3	1000	
2803	GALLIUM	Nil	6 kg	30 kg	2 kg	20 kg	LQ24/3	1000	
2805	LITHIUM HYDRIDE, FUSED SOLID	30/500	500 g	30 kg	500 g	20 kg	LQ11/2	333	
2806	LITHIUM NITRIDE	Nil	Nil	Nil	Nil	Nil	LQ0/1	20	
2807	MAGNETISED MATERIAL	Not	Subject	To ADR	-	-	Not Subject	to	ADR
2809	MERCURY	Nil	5 kg	30 kg	5 kg	20 kg	LQ19/3	1000	599
2810	TOXIC LIQUID, ORGANIC, N.O.S., PG1	1/300	Nil	Nil	Nil	Nil	LQ0/1	20	274, 315, 614
2810	TOXIC LIQUID, ORGANIC, N.O.S., PG11	1/500	500 ml	2 litres	100 ml	2 litres	LQ17/2	333	274, 614
2810	TOXIC LIQUID, ORGANIC, N.O.S., PG111	30/1000	5 litres	30 kg	5 litres	20 kg	LQ7/2	333	274, 614
2811	TOXIC SOLID, ORGANIC, N.O.S., PG1	1/300	Nil	Nil	Nil	Nil	LQ0/1	20	274, 614

UN	Substance	Excepted Quantities	LQ Packages		LQ Shrink Wrapped Trays		Limited Quantity Value/Transport Category	Max Load	Special Provisions
			Receptacle Size	Gross Package	Receptacle Size	Gross Package			
2811	TOXIC SOLID, ORGANIC, N.O.S., PG11	1/500	1 kg	4 kg	500 g	4 kg	LQ18/2	333	274, 614
2811	TOXIC SOLID, ORGANIC, N.O.S., PG111	30/1000	6 kg	30 kg	3 kg	20 kg	LQ9/2	333	274, 614
2812	SODIUM ALUMINATE, SOLID	Not	Subject	To ADR	-	-	Not Subject	to	ADR
2813	WATER-REACTIVE SOLID, N.O.S., PG1	Nil	Nil	Nil	Nil	Nil	LQ0/0	Nil	274
2813	WATER-REACTIVE SOLID, N.O.S., PG11	30/500	500 g	30 kg	500 g	20 kg	LQ11/0	Nil	274
2813	WATER-REACTIVE SOLID, N.O.S., PG111	30/1000	1 kg	30 kg	1 kg	20 kg	LQ12/0	Nil	274
2814	INFECTIOUS SUBSTANCE, AFFECTING HUMANS	Nil	Nil	Nil	Nil	Nil	LQ0/0	Nil	318
2814	INFECTIOUS SUBSTANCE, AFECTING HUMANS, IN REFRIGERATED LIQUID NITROGEN	Nil	Nil	Nil	Nil	Nil	LQ0/0	Nil	318
2814	INFECTIOUS SUBSTANCE, AFFECTING HUMANS (ANIMAL MATERIAL ONLY)	Nil	Nil	Nil	Nil	Nil	LQ0/0	Nil	318
2815	N-AMINOETHYLPIPERAZINE	30/1000	5 litres	30 kg	5 litres	20 kg	LQ7/3	1000	
2817	AMMONIUM HYDROGENDIFLUORIDE SOLUTION, PG11	30/500	1 litre	30 kg	500 ml	20 kg	LQ22/2	333	
2817	AMMONIUM HYDROGENDIFLUORIDE SOLUTION, PG111	30/1000	5 litres	30 kg	5 litres	20 kg	LQ7/3	1000	

UN	Name								
2818	AMMONIUM POLYSULPHIDE SOLUTION, PG11	30/500	1 litre	30 kg	500 ml	20 kg	LQ22/2	333	
2818	AMMONIUM POLYSULPHIDE SOLUTION, PG111	30/1000	5 litres	30 kg	5 litres	20 kg	LQ7/3	1000	
2819	AMYL ACID PHOSPHATE	30/1000	5 litres	30 kg	5 litres	20 kg	LQ7/3	1000	
2820	BUTYRIC ACID	30/1000	5 litres	30 kg	5 litres	20 kg	LQ7/3	1000	
2821	PHENOL SOLUTION, PG11	1/500	500 ml	2 litres	100 ml	2 litres	LQ17/2	333	
2821	PHENOL SOLUTION, PG111	30/1000	5 litres	30 kg	5 litre	20 kg	LQ7/2	333	
2822	2-CHLOROPYRIDINE	1/500	500 ml	2 litres	100 ml	2 litres	LQ17/2	333	
2823	CROTONIC ACID	30/1000	6 kg	30 kg	2 kg	20 kg	LQ24/3	1000	
2826	ETHYL CHLOROTHIOFORMATE	30/500	1 litre	30 kg	500 ml	20 kg	LQ22/2	333	
2829	CAPROIC ACID	30/1000	5 litres	30 kg	5 litres	20 kg	LQ7/3	1000	
2830	LITHIUM FERROSILICON	30/500	500 g	30 kg	500 g	20 kg	LQ11/2	333	
2831	1,1,1-TRICHLOROETHANE	30/1000	5 litres	30 kg	5 litres	20 kg	LQ7/2	333	
2834	PHOSPHOROUS ACID	30/1000	6 kg	24 kg	2 kg	20 kg	LQ24/3	1000	
2835	SODIUM ALUMINIUM HYDRIDE	30/500	500 g	30 kg	500 g	20 kg	LQ11/2	333	
2837	BISULPHATES, AQUEOUS SOLUTION, PG11	30/500	1 litre	30 kg	500 ml	20 kg	LQ22/2	333	274
2837	BISULPHATES, AQUEOUS SOLUTION, PG111	30/1000	5 litres	30 kg	5 litres	20 kg	LQ7/3	1000	274
2838	VINYL BUTYRATE, STABILISED	30/500	3 litres	30 kg	1 litre	20 kg	LQ4/2	333	
2839	ALDOL	1/500	500 ml	2 litres	100 ml	2 litres	LQ17/2	333	
2840	BUTYRALDOXIME	30/1000	5 litres	30 kg	5 litres	20 kg	LQ7/3	1000	

UN	Substance	Excepted Quantities	LQ Packages		LQ Shrink Wrapped Trays		Limited Quantity Value/Transport Category	Max Load	Special Provisions
			Receptacle Size	Package Gross	Receptacle Size	Package Gross			
2841	DI-N-AMYLAMINE	30/1000	5 litres	30 kg	5 litres	20 kg	LQ7/3	1000	
2842	NITROETHANE	30/1000	5 litres	30 kg	5 litres	20 kg	LQ7/3	1000	
2844	CALCIUM MANGANESE SILICON	30/1000	1 kg	30 kg	1 kg	20 kg	LQ12/3	1000	
2845	PYROPHORIC LIQUID, ORGANIC, N.O.S.	Nil	Nil	Nil	Nil	Nil	LQ0/0	Nil	274
2846	PYROPHORIC SOLID, ORGANIC, N.O.S.	Nil	Nil	Nil	Nil	Nil	LQ0/0	Nil	274
2849	3-CHLOROPROPANOL-1	30/1000	5 litres	30 kg	5 litres	20 kg	LQ7/2	333	
2850	PROPYLENE TETRAMER	30/1000	5 litres	30 kg	5 litres	20 kg	LQ7/3	1000	
2851	BORON TRIFLUORIDE DIHYDRATE	30/500	1 litre	30 kg	500 ml	20 kg	LQ22/2	1000	
2852	DIPICRYL SULPHIDE, WETTED WITH NOT LESS THAN 10% WATER, BY MASS	Nil	Nil	Nil	Nil	Nil	LQ0/1	20	545
2853	MAGNESIUM FLUOROSILICATE	30/1000	6 kg	30 kg	3 kg	20 kg	LQ9/2	333	
2854	AMMONIUM FLUOROSILICATE	30/1000	6 kg	30 kg	3 kg	20 kg	LQ9/2	333	
2855	ZINC FLUOROSILICATE	30/1000	6 kg	30 kg	3 kg	20 kg	LQ9/2	333	
2856	FLUOROSILICATES, N.O.S.	30/1000	6 kg	30 kg	3 kg	20 kg	LQ9/2	333	274
2857	REFRIGERATING MACHINES, CONTAINING NON-FLAMMABLE, NON-TOXIC, LIQUEFIED GAS OR AMMONIA SOLUTIONS (UN 2672)	Nil	Nil	Nil	Nil	Nil	LQ0/3	1000	119

		30/1000	6 kg	30 kg	3 kg	20 kg	LQ9/3	1000	546
2858	ZIRCONIUM, DRY, COILED WIRE, FINISHED METAL SHEETS, STRIP	30/1000	6 kg	30 kg	3 kg	20 kg	LQ9/3	1000	546
2859	AMMONIUM METAVANADATE	1/500	1 kg	4 kg	500 g	4 kg	LQ18/2	333	
2861	AMMONIUM POLYVANADATE	1/500	1 kg	4 kg	500 g	4 kg	LQ18/2	333	
2862	VANADIUM PENTOXIDE, NON-FUSED FORM	30/1000	6 kg	30 kg	3 kg	20 kg	LQ9/2	333	600
2863	SODIUM AMMONIUM VANADATE	1/500	1 kg	4 kg	500 g	4 kg	LQ18/2	333	
2864	POTASSIUM METAVANADATE	1/500	1 kg	4 kg	500 g	4 kg	LQ18/2	333	
2865	HYDROXYLAMINE SULPHATE	30/1000	6 kg	30 kg	2 kg	20 kg	LQ24/3	1000	
2869	TITANIUM TRICHLORIDE, MIXTURE, PG11	30/500	3 kg	30 kg	1 kg	20 kg	LQ23/2	333	
2869	TITANIUM TRICHLORIDE, MIXTURE, PG111	30/1000	6 kg	30 kg	2 kg	20 kg	LQ24/3	1000	
2870	ALUMINIUM BOROHYDRIDE	Nil	Nil	Nil	Nil	Nil	LQ0/0	Nil	
2870	ALUMINIUM BOROHYDRIDE IN DEVICES	Nil	Nil	Nil	Nil	Nil	LQ0/0	Nil	
2871	ANTIMONY POWDER	30/1000	6 kg	30 kg	3 kg	20 kg	LQ9/2	333	
2872	DIBROMOCHLOROPROPANES, PG11	1/500	500 ml	2 litres	100 ml	2 litres	LQ17/2	333	
2872	DIBROMOCHLOROPROPANES, PG111	30/1000	5 litres	30 kg	5 litres	20 kg	LQ7/2	333	
2873	DIBUTYLAMINOETHANOL	30/1000	5 litres	30 kg	5 litres	20 kg	LQ7/2	333	
2874	FURFURYL ALCOHOL	30/1000	5 litres	30 kg	5 litres	20 kg	LQ7/2	333	
2875	HEXACHLOROPHENE	30/1000	6 kg	30 kg	3 kg	20 kg	LQ9/2	333	
2876	RESORCINOL	30/1000	6 kg	30 kg	3 kg	20 kg	LQ9/2	333	
2878	TITANIUM SPONGE GRANULES OR TITANIUM SPONGE POWDERS	30/1000	6 kg	30 kg	3 kg	20 kg	LQ9/3	1000	

UN	Substance	Excepted Quantities	LQ Packages		LQ Shrink Wrapped Trays		Limited Quantity Value/Transport Category	Max Load	Special Provisions
			Receptacle Size	Package Gross	Receptacle Size	Package Gross			
2879	SELENIUM OXYCHLORIDE	Nil	Nil	Nil	Nil	Nil	LQ0/1	20	
2880	CALCIUM HYPOCHLORITE, HYDRATED, OR CALCIUM HYPOCHLORITE, HYDRATED MIXTURE WITH NOT LESS THAN 5.5% BUT NOT MORE THAN 16% WATER, PG11	30/500	500 g	30 kg	500 g	20 kg	LQ11/2	333	313, 314,322
2880	CALCIUM HYPOCHLORITE, HYDRATED, OR CALCIUM HYPOCHLORITE, HYDRATED MIXTURE WITH NOT LESS THAN 5.5% BUT NOT MORE THAN 16% WATER, PG111	30/1000	1 kg	30 kg	1 kg	20 kg	LQ12/3	1000	313,314
2881	METAL CATALYST, DRY, PG1	Nil	Nil	Nil	Nil	Nil	LQ0/0	Nil	274
2881	METAL CATALYST, DRY, PG11	30/500	Nil	Nil	Nil	Nil	LQ0/2	333	274
2881	METAL CATALYST, DRY, PG111	30/1000	Nil	Nil	Nil	Nil	LQ0/3	1000	274
2900	INFECTIOUS SUBSTANCE, AFFECTING ANIMALS ONLY	Nil	Nil	Nil	Nil	Nil	LQ0/0	Nil	318
2900	INFECTIOUS SUBSTANCES, AFFECTING ANIMALS ONLY IN REFRIGERATED LIQUID NITROGEN	Nil	Nil	Nil	Nil	Nil	LQ0/0	Nil	318
2901	BROMINE CHLORIDE	Nil	Nil	Nil	Nil	Nil	LQ0/1	20	
2902	PESTICIDE, LIQUID, TOXIC, N.O.S., PG1	1/300	Nil	Nil	Nil	Nil	LQ0/1	20	61,274, 648
2902	PESTICIDE, LIQUID, TOXIC, N.O.S., PG11	1/500	500 ml	2 litres	100 ml	2 litres	LQ17/2	333	61, 274, 648

2902	PESTICIDE, LIQUID, TOXIC, N.O.S., PG111	30/1000	5 litres	30 kg	5 litres	20 kg	LQ7/2	333	61, 274, 648
2903	PESTICIDE, LIQUID, TOXIC, FLAMMABLE, N.O.S., PG1	1/300	Nil	Nil	Nil	Nil	LQ0/1	20	61, 274
2903	PESTICIDE, LIQUID, TOXIC, FLAMMABLE, N.O.S., PG11	1/500	500 ml	2 litres	100 ml	2 litres	LQ17/2	333	61, 274
2903	PESTICIDE, LIQUID, TOXIC, FLAMMABLE, N.O.S., PG111	30/1000	5 litres	30 kg	5 litres	20 kg	LQ7/2	333	61, 274
2904	CHLOROPHENOLATES, LIQUID OR PHENOLATES, LIQUID	30/1000	5 litres	30 kg	5 litres	20 kg	LQ7/3	1000	
2905	CHLOROPHENOLATES, SOLID OR PHENOLATES, SOLID	30/1000	6 kg	30 kg	2 kg	20 kg	LQ24/3	1000	
2907	ISOSORBIDE DINITRATE MIXTURE WITH NOT LESS THAN 60% LACTOSE, MANNOSE, STARCH, OR CALCIUM HYDROGEN PHOSPHATE	Nil	3 kg	30 kg	500 g	20 kg	LQ8/2	333	127
2908	RADIOACTIVE MATERIAL, EXCEPTED PACKAGE – EMPTY PACKAGING	Nil	Nil	Nil	Nil	Nil	LQ0/4	Unlimited	290
2909	RADIOACTIVE MATERIALS, EXCEPTED PACKAGE – ARTICLES MANUFACTURED FROM NATURAL URANIUM OR DEPLETED URANIUM OR NATURAL THORIUM	Nil	Nil	Nil	Nil	Nil	LQ0/4	Unlimited	290
2910	RADIOACTIVE MATERIAL, EXCEPTED PACKAGE – LIMITED QUANTITY OF MATERIAL	Nil	Nil	Nil	Nil	Nil	LQ0/4	Unlimited	290
2911	RADIOACTIVE MATERIAL, EXCEPTED PACKAGE – INSTRUMENTS OR ARTICLES	Nil	Nil	Nil	Nil	Nil	LQ0/4	Unlimited	290
2912	RADIOACTIVE MATERIAL, LOW SPECIFIC ACTIVITY (LSA-I), NON FISSILE OR FISSILE EXCEPTED	Nil	Nil	Nil	Nil	Nil	LQ0/0	Nil	172, 317

UN	Substance	Excepted Quantities	LQ Packages Receptacle Size	LQ Packages Package Gross	LQ Shrink Wrapped Trays Receptacle Size	LQ Shrink Wrapped Trays Package Gross	Limited Quantity Value/Transport Category	Max Load	Special Provisions
2913	RADIOACTIVE MATERIAL, SURFACE CONTAMINATED OBJECTS (SCO-I OR SCO-II), NON-FISSILE OR FISSILE EXCEPTED	Nil	Nil	Nil	Nil	Nil	LQ0/0	Nil	172, 317, 336
2915	RADIOACTIVE MATERIAL, TYPE A PACKAGE, NON SPECIAL FORM, NON-FISSILE OR FISSILE EXCEPTED	Nil	Nil	Nil	Nil	Nil	LQ0/0	Nil	172, 317
2916	RADIOACTIVE MATERIAL, TYPE B (U) PACKAGE, NON-FISSILE OR FISSILE EXCEPTED	Nil	Nil	Nil	Nil	Nil	LQ0/0	Nil	172, 317, 337
2917	RADIOACTIVE MATERIAL, TYPE B (M), NON-FISSILE OR FISSILE EXCEPTED	Nil	Nil	Nil	Nil	Nil	LQ0/0	Nil	172, 317, 337
2919	RADIOACTIVE MATERIAL TRANSPORTED UNDER SPECIAL ARRANGEMENT, NON-FISSILE OR FISSILE EXCEPTED	Nil	Nil	Nil	Nil	Nil	LQ0/0	Nil	172, 317
2920	CORROSIVE LIQUID, FLAMMABLE, N.O.S., PG1	Nil	Nil	Nil	Nil	Nil	LQ0/1	20	274
2920	CORROSIVE LIQUID, FLAMMABLE, N.O.S., PG11	30/500	1 litre	30 kg	500 ml	20 kg	LQ22/2	333	274
2921	CORROSIVE SOLID, FLAMMABLE, N.O.S., PG1	Nil	Nil	Nil	Nil	Nil	LQ0/1	20	274
2921	CORROSIVE SOLID, FLAMMABLE, N.O.S., PG11	30/500	3 kg	30 kg	1 kg	20 kg	LQ23/2	333	274

UN	Name						LQ		
2922	CORROSIVE LIQUID, TOXIC, N.O.S., PG1	Nil	Nil	Nil	Nil	Nil	LQ0/1	20	274
2922	CORROSIVE LIQUID, TOXIC, N.O.S., PG11	30/500	1 litre	30 kg	500 ml	20 kg	LQ22/2	333	274
2922	CORROSIVE LIQUID, TOXIC, N.O.S., PG111	30/1000	5 litres	30 kg	5 litres	20 kg	LQ7/3	1000	274
2923	CORROSIVE SOLID, TOXIC, N.O.S., PG1	Nil	Nil	Nil	Nil	Nil	LQ0/1	20	274
2923	CORROSIVE SOLID, TOXIC, N.O.S., PG11	30/500	3 kg	30 kg	1 kg	20 kg	LQ23/2	333	274
2923	CORROSIVE SOLID, TOXIC, N.O.S., PG111	30/1000	6 kg	30 kg	2 kg	20 kg	LQ24/3	1000	274
2924	FLAMMABLE LIQUID, CORROSIVE, N.O.S., PG1	Nil	500 ml	1 litre	Not	Allowed	LQ3/1	20	274
2924	FLAMMABLE LIQUID, CORROSIVE, N.O.S., PG11	30/500	3 litres	30 kg	1 litre	20 kg	LQ4/2	333	274
2924	CORROSIVE SOLID, TOXIC, N.O.S., PG111	30/1000	5 litres	30 kg	5 litres	20 kg	LQ7/3	1000	274
2925	FLAMMABLE SOLID, CORROSIVE, ORGANIC, N.O.S., PG11	30/500	Nil	Nil	Nil	Nil	LQ0/2	333	274
2925	FLAMMABLE SOLID, CORROSIVE, ORGANIC, N.O.S., PG111	30/1000	Nil	Nil	Nil	Nil	LQ0/3	1000	274
2926	FLAMMABLE SOLID, TOXIC, ORGANIC, N.O.S., PG11	30/500	Nil	Nil	Nil	Nil	LQ0/2	333	274
2926	FLAMMABLE SOLID, TOXIC, ORGANIC, N.O.S., PG111	30/1000	Nil	Nil	Nil	Nil	LQ0/3	1000	274
2927	TOXIC LIQUID, CORROSIVE, ORGANIC, N.O.S., PG1	1/300	Nil	Nil	Nil	Nil	LQ0/1	20	274, 315
2927	TOXIC LIQUID, CORROSIVE, ORGANIC, N.O.S., PG11	1/500	500 ml	2 litres	100 ml	2 litres	LQ17/2	333	274

UN	Substance	Excepted Quantities	LQ Packages		LQ Shrink Wrapped Trays		Limited Quantity Value/Transport Category	Max Load	Special Provisions
			Receptacle Size	Package Gross	Receptacle Size	Package Gross			
2928	TOXIC SOLID, CORROSIVE, ORGANIC, N.O.S., PG1	1/300	Nil	Nil	Nil	Nil	LQ0/1	20	274
2928	TOXIC SOLID, CORROSIVE, ORGANIC, N.O.S., PG11	1/500	1 kg	4 kg	500 g	4 kg	LQ18/2	333	274
2929	TOXIC LIQUID, FLAMMABLE, ORGANIC, N.O.S., PG1	1/300	Nil	Nil	Nil	Nil	LQ0/1	20	274, 315
2929	TOXIC LIQUID, FLAMMABLE, ORGANIC, N.O.S., PG11	1/500	500 ml	2 litres	100 ml	2 litres	LQ17/2	333	274
2930	TOXIC SOLID, FLAMMABLE, ORGANIC, N.O.S., PG1	1/300	Nil	Nil	Nil	Nil	LQ0/1	20	274
2930	TOXIC SOLID, FLAMMABLE, ORGANIC, N.O.S., PG11	1/500	1 kg	4 kg	500 g	4 kg	LQ18/2	333	274
2931	VANADYL SULPHATE	1/500	1 kg	4 kg	500 g	4 kg	LQ18/2	333	
2933	METHYL 2-CHLOROPROPIONATE	30/1000	5 litres	30 kg	5 litres	20 kg	LQ7/3	1000	
2934	ISOPROPYL 2-CHLOROPROPIONATE	30/1000	5 litres	30 kg	5 litres	20 kg	LQ7/3	1000	
2935	ETHYL 2-CHLOROPROPIONATE	30/1000	5 litres	30 kg	5 litres	20 kg	LQ7/3	1000	
2936	THIOLACTIC ACID	1/500	500 ml	2 litres	100 ml	2 litres	LQ17/2	333	
2937	ALPHA-METHYLBENZYL ALCOHOL	30/1000	5 litres	30 kg	5 litres	20 kg	LQ7/2	333	

2940	9-PHOSPHABICYCLONONANES (CYCLOOCTADIENE PHOSPHINES)	30/500	Nil	Nil	Nil	Nil	Nil	333	LQ0/2	
2941	FLUOROANILINES	30/1000	5 litres	30 kg	5 litres	5 litres	20 kg	333	LQ7/2	
2942	2-TRIFLUOROMETHYLANILINE	30/1000	5 litres	30 kg	5 litres	5 litres	20 kg	333	LQ7/2	
2943	TETRAHYDROFURFURYLAMINE	30/1000	5 litres	30 kg	5 litres	5 litres	20 kg	1000	LQ7/3	
2945	N-METHYLBUTYLAMINE	30/500	3 litres	30 kg	1 litre	1 litre	20 kg	333	LQ4/2	
2946	2-AMINO-5-DIETHYLAMINOPENTANE	30/1000	5 litres	30 kg	5 litres	5 litres	20 kg	333	LQ7/2	
2947	ISOPROPYL CHOROACETATE	30/1000	5 litres	30 kg	5 litres	5 litres	20 kg	1000	LQ7/3	
2948	3-TRIFLUOROMETHYLANILINE	1/500	500 ml	2 litres	100 ml	100 ml	2 litres	333	LQ17/2	
2949	SODIUM HYDROSULPHIDE WITH NOT LESS THAN 25% WATER OF CRYSTALLISATION	30/500	1 kg	30 kg	1 kg	1 kg	20 kg	333	LQ23/2	523
2950	MAGNESIUM GRANULES, COATED	30/1000	1 kg	30 kg	1 kg	1 kg	20 kg	1000	LQ12/3	
2956	5-TERT-BUTYL-2,4,6-TRINITRO-M-XYLENE, (MUSK XYLENE)	30/1000	Nil	Nil	Nil	Nil	Nil	1000	LQ0/3	638
2965	BORON TRIFLUORIDE DIMETHYL ETHERATE	Nil	Nil	Nil	Nil	Nil	Nil	Nil	LQ0/0	
2966	THIOGLYCOL	1/500	500 ml	2 litres	100 ml	100 ml	2 litres	333	LQ17/2	
2967	SULPHAMIC ACID	30/1000	6 kg	30 kg	2 kg	2 kg	20 kg	1000	LQ24/3	
2968	MANEB, STABILISED OR MANEB PREPARATIONS, STABILISED AGAINST SELF-HEATING	30/1000	1 kg	30 kg	1 kg	1 kg	20 kg	Nil	LQ12/0	547
2969	CASTOR BEANS OR CASTOR MEAL OR CASTOR POMACE OR CASTOR FLAKE	30/500	1 kg	30 kg	1 kg	1 kg	20 kg	333	LQ25/2	141

UN	Substance	Excepted Quantities	LQ Packages		LQ Shrink Wrapped Trays		Limited Quantity Value/Transport Category	Max Load	Special Provisions
			Receptacle Size	Package Gross	Receptacle Size	Package Gross			
2977	RADIOACTIVE MATERIAL, URANIUM HEXAFLUORIDE, FISSILE	Nil	Nil	Nil	Nil	Nil	LQ0/0	Nil	172
2978	RADIOACTIVE MATERIAL, URANIUM HEXAFLUORIDE, NON-FISSILE OR FISSILE EXCEPTED	Nil	Nil	Nil	Nil	Nil	LQ0/0	Nil	172
2983	ETHYLENE OXIDE AND PROPYLENE OXIDE MIXTURE NOT MORE THAN 30% ETHYLENE OXIDE	Nil	Nil	Nil	Nil	Nil	LQ0/1	20	
2984	HYDROGEN PEROXIDE, AQUEOUS SOLUTION, WITH NOT LESS THAN 8% BUT LESS THAN 20% HYDROGEN PEROXIDE (STABILISED AS NECESSARY)	30/1000	1 litre	30 kg	1 litre	20 kg	LQ13/3	1000	65
2985	CHLOROSILANES, FLAMMABLE, CORROSIVE, N.O.S.	30/500	3 litres	30 kg	1 litre	20 kg	LQ4/2	333	274, 548
2986	CHLOROSILANES, CORROSIVE, FLAMMABLE, N.O.S.	30/500	1 litre	30 kg	500 ml	20 kg	LQ22/2	333	274, 548
2987	CHLOROSILANES, CORROSIVE, N.O.S.	30/500	1 litre	30 kg	500 ml	20 kg	LQ22/2	333	274, 548
2988	CHLOROSILANES, WATER-REACTIVE, FLAMMABLE, CORROSIVE, N.O.S.	Nil	Nil	Nil	Nil	Nil	LQ0/0	Nil	274, 549
2989	LEAD PHOSPHITE DIBASIC, PG11	30/500	3 kg	30 kg	500 g	20 kg	LQ8/2	333	
2989	LEAD PHOSPHITE DIBASIC, PG111	30/1000	6 kg	30 kg	3 kg	20 kg	LQ9/3	1000	

UN	Name									
2990	LIFE-SAVING APPLIANCES, SELF-INFLATING	Nil	Nil	Nil	Nil	Nil	LQ0/3	1000	296, 635
2991	CARBAMATE PESTICIDE, LIQUID, TOXIC, FLAMMABLE, PG1	1/300	Nil	Nil	Nil	Nil	LQ0/1	20	61,274
2991	CARBAMATE PESTICIDE, LIQUID, TOXIC, FLAMMABLE, PG11	1/500	500 ml	2 litres	100 ml	2 litres	LQ17/2	333	61, 274
2991	CARBAMATE PESTICIDE, LIQUID, TOXIC, FLAMMABLE, PG111	30/1000	5 litres	30 kg	5 litres	20 kg	LQ7/2	333	61, 274
2992	CARBAMATE PESTICIDE, LIQUID, TOXIC, PG1	1/300	Nil	Nil	Nil	Nil	LQ0/1	20	61, 274, 648
2992	CARBAMATE PESTICIDE, LIQUID, TOXIC, PG11	1/500	500 ml	2 litres	100 ml	2 litres	LQ17/2	333	61,274, 648
2992	CARBAMATE PESTICIDE, LIQUID, TOXIC, PG111	30/1000	5 litres	30 kg	5 litres	20 kg	LQ7/2	333	61, 274, 648
2993	ARSENICAL PESTICIDE, LIQUID, TOXIC, FLAMMABLE, PG1	1/300	Nil	Nil	Nil	Nil	LQ0/1	20	61, 274
2993	ARSENICAL PESTICIDE, LIQUID, TOXIC, FLAMMABLE, PG11	1/500	500 ml	2 litres	100 ml	2 litres	LQ17/2	333	61, 274
2993	ARSENICAL PESTICIDE, LIQUID, TOXIC, FLAMMABLE, PG111	30/1000	5 litres	30 kg	5 litres	20 kg	LQ7/2	333	61, 274
2994	ARSENICAL PESTICIDE, LIQUID, TOXIC, PG1	1/300	Nil	Nil	Nil	Nil	LQ0/1	20	61, 274, 648
2994	ARSENICAL PESTICIDE, LIQUID, TOXIC, PG11	1/500	500 ml	2 litres	100 ml	2 litres	LQ17/2	333	61, 274, 648
2994	ARSENICAL PESTICIDE, LIQUID, TOXIC, PG111	30/1000	5 litres	30 kg	5 litres	20 kg	LQ7/2	333	61, 274, 648

UN	Substance	Excepted Quantities	LQ Packages Receptacle Size	LQ Packages Package Gross	LQ Shrink Wrapped Trays Receptacle Size	LQ Shrink Wrapped Trays Package Gross	Limited Quantity Value/Transport Category	Max Load	Special Provisions
2995	ORGANOCHLORINE PESTICIDE, LIQUID, TOXIC, FLAMMABLE, PG1	1/300	Nil	Nil	Nil	Nil	LQ0/1	20	61, 274
2995	ORGANOCHLORINE PESTICIDE, LIQUID, TOXIC, FLAMMABLE, PG11	1/500	500 ml	2 litres	100 ml	2 litres	LQ17/2	333	61, 274
2995	ORGANOCHLORINE PESTICIDE, LIQUID, TOXIC, FLAMMABLE, PG111	30/1000	5 litres	30 kg	5 litres	20 kg	LQ7/2	333	61, 274
2996	ORGANOCHLORINE PESTICIDE, LIQUID, TOXIC, PG1	1/300	Nil	Nil	Nil	Nil	LQ0/1	20	61, 274, 648
2996	ORGANOCHLORINE PESTICIDE, LIQUID, TOXIC, PG11	1/500	500 ml	2 litres	100 ml	2 litres	LQ17/2	333	61, 274, 648
2996	ORGANOCHLORINE PESTICIDE, LIQUID, TOXIC, PG111	30/1000	5 litres	30 kg	5 litres	20 kg	LQ7/2	333	61, 274, 648
2997	TRIAZINE PESTICIDE, LIQUID, TOXIC, FLAMMABLE, PG1	1/300	Nil	Nil	Nil	Nil	LQ0/1	20	61, 274
2997	TRIAZINE PESTICIDE, LIQUID, TOXIC, FLAMMABLE, PG11	1/500	500 ml	2 litres	100 ml	2 litres	LQ17/2	333	61, 274
2997	TRIAZINE PESTICIDE, LIQUID, TOXIC, FLAMMABLE, PG111	30/1000	5 litres	30 kg	5 litres	20 kg	LQ7/2	333	61, 274
2998	TRIAZINE PESTICIDE, LIQUID, TOXIC, PG1	1/300	Nil	Nil	Nil	Nil	LQ0/1	20	61, 274, 648
2998	TRIAZINE PESTICIDE, LIQUID, TOXIC, PG11	1/500	500 ml	2 litres	100 ml	2 litres	LQ17/2	333	61, 274, 648

UN	Name								
2998	TRIAZINE PESTICIDE, LIQUID, TOXIC, PG111	30/1000	5 litres	30 kg	5 litres	20 kg	LQ7/2	333	61, 274, 648
3005	THIOCARBAMATE PESTICIDE, LIQUID, TOXIC, FLAMMABLE, PG1	1/300	Nil	Nil	Nil	Nil	LQ0/1	20	61, 274
3005	THIOCARBAMATE PESTICIDE, LIQUID, TOXIC, FLAMMABLE, PG11	1/500	500 ml	2 litres	100 ml	2 litres	LQ17/2	333	61, 274
3005	THIOCARBAMATE PESTICIDE, LIQUID, TOXIC, FLAMMABLE, PG111	30/1000	5 litres	30 kg	5 litres	20 kg	LQ7/2	333	61, 274
3006	THIOCARBAMATE PESTICIDE, LIQUID, TOXIC, PG1	1/300	Nil	Nil	Nil	Nil	LQ0/1	20	61,274, 648
3006	THIOCARBAMATE PESTICIDE, LIQUID, TOXIC, PG11	1/500	500 ml	2 litres	100 ml	2 litres	LQ17/2	333	61, 274, 648
3006	THIOCARBAMATE PESTICIDE, LIQUID, TOXIC, PG111	30/1000	5 litres	30 kg	5 litres	20 kg	LQ7/2	333	61, 274, 648
3009	COPPER BASED PESTICIDE, LIQUID, TOXIC, FLAMMABLE, PG1	1/300	Nil	Nil	Nil	Nil	LQ0/1	20	61, 274
3009	COPPER BASED PESTICIDE, LIQUID, TOXIC, FLAMMABLE, PG11	1/500	500 ml	2 litres	100 ml	2 litres	LQ17/2	333	61, 274
3009	COPPER BASED PESTICIDE, LIQUID, TOXIC, FLAMMABLE, PG111	30/1000	5 litres	30 kg	5 litres	20 kg	LQ7/2	333	61, 274
3010	COPPER BASED PESTICIDE, LIQUID, TOXIC, PG1	1/300	Nil	Nil	Nil	Nil	LQ0/1	20	61, 274, 648
3010	COPPER BASED PESTICIDE, LIQUID, TOXIC, PG11	1/500	500 ml	2 litres	100 ml	2 litres	LQ17/2	333	61, 274, 648
3010	COPPER BASED PESTICIDE, LIQUID, TOXIC, PG111	30/1000	5 litres	30 kg	5 litres	20 kg	LQ7/2	333	61, 274, 648

UN	Substance	Excepted Quantities	LQ Packages		LQ Shrink Wrapped Trays		Limited Quantity Value/Transport Category	Max Load	Special Provisions
			Receptacle Size	Package Gross	Receptacle Size	Package Gross			
3011	MERCURY BASED PESTICIDE, LIQUID, TOXIC, FLAMMABLE, PG1	1/300	Nil	Nil	Nil	Nil	LQ0/1	20	61, 274
3011	MERCURY BASED PESTICIDE, LIQUID, TOXIC, FLAMMABLE, PG11	1/500	500 ml	2 litres	100 ml	2 litre	LQ17/2	333	61, 274
3011	MERCURY BASED PESTICIDE, LIQUID, TOXIC, FLAMMABLE, PG111	30/1000	5 litres	30 kg	5 litres	20 kg	LQ7/2	333	61, 274
3012	MERCURY BASED PESTICIDE, LIQUID, TOXIC, PG1	1/300	Nil	Nil	Nil	Nil	LQ0/1	20	61, 274, 648
3012	MERCURY BASED PESTICIDE, LIQUID, TOXIC, PG11	1/500	500 ml	2 litres	100 ml	2 litres	LQ17/2	333	61, 274, 648
3012	MERCURY BASED PESTICIDE, LIQUID, TOXIC, PG111	30/1000	5 litres	30 kg	5 litres	20 kg	LQ7/2	333	61, 274, 648
3013	SUBSTITUTED NITROPHENOL PESTICIDE, LIQUID, TOXIC, FLAMMABLE, PG1	1/300	Nil	Nil	Nil	Nil	LQ0/1	20	61, 274
3013	SUBSTITUTED NITROPHENOL PESTICIDE, LIQUID, TOXIC, FLAMMABLE, PG11	1/500	500 ml	2 litres	100 ml	2 litres	LQ17/2	333	61, 274
3013	SUBSTITUTED NITROPHENOL PESTICIDE, LIQUID, TOXIC, FLAMMABLE, PG111	30/1000	5 litres	30 kg	5 litres	20 kg	LQ7/2	333	61, 274
3014	SUBSTITUTED NITROPHENOL PESTICIDE, LIQUID, TOXIC, PG1	1/300	Nil	Nil	Nil	Nil	LQ0/1	20	61, 274, 648

UN	Name								
3014	SUBSTITUTED NITROPHENOL PESTICIDE, LIQUID, TOXIC, PG11	1/500	500 ml	2 litres	100 ml	2 litres	LQ17/2	333	61, 274, 648
3014	SUBSTITUTED NITROPHENOL PESTICIDE, LIQUID, TOXIC, PG111	30/1000	5 litres	30 kg	5 litres	20 kg	LQ7/2	333	61, 274, 648
3015	BIPYRIDILIUM PESTICIDE, LIQUID, TOXIC, FLAMMABLE, PG1	1/300	Nil	Nil	Nil	Nil	LQ0/1	20	61, 274
3015	BIPYRIDILIUM PESTICIDE, LIQUID, TOXIC, FLAMMABLE, PG11	1/500	500 ml	2 litres	100 ml	2 litres	LQ17/2	333	61, 274
3015	BIPYRIDILIUM PESTICIDE, LIQUID, TOXIC, FLAMMABLE, PG111	30/1000	5 litres	30 kg	5 litres	20 kg	LQ7/2	333	61, 274
3016	BIPYRIDILIUM PESTICIDE, LIQUID, TOXIC, PG1	1/300	Nil	Nil	Nil	Nil	LQ0/1	20	61, 274, 648
3016	BIPYRIDILIUM PESTICIDE, LIQUID, TOXIC, PG11	1/500	500 ml	2 litres	100 ml	2 litres	LQ17/2	333	61, 274, 648
3016	BIPYRIDILIUM PESTICIDE, LIQUID, TOXIC, PG111	30/1000	5 litres	30 kg	5 litres	20 kg	LQ7/2	333	61, 274, 648
3017	ORGANOPHOSPHORUS PESTICIDE, LIQUID, TOXIC, FLAMMABLE, PG1	1/300	Nil	Nil	Nil	Nil	LQ0/1	20	61, 274
3017	ORGANOPHOSPHORUS PESTICIDE, LIQUID, TOXIC, FLAMMABLE, PG11	1/500	500 ml	2 litres	100 ml	2 litres	LQ17/2	333	61, 274
3017	ORGANOPHOSPHORUS PESTICIDE, LIQUID, TOXIC, FLAMMABLE, PG111	30/1000	5 litres	30 kg	5 litres	20 kg	LQ7/2	333	61, 274
3018	ORGANOPHOSPHORUS PESTICIDE, LIQUID, TOXIC, PG1	1/300	Nil	Nil	Nil	Nil	LQ0/1	20	61, 274, 648
3018	ORGANOPHOSPHORUS PESTICIDE, LIQUID, TOXIC, PG11	1/500	500 ml	2 litres	100 ml	2 litres	LQ17/2	333	61, 274, 648

UN	Substance	Excepted Quantities	LQ Packages Receptacle Size	LQ Packages Package Gross	LQ Shrink Wrapped Trays Receptacle Size	LQ Shrink Wrapped Trays Package Gross	Limited Quantity Value/Transport Category	Max Load	Special Provisions
3018	ORGANOPHOSPHORUS PESTICIDE, LIQUID, TOXIC, PG111	30/1000	5 litres	30 kg	5 litres	20 kg	LQ7/2	333	61, 274, 648
3019	ORGANOTIN PESTICIDE, LIQUID, TOXIC, FLAMMABLE, PG1	1/300	Nil	Nil	Nil	Nil	LQ0/1	20	61, 274
3019	ORGANOTIN PESTICIDE, LIQUID, TOXIC, FLAMMABLE, PG11	1/500	500 ml	2 litres	100 ml	2 litres	LQ17/2	333	61, 274
3019	ORGANOTIN PESTICIDE, LIQUID, TOXIC, FLAMMABLE, PG111	30/1000	5 litres	30 kg	5 litres	20 kg	LQ7/2	333	61, 274
3020	ORGANOTIN PESTICIDE, LIQUID, TOXIC, PG1	1/300	Nil	Nil	Nil	Nil	LQ0/1	20	61, 274, 648
3020	ORGANOTIN PESTICIDE, LIQUID, TOXIC, PG11	1/500	500 ml	2 litres	100 ml	2 litres	LQ17/2	333	61, 274, 648
3020	ORGANOTIN PESTICIDE, LIQUID, TOXIC, PG111	30/1000	5 litres	30 kg	5 litres	20 kg	LQ7/2	333	61, 274, 648
3021	PESTICIDE, LIQUID, FLAMMABLE, TOXIC, N.O.S., PG1	Nil	500 ml	1 litre	Not	Allowed	LQ3/1	20	61, 274
3021	PESTICIDE, LIQUID, FLAMMABLE, TOXIC, N.O.S., PG11	30/500	3 litres	30 kg	1 litre	20 kg	LQ4/2	333	61, 274
3022	1,2-BUTYLENE OXIDE, STABILISED	30/500	3 litres	30 kg	1 litre	20 kg	LQ4/2	333	
3023	2-METHYL-2-HEPTANETHIOL	1/300	Nil	Nil	Nil	Nil	LQ0/1	20	

UN No	Name and description				Not	Allowed			
3024	COUMARIN DERIVATIVE PESTICIDE, LIQUID, FLAMMABLE, TOXIC, PG1	Nil	500 ml	1 litre	Nil	Nil	LQ3/1	20	61, 274
3024	COUMARIN DERIVATIVE PESTICIDE, LIQUID, FLAMMABLE, TOXIC, PG11	30/500	3 litres	30 kg	1 litre	20 kg	LQ4/2	333	61, 274
3025	COUMARIN DERIVATIVE PESTICIDE, LIQUID, TOXIC, FLAMMABLE, PG1	1/300	Nil	Nil	Nil	Nil	LQ0/1	20	61, 274
3025	COUMARIN DERIVATIVE PESTICIDE, LIQUID, TOXIC, FLAMMABLE, PG11	1/500	500 ml	2 litres	100 ml	2 litres	LQ17/2	333	61, 274
3025	COUMARIN DERIVATIVE PESTICIDE, LIQUID, TOXIC, FLAMMABLE, PG111	30/1000	5 litres	30 kg	1 litre	20 kg	LQ7/2	333	61, 274
3026	COUMARIN DERIVATIVE PESTICIDE, LIQUID, TOXIC, PG1	1/300	Nil	Nil	Nil	Nil	LQ0/1	20	61, 274, 648
3026	COUMARIN DERIVATIVE PESTICIDE, LIQUID, TOXIC, PG11	1/500	500 ml	2 litres	100 ml	2 litres	LQ17/2	333	61, 274, 648
3026	COUMARIN DERIVATIVE PESTICIDE, LIQUID, TOXIC, PG111	30/1000	5 litres	30 kg	5 litres	20 kg	LQ7/2	333	61, 274, 648
3027	COUMARIN, DERIVATIVE PESTICIDE, SOLID, TOXIC, PG1	1/300	Nil	Nil	Nil	Nil	LQ0/1	20	61, 274, 648
3027	COUMARIN, DERIVATIVE PESTICIDE, SOLID, TOXIC, PG11	1/500	1 kg	4 kg	500 g	4 kg	LQ18/2	333	61, 274, 648
3027	COUMARIN, DERIVATIVE PESTICIDE, SOLID, TOXIC, PG111	30/100	6 kg	30 kg	3 kg	20 kg	LQ9/2	333	61, 274, 648
3028	BATTERIES, DRY, CONTAINING POTASSIUM HYDROXIDE SOLID, ELECTRIC, STORAGE	Nil	Nil	Nil	Nil	Nil	LQ0/3	1000	295, 304, 598
3048	ALUMINIUM PHOSPHIDE PESTICIDES	1/300	Nil	Nil	Nil	Nil	LQ0/1	20	153, 648
3054	CYCLOHEXYL MERCAPTAN	30/1000	5 litres	30 kg	5 litres	20 kg	LQ7/3	1000	

UN	Substance	Excepted Quantities	LQ Packages Receptacle Size	LQ Packages Package Gross	LQ Shrink Wrapped Trays Receptacle Size	LQ Shrink Wrapped Trays Package Gross	Limited Quantity Value/Transport Category	Max Load	Special Provisions
3055	2-(2-AMINOETHOXY)ETHANOL	30/1000	5 litres	30 kg	5 litres	20 kg	LQ7/3	1000	
3056	N-HEPTALDEHYDE	30/1000	5 litres	30 kg	5 litres	20 kg	LQ7/3	1000	
3057	TRIFLUOROACETYL CHLORIDE	Nil	Nil	Nil	Nil	Nil	LQ0/1	20	
3064	NITROGLYCERIN, SOLUTION IN ALCOHOL, WITH MORE THAN 1% BUT NOT MORE THAN 5% NITRO-GLYCERINE	Nil	Nil	Nil	Nil	Nil	LQ0/2	333	
3065	ALCOHOLIC BEVERAGES, WITH MORE THAN 70% ALCOHOL BY VOLUME, PG11	30/500	5 litres	Unlimited	1 litre	20 kg	LQ5/2	333	
3065	ALCOHOLIC BEVERAGES, WITH MORE THAN 24% AND NOT MORE THAN 70% ALCOHOL BY VOLUME, PG111	30/1000	5 litres	30 kg	5 litres	20 kg	LQ7/3	1000	144, 145, 247
3066	PAINT (INCLUDING PAINT, LACQUER, ENAMEL, STAIN, SHELLAC, VARNISH, POLISH, LIQUID FILLER AND LIQUID LACQUER BASE) OR, PAINT RELATED MATERIAL (INCLUDING PAINT-THINNING OR REDUCING COMPOUND), PG11	30/500	1 litre	30 kg	500 ml	20 kg	LQ22/2	333	163
3066	PAINT (INCLUDING PAINT, LACQUER, ENAMEL, STAIN, SHELLAC, VARNISH, POLISH, LIQUID FILLER AND LIQUID LACQUER BASE) OR, PAINT RELATED MATERIAL (INCLUDING PAINT-THINNING OR REDUCING COMPOUND), PG111	30/1000	5 litres	30 kg	5 litres	20 kg	LQ7/3	1000	163

3070	ETHYLENE OXIDE AND DICHLORODIFLUOROMETHANE MIXTURE WITH NOT MORE THAN 12.5% ETHYLENE OXIDE	30/1000	120 ml	30 kg	120 ml	20 kg	LQ1/3	1000	
3071	MERCAPTANS, LIQUID, TOXIC, FLAMMABLE, N.O.S. OR MERCAPTAN MIXTURE, LIQUID, TOXIC, FLAMMABLE, N.O.S.	1/500	500 ml	2 litres	100 ml	2 litres	LQ17/2	333	274
3072	LIFE SAVING APPLIANCES NOT SELF-INFLATING, CONTAINING DANGEROUS GOODS AS EQUIPMENT	Nil	Nil	Nil	Nil	Nil	LQ0/3	1000	296, 635
3073	VINYLPYRIDINES, STABILISED	1/500	500 ml	2 litres	100 ml	2 litres	LQ17/2	333	
3077	ENVIRONMENTALLY HAZARDOUS SUBSTANCE, SOLID, N.O.S.	30/1000	6 kg	30 kg	6 kg	20 kg	LQ27/3	1000	274, 335, 601
3078	CERIUM, TURNINGS OR GRITTY POWDER	30/500	500 g	30 kg	500 g	20 kg	LQ11/2	333	550
3079	METHACRYLONITRILE, STABILISED	Nil	Nil	Nil	Nil	Nil	LQ0/1	20	
3080	ISOCYANATES, TOXIC, FLAMMABLE, N.O.S. OR ISOCYANATE SOLUTION, TOXIC, FLAMMABLE, N.O.S.	1/500	500 ml	2 litres	100 ml	2 litres	LQ17/2	333	274, 551
3082	ENVIRONMENTALLY HAZARDOUS SUBSTANCE, LIQUID, N.O.S.	30/1000	5 litres	30 kg	5 litres	20 kg	LQ7/3	1000	274, 601, 335
3083	PERCHLORYL FLUORIDE	Nil	Nil	Nil	Nil	Nil	LQ0/1	20	
3084	CORROSIVE SOLID, OXIDISING, N.O.S., PG1	Nil	Nil	Nil	Nil	Nil	LQ0/1	20	274
3084	CORROSIVE SOLID, OXIDISING, N.O.S., PG11	30/500	3 kg	30 kg	1 kg	20 kg	LQ23/2	333	274
3085	OXIDISING SOLID, CORROSIVE, N.O.S., PG1	Nil	Nil	Nil	Nil	Nil	LQ0/1	20	274

UN	Substance	Excepted Quantities	LQ Packages		LQ Shrink Wrapped Trays		Limited Quantity Value/Transport Category	Max Load	Special Provisions
			Receptacle Size	Package Gross	Receptacle Size	Package Gross			
3085	OXIDISING SOLID, CORROSIVE, N.O.S., PG11	30/500	500 g	30 kg	500 g	20 kg	LQ11/2	333	274
3085	OXIDISING SOLID, CORROSIVE, N.O.S., PG111	30/1000	1 kg	30 kg	1 kg	20 kg	LQ12/3	1000	274
3086	TOXIC SOLID, OXIDISING, N.O.S., PG1	1/300	Nil	Nil	Nil	Nil	LQ0/1	20	274
3086	TOXIC SOLID, OXIDISING, N.O.S., PG11	1/500	1 kg	4 kg	500 g	4 kg	LQ18/2	333	274
3087	OXIDISING SOLID, TOXIC, N.O.S., PG1	Nil	Nil	Nil	Nil	Nil	LQ0/1	20	274
3087	OXIDISING SOLID, TOXIC, N.O.S., PG11	30/500	500 g	30 kg	500 g	20 kg	LQ11/2	333	274
3087	OXIDISING SOLID, TOXIC, N.O.S., PG111	30/1000	1 kg	30 kg	1 kg	20 kg	LQ12/3	1000	274
3088	SELF-HEATING SOLID, ORGANIC, N.O.S., PG11	30/500	Nil	Nil	Nil	Nil	LQ0/2	333	274
3088	SELF-HEATING SOLID, ORGANIC, N.O.S., PG111	30/1000	Nil	Nil	Nil	Nil	LQ0/3	1000	274
3089	METAL POWDER, FLAMMABLE, N.O.S., PG11	30/500	3 kg	30 kg	500 g	20 kg	LQ8/2	333	274, 552
3089	METAL POWDER, FLAMMABLE, N.O.S., PG111	30/1000	6 kg	30 kg	3 kg	20 kg	LQ9/3	1000	274, 552
3090	LITHIUM BATTERIES	Nil	Nil	Nil	Nil	Nil	LQ0/2	333	188, 230, 310, 636

UN	Name						LQ		
3091	LITHIUM BATTERIES CONTAINED IN EQUIPMENT OR LITHIUM BATTERIES PACKED WITH EQUIPMENT	Nil	Nil	Nil	Nil	Nil	LQ0/2	333	188, 230, 636
3092	1-METHOXY-2-PROPANOL	30/1000	5 litres	30 kg	5 litres	20 kg	LQ7/3	1000	
3093	CORROSIVE LIQUID, OXIDISING, N.O.S., PG1	Nil	Nil	Nil	Nil	Nil	LQ0/1	20	274
3093	CORROSIVE LIQUID, OXIDISING, N.O.S., PG11	30/500	1 litre	30 kg	500 ml	20 kg	LQ22/2	333	274
3094	CORROSIVE LIQUID, WATER-REACTIVE, N.O.S., PG1	Nil	Nil	Nil	Nil	Nil	LQ0/1	20	274
3094	CORROSIVE LIQUID, WATER-REACTIVE, N.O.S., PG11	30/500	1 litre	30 kg	500 ml	20 kg	LQ22/2	333	274
3095	CORROSIVE SOLID, SELF-HEATING, N.O.S., PG1	Nil	Nil	Nil	Nil	Nil	LQ0/1	20	274
3095	CORROSIVE SOLID, SELF-HEATING, N.O.S., PG11	30/500	3 kg	30 kg	1 kg	20 kg	LQ23/2	333	274
3096	CORROSIVE SOLID, WATER-REACTIVE, N.O.S., PG1	Nil	Nil	Nil	Nil	Nil	LQ0/1	20	274
3096	CORROSIVE SOLID, WATER-REACTIVE, N.O.S., PG11	30/500	3 kg	30 kg	1 kg	20 kg	LQ23/2	333	274
3097	FLAMMABLE SOLID, OXIDISING, N.O.S.	Carriage	Prohibited		–	–	Carriage		Prohibited
3098	OXIDISING LIQUID, CORROSIVE, N.O.S., PG1	Nil	Nil	Nil	Nil	Nil	LQ0/1	20	274
3098	OXIDISING LIQUID, CORROSIVE, N.O.S., PG11	30/500	500 ml	30 kg	500 ml	20 kg	LQ10/2	333	274

UN	Substance	Excepted Quantities	LQ Packages		LQ Shrink Wrapped Trays		Limited Quantity Value/Transport Category	Max Load	Special Provisions
			Receptacle Size	Gross Package	Receptacle Size	Gross Package			
3098	OXIDISING LIQUID, CORROSIVE, N.O.S., PG111	30/1000	1 litre	30 kg	1 litre	20 kg	LQ13/3	1000	274
3099	OXIDISING LIQUID, TOXIC, N.O.S, PG1	Nil	Nil	Nil	Nil	Nil	LQ0/1	20	274
3099	OXIDISING LIQUID, TOXIC, N.O.S., PG11	30/500	500 ml	30 kg	500 ml	20 kg	LQ10/2	333	274
3099	OXIDISING LIQUID, TOXIC, N.O.S., PG111	30/1000	1 litre	30 kg	1 litre	20 kg	LQ13/3	1000	274
3100	OXIDISING SOLID, SELF-HEATING, N.O.S.	Carriage	Prohibited		-	-	Carriage		Prohibited
3101	ORGANIC PEROXIDE TYPE B, LIQUID	Nil	25 ml	30 kg	25 ml	20 kg	LQ14/1	20	122, 181, 274
3102	ORGANIC PEROXIDE TYPE B, SOLID	Nil	100 g	30 kg	100 g	20 kg	LQ15/1	20	122, 181, 274
3103	ORGANIC PEROXIDE TYPE C, LIQUID	Nil	25 ml	30 kg	25 ml	20 kg	LQ14/1	20	122, 274
3104	ORGANIC PEROXIDE TYPE C, SOLID	Nil	100 g	30 kg	100 g	20 kg	LQ15/1	20	122, 274
3105	ORGANIC PEROXIDE TYPE D, LIQUID	Nil	125 ml	30 kg	125 ml	20 kg	LQ16/2	333	122, 274
3106	ORGANIC PEROXIDE TYPE D, SOLID	Nil	500 g	30 kg	500 g	20 kg	LQ11/2	333	122, 274
3107	ORGANIC PEROXIDE TYPE E, LIQUID	Nil	125 ml	30 kg	125 ml	20 kg	LQ16/2	333	122, 274
3108	ORGANIC PEROXIDE TYPE E, SOLID	Nil	500 g	30 kg	500 g	20 kg	LQ11/2	333	122, 274
3109	ORGANIC PEROXIDE TYPE F, LIQUID	Nil	125 ml	30 kg	125 ml	20 kg	LQ16/2	333	122, 274
3110	ORGANIC PEROXIDE TYPE F, SOLID	Nil	500 g	30 kg	500 g	20 kg	LQ11/2	333	122, 274

UN No.	Name								
3111	ORGANIC PEROXIDE TYPE B, LIQUID, TEMPERATURE CONTROLLED	Nil	Nil	Nil	Nil	Nil	LQ0/1	20	122, 181, 274
3112	ORGANIC PEROXIDE TYPE B, SOLID, TEMPERATURE CONTROLLED	Nil	Nil	Nil	Nil	Nil	LQ0/1	20	122, 181, 274
3113	ORGANIC PEROXIDE TYPE C, LIQUID, TEMPERATURE CONTROLLED	Nil	Nil	Nil	Nil	Nil	LQ0/1	20	122, 274
3114	ORGANIC PEROXIDE TYPE C, SOLID, TEMPERATURE CONTROLLED	Nil	Nil	Nil	Nil	Nil	LQ0/1	20	122, 274
3115	ORGANIC PEROXIDE TYPE D, LIQUID, TEMPERATURE CONTROLLED	Nil	Nil	Nil	Nil	Nil	LQ0/1	20	122, 274
3116	ORGANIC PEROXIDE TYPE D, SOLID, TEMPERATURE CONTROLLED	Nil	Nil	Nil	Nil	Nil	LQ0/1	20	122, 274
3117	ORGANIC PEROXIDE TYPE E, LIQUID, TEMPERATURE CONTROLLED	Nil	Nil	Nil	Nil	Nil	LQ0/1	20	122, 274
3118	ORGANIC PEROXIDE TYPE E, SOLID, TEMPERATURE CONTROLLED	Nil	Nil	Nil	Nil	Nil	LQ0/1	20	122, 274
3119	ORGANIC PEROXIDE TYPE F, LIQUID, TEMPERATURE CONTROLLED	Nil	Nil	Nil	Nil	Nil	LQ0/1	20	122, 274
3120	ORGANIC PEROXIDE TYPE F, SOLID, TEMPERATURE CONTROLLED	Nil	Nil	Nil	Nil	Nil	LQ0/1	20	122, 274
3121	OXIDISING SOLID, WATER-REACTIVE, N.O.S.	Carriage	Prohibited	–	–		Carriage		Prohibited
3122	TOXIC LIQUID, OXIDISING, N.O.S., PG1	30/1000	Nil	Nil	Nil	Nil	LQ0/1	20	274, 315
3122	TOXIC LIQUID, OXIDISING, N.O.S., PG11	1/500	500 ml	2 litres	100 ml	2 litres	LQ17/2	333	274
3123	TOXIC LIQUID, WATER-REACTIVE, N.O.S., PG1	1/300	Nil	Nil	Nil	Nil	LQ0/1	20	274, 315

UN	Substance	Excepted Quantities	LQ Packages Receptacle Size	LQ Packages Gross Package	LQ Shrink Wrapped Trays Receptacle Size	LQ Shrink Wrapped Trays Gross Package	Limited Quantity Value/Transport Category	Max Load	Special Provisions
3123	TOXIC LIQUID, WATER-REACTIVE, N.O.S., PG11	1/500	500 ml	2 litres	100 ml	2 litres	LQ17/2	333	274
3124	TOXIC SOLID, SELF-HEATING, N.O.S., PG1	1/300	Nil	Nil	Nil	Nil	LQ0/1	20	274
3124	TOXIC SOLID, SELF-HEATING, N.O.S., PG11	1/500	1 kg	4 kg	500 g	4 kg	LQ18/2	333	274
3125	TOXIC SOLID, WATER-REACTIVE, N.O.S., PG1	1/300	Nil	Nil	Nil	Nil	LQ0/1	20	274
3125	TOXIC SOLID, WATER-REACTIVE, N.O.S., PG11	1/500	1 kg	4 kg	500 g	4 kg	LQ18/2	333	274
3126	SELF-HEATING SOLID, CORROSIVE, ORGANIC, N.O.S., PG11	30/500	Nil	Nil	Nil	Nil	LQ0/2	333	274
3126	SELF-HEATING SOLID, CORROSIVE, ORGANIC, N.O.S., PG111	30/1000	Nil	Nil	Nil	Nil	LQ0/3	1000	274
3127	SELF-HEATING SOLID, OXIDISING, N.O.S.	Carriage	Prohibited		–	–	Carriage		Prohibited
3128	SELF-HEATING SOLID, TOXIC, ORGANIC, N.O.S., PG11	30/500	Nil	Nil	Nil	Nil	LQ0/2	333	274
3128	SELF-HEATING SOLID, TOXIC, ORGANIC, N.O.S., PG111	30/1000	Nil	Nil	Nil	Nil	LQ0/3	1000	274
3129	WATER-REACTIVE LIQUID, CORROSIVE, N.O.S., PG1	Nil	Nil	Nil	Nil	Nil	LQ0/0	Nil	274

3129	WATER-REACTIVE LIQUID, CORROSIVE, N.O.S., PG11	30/500	500 ml	30 kg	500 ml	20 kg	LQ10/0	Nil	274
3129	WATER-REACTIVE LIQUID, CORROSIVE, N.O.S., PG111	30/1000	1 litre	30 kg	1 litre	20 kg	LQ13/0	Nil	274
3130	WATER-REACTIVE LIQUID, TOXIC, N.O.S., PG1	Nil	Nil	Nil	Nil	Nil	LQ0/0	Nil	274
3130	WATER-REACTIVE LIQUID, TOXIC, N.O.S., PG11	30/500	500 ml	30 kg	500 ml	20 kg	LQ10/0	Nil	274
3130	WATER-REACTIVE LIQUID, TOXIC, N.O.S., PG111	30/1000	1 litre	30 kg	1 litre	20 kg	LQ13/0	Nil	274
3131	WATER-REACTIVE SOLID, CORROSIVE, N.O.S., PG1	Nil	Nil	Nil	Nil	Nil	LQ0/0	Nil	274
3131	WATER-REACTIVE SOLID, CORROSIVE, N.O.S., PG11	30/500	500 g	30 kg	500 g	20 kg	LQ11/0	Nil	274
3131	WATER-REACTIVE SOLID, CORROSIVE, N.O.S., PG111	30/1000	1 kg	30 kg	1 kg	20 kg	LQ12/0	Nil	274
3132	WATER-REACTIVE SOLID, FLAMMABLE, N.O.S., PG1	Nil	Nil	Nil	Nil	Nil	LQ0/0	Nil	274
3132	WATER-REACTIVE SOLID, FLAMMABLE, N.O.S., PG11	30/500	500 g	30 kg	500 g	20 kg	LQ11/0	Nil	274
3132	WATER-REACTIVE SOLID, FLAMMABLE, N.O.S., PG111	30/1000	1 kg	30 kg	1 kg	20 kg	LQ12/0	Nil	274
3133	WATER-REACTIVE SOLID, OXIDISING, N.O.S.	Carriage	Prohibited		-	-	Carriage		Prohibited
3134	WATER-REACTIVE SOLID, TOXIC, N.O.S., PG1	Nil	Nil	Nil	Nil	Nil	LQ0/0	Nil	274

UN	Substance	Excepted Quantities	LQ Packages		LQ Shrink Wrapped Trays		Limited Quantity Value/Transport Category	Max Load	Special Provisions
			Receptacle Size	Gross Package	Receptacle Size	Gross Package			
3134	WATER-REACTIVE SOLID, TOXIC, N.O.S., PG11	30/500	500 g	30 kg	500 g	20 kg	LQ11/0	Nil	274
3134	WATER-REACTIVE SOLID, TOXIC, N.O.S., PG111	30/1000	1 kg	30 kg	1 kg	20 kg	LQ12/0	Nil	274
3135	WATER-REACTIVE SOLID, SELF-HEATING, N.O.S., PG1	Nil	Nil	Nil	Nil	Nil	LQ0/1	20	274
3135	WATER-REACTIVE SOLID, SELF-HEATING, N.O.S., PG11	30/500	500 g	30 kg	500 g	20 kg	LQ11/2	333	274
3135	WATER-REACTIVE SOLID, SELF-HEATING, N.O.S., PG111	30/1000	1 kg	30 kg	1 kg	20 kg	LQ12/3	1000	274
3136	TRIFLUOROMETHANE, REFRIGERATED LIQUID	30/1000	120 ml	30 kg	120 ml	20 kg	LQ1/3	1000	593
3137	OXIDISING SOLID, FLAMMABLE, N.O.S.	Carriage	Prohibited		–	–	Carriage		Prohibited
3138	ETHYLENE, ACETYLENE AND PROPYLENE MIXTURE, REFRIGERATED LIQUID, CONTAINING AT LEAST 71.5% ETHYLENE WITH NOT MORE THAN 22.5% ACETYLENE AND NOT MORE THAN 6% PROPYLENE	Nil	Nil	Nil	Nil	Nil	LQ0/2	333	
3139	OXIDISING LIQUID, N.O.S., PG1	Nil	Nil	Nil	Nil	Nil	LQ0/1	20	274
3139	OXIDISING LIQUID, N.O.S., PG11	30/500	500 ml	30 kg	500 ml	20 kg	LQ10/2	333	274
3139	OXIDISING LIQUID, N.O.S., PG111	30/1000	1 litre	30 kg	1 litre	20 kg	LQ13/3	1000	274

3140	ALKALOIDS, LIQUID, N.O.S. OR ALKALOID SALTS, LIQUID, N.O.S., PG1	1/300	Nil	Nil	Nil	Nil	LQ0/1	20	43, 274
3140	ALKALOIDS, LIQUID, N.O.S. OR ALKALOID SALTS, LIQUID, N.O.S., PG11	1/500	500 ml	2 litres	100 ml	2 litres	LQ17/2	333	274, 43
3140	ALKALOIDS, LIQUID, N.O.S. OR ALKALOID SALTS, LIQUID, N.O.S., PG111	30/1000	5 litres	30 kg	5 litres	20 kg	LQ7/2	333	274, 43
3141	ANTIMONY COMPOUND, INORGANIC, LIQUID, N.O.S.	30/1000	5 litres	30 kg	5 litres	20 kg	LQ7/2	333	45, 274, 512
3142	DISINFECTANT, LIQUID, TOXIC, N.O.S., PG1	1/300	Nil	Nil	Nil	Nil	LQ0/1	20	274
3142	DISINFECTANT, LIQUID, TOXIC, N.O.S., PG11	1/500	500 ml	2 litres	100 ml	2 litres	LQ17/2	333	274
3142	DISINFECTANT, LIQUID, TOXIC, N.O.S., PG111	30/1000	5 litres	30 kg	5 litres	20 kg	LQ7/2	333	274
3143	DYE, SOLID, TOXIC, N.O.S. OR DYE INTERMEDIATE, SOLID, TOXIC, N.O.S., PG1	1/300	Nil	Nil	Nil	Nil	LQ0/1	20	274
3143	DYE, SOLID, TOXIC, N.O.S. OR DYE INTERMEDIATE, SOLID, TOXIC, N.O.S., PG11	1/500	1 kg	4 kg	500 g	4 kg	LQ18/2	333	274
3143	DYE, SOLID, TOXIC, N.O.S. OR DYE INTERMEDIATE, SOLID, TOXIC, N.O.S., PG111	30/1000	6 kg	30 kg	3 kg	20 kg	LQ9/2	333	274
3144	NICOTINE COMPOUND, LIQUID, N.O.S. OR NICOTINE PREPARATION, LIQUID, N.O.S., PG1	1/300	Nil	Nil	Nil	Nil	LQ0/1	20	43, 274
3144	NICOTINE COMPOUND, LIQUID, N.O.S. OR NICOTINE PREPARATION, LIQUID, N.O.S., PG11	1/500	500 ml	2 litres	100 ml	2 litres	LQ17/2	333	43, 274

UN	Substance	Excepted Quantities	LQ Packages Receptacle Size	LQ Packages Gross Package	LQ Shrink Wrapped Trays Receptacle Size	LQ Shrink Wrapped Trays Gross Package	Limited Quantity Value/Transport Category	Max Load	Special Provisions
3144	NICOTINE COMPOUND, LIQUID, N.O.S. OR NICOTINE PREPARATION, LIQUID, N.O.S., PG111	30/1000	5 litres	30 kg	5 litres	20 kg	LQ7/2	333	43, 274
3145	ALKYLPHENOLS, LIQUID, N.O.S. (INCLUDING C2-C12 HOMOLOGUES), PG1	Nil	Nil	Nil	Nil	Nil	LQ0/1	20	274
3145	ALKYPHENOLS, LIQUID, N.O.S. (INCLUDING C2-C12 HOMOLOGUES), PG11	30/500	1 litre	30 kg	500 ml	20 kg	LQ22/2	333	274
3145	ALKYPHENOLS, LIQUID, N.O.S. (INCLUDING C2-C12 HOMOLOGUES), PG111	30/1000	5 litres	30 kg	5 litres	20 kg	LQ7/3	1000	274
3146	ORGANOTIN COMPOUND, SOLID, TOXIC, N.O.S., PG1	1/300	Nil	Nil	Nil	Nil	LQ0/1	20	43, 274
3146	ORGANOTIN COMPOUND, SOLID, TOXIC, N.O.S., PG11	1/500	1 kg	4 kg	500 g	4 kg	LQ18/2	333	43, 274
3146	ORGANOTIN COMPOUND, SOLID, TOXIC, N.O.S., PG111	30/1000	6 kg	30 kg	3 kg	20 kg	LQ9/2	333	43, 274
3147	DYE, SOLID, CORROSIVE, N.O.S. OR DYE INTERMEDIATE, SOLID, CORROSIVE, N.O.S., PG1	Nil	Nil	Nil	Nil	Nil	LQ0/1	20	274
3147	DYE, SOLID, CORROSIVE, N.O.S. OR DYE INTERMEDIATE, SOLID, CORROSIVE, N.O.S., PG11	30/500	3 kg	30 kg	1 kg	20 kg	LQ23/2	333	274

UN No.	Name and description								
3147	DYE, SOLID, CORROSIVE, N.O.S. OR DYE INTERMEDIATE, SOLID, CORROSIVE, N.O.S., PG111	30/1000	6 kg	30 kg	2 kg	20 kg	LQ24/3	1000	274
3148	WATER-REACTIVE LIQUID, N.O.S., PG1	Nil	Nil	Nil	Nil	Nil	LQ0/0	Nil	274
3148	WATER-REACTIVE LIQUID, N.O.S., PG11	30/500	500 ml	30 kg	500 ml	20 kg	LQ10/0	Nil	274
3148	WATER-REACTIVE LIQUID, N.O.S., PG111	30/1000	1 litre	30 kg	1 litre	20 kg	LQ13/0	Nil	274
3149	HYDROGEN PEROXIDE AND PEROXYACETIC ACID MIXTURE, WITH ACID(S), WATER AND NOT MORE THAN 5% PEROXYACETIC ACID, STABILISED	30/500	500 ml	30 kg	500 ml	20 kg	LQ10/2	333	196, 553
3150	DEVICES, SMALL, HYDROCARBON GAS POWERED OR HYDROCARBON GAS REFILLS FOR SMALL DEVICES, WITH RELEASE DEVICE	Nil	Nil	Nil	Nil	Nil	LQ0/2	333	
3151	POLYHALOGENATED BIPHENYLS, LIQUID OR POLYHALOGENATED TERPHENYLS, LIQUID	30/500	500 ml	2 litre	500 ml	2 litres	LQ26/0	Nil	203,305
3152	POLYHALOGENATED BIPHENYLS, SOLID OR POLYHALOGENATED TERPHENYLS, SOLID	30/500	1 kg	30 kg	1 kg	20 kg	LQ25/0	Nil	203, 305
3153	PERFLUORO (METHYL VINYL ETHER)	Nil	Nil	Nil	Nil	Nil	LQ0/2	333	
3154	PERFLUORO (ETHYL VINYL ETHER)	Nil	Nil	Nil	Nil	Nil	LQ0/2	333	
3155	PENTACHLOROPHENOL	1/500	1 kg	4 kg	500 g	4 kg	LQ18/2	333	43
3156	COMPRESSED GAS, OXIDISING, N.O.S.	Nil	Nil	Nil	Nil	Nil	LQ0/3	1000	274
3157	LIQUEFIED GAS, OXIDISING, N.O.S.	Nil	Nil	Nil	Nil	Nil	LQ0/3	1000	274

UN	Substance	Excepted Quantities	LQ Packages		LQ Shrink Wrapped Trays		Limited Quantity Value/Transport Category	Max Load	Special Provisions
			Receptacle Size	Package Gross	Receptacle Size	Package Gross			
3158	GAS, REFRIGERATED LIQUID, N.O.S.	30/1000	120 ml	30 kg	120 ml	20 kg	LQ1/3	1000	274, 593
3159	1,1,1,2-TETRAFLUOROETHANE (REFRIGERANT GAS R134A)	30/1000	120 ml	30 kg	120 ml	20 kg	LQ1/3	1000	
3160	LIQUEFIED GAS, TOXIC, FLAMMABLE, N.O.S.	Nil	Nil	Nil	Nil	Nil	LQ0/1	20	274
3161	LIQUEFIED GAS, FLAMMABLE, N.O.S.	Nil	Nil	Nil	Nil	Nil	LQ0/2	333	274
3162	LIQUEFIED GAS, TOXIC, N.O.S.	Nil	Nil	Nil	Nil	Nil	LQ0/1	20	274
3163	LIQUEFIED GAS, N.O.S.	30/1000	120 ml	30 kg	120 ml	20 kg	LQ1/3	1000	274
3164	ARTICLES, PRESSURISED PNEUMATIC OR HYDRAULIC (CONTAINING NON-FLAMMABLE GAS)	Nil	Nil	Nil	Nil	Nil	LQ0/3	1000	283, 594
3165	AIRCRAFT HYDRAULIC POWER UNIT FUEL TANK (CONTAINING A MIXTURE OF ANHYDROUS HYDRAZINE AND METHYLHYDRAZINE) (M86 FUEL)	Nil	Nil	Nil	Nil	Nil	LQ0/1	20	
3166	ENGINES, INTERNAL COMBUSTION, INCLUDING WHEN FITTED IN MACHINERY OR VEHICLES	Not	Subject	To ADR	-	-	Not Subject	to	ADR
3167	GAS SAMPLE, NON-PRESSURISED, FLAMMABLE, N.O.S. NOT REFRIGERATED LIQUID	Nil	Nil	Nil	Nil	Nil	LQ0/2	333	274

UN No.	Name								
3168	GAS SAMPLE, NON-PRESSURISED, TOXIC, FLAMMABLE, N.O.S., NOT REFRIGERATED LIQUID	Nil	Nil	Nil	Nil	Nil	LQ0/1	20	274
3169	GAS SAMPLE, NON-PRESSURISED, TOXIC, N.O.S., NOT REFRIGERATED LIQUID	Nil	Nil	Nil	Nil	Nil	LQ0/1	20	274
3170	ALUMINIUM SMELTING BY-PRODUCTS OR ALUMINIUM REMELTING BY-PRODUCTS, PG11	30/500	500 g	30 kg	500 g	20 kg	LQ11/2	333	274
3170	ALUMINIUM SMELTING BY-PRODUCTS OR ALUMINIUM REMELTING BY-PRODUCTS, PG111	30/1000	1 kg	30 kg	1 kg	20 kg	LQ12/3	1000	244
3171	BATTERY-POWERED VEHICLE OR BATTERY-POWERED EQUIPMENT	Not Subject	Subject	To ADR	–	–	Not Subject	to	ADR
3172	TOXINS, EXTRACTED FROM LIVING SOURCES, TOXIC, N.O.S., PG1	1/300	Nil	Nil	Nil	Nil	LQ0/1	20	210, 274
3172	TOXINS, EXTRACTED FROM LIVING SOURCES, TOXIC, N.O.S., PG11	1/500	500 ml	2 litres	100 ml	2 litres	LQ17/2	333	210, 274
3172	TOXINS, EXTRACTED FROM LIVING SOURCES, TOXIC, N.O.S., PG111	30/1000	5 litres	30 kg	5 litres	20 kg	LQ7/2	333	210, 274
3174	TITANIUM DISULPHIDE	30/1000	Nil	Nil	Nil	Nil	LQ0/3	1000	
3175	SOLIDS CONTAINING FLAMMABLE LIQUID, N.O.S.	30/500	3 kg	30 kg	500 g	20 kg	LQ8/2	333	216, 274
3176	FLAMMABLE SOLID, ORGANIC, MOLTEN, N.O.S., PG11	Nil	Nil	Nil	Nil	Nil	LQ0/2	333	274
3176	FLAMMABLE SOLID, ORGANIC, MOLTEN, N.O.S., PG111	Nil	Nil	Nil	Nil	Nil	LQ0/3	1000	274

UN	Substance	Excepted Quantities	LQ Packages Receptacle Size	LQ Packages Package Gross	LQ Shrink Wrapped Trays Receptacle Size	LQ Shrink Wrapped Trays Package Gross	Limited Quantity Value/Transport Category	Max Load	Special Provisions
3178	FLAMMABLE SOLID, INORGANIC, N.O.S., PG11	30/500	3 kg	30 kg	500 g	20 kg	LQ8/2	333	274
3178	FLAMMABLE SOLID, INORGANIC, N.O.S., PG111	30/1000	6 kg	30 kg	3 kg	20 kg	LQ9/3	1000	274
3179	FLAMMABLE SOLID, TOXIC, INORGANIC, N.O.S., PG11	30/500	Nil	Nil	Nil	Nil	LQ0/2	333	274
3179	FLAMMABLE SOLID, TOXIC, INORGANIC, N.O.S., PG111	30/1000	Nil	Nil	Nil	Nil	LQ0/3	1000	274
3180	FLAMMABLE SOLID, CORROSIVE, INORGANIC, N.O.S., PG11	30/500	Nil	Nil	Nil	Nil	LQ0/2	333	274
3180	FLAMMABLE SOLID, CORROSIVE, INORGANIC, N.O.S., PG111	30/1000	Nil	Nil	Nil	Nil	LQ0/3	1000	274
3181	METAL SALTS OF ORGANIC COMPOUNDS, FLAMMABLE, N.O.S., PG11	30/500	3 kg	30 kg	500 g	20 kg	LQ8/2	333	274
3181	METAL SALTS OF ORGANIC COMPOUNDS, FLAMMABLE, N.O.S., PG111	30/1000	6 kg	30 kg	3 kg	20 kg	LQ9/3	1000	274
3182	METAL HYDRIDES, FLAMMABLE, N.O.S., PG11	30/500	3 kg	30 kg	500 g	20 kg	LQ8/2	333	274, 554
3182	METAL HYDRIDES, FLAMMABLE, N.O.S., PG111	30/1000	6 kg	30 kg	3 kg	20 kg	LQ9/3	1000	274, 554

UN	Name								
3183	SELF-HEATING LIQUID, ORGANIC, N.O.S., PG11	30/500	Nil	Nil	Nil	Nil	LQ0/2	333	274
3183	SELF-HEATING LIQUID, ORGANIC, N.O.S., PG111	30/1000	Nil	Nil	Nil	Nil	LQ0/3	1000	274
3184	SELF-HEATING LIQUID, TOXIC, ORGANIC, N.O.S., PG11	30/500	Nil	Nil	Nil	Nil	LQ0/2	333	274
3184	SELF-HEATING LIQUID, TOXIC, ORGANIC, N.O.S., PG111	30/1000	Nil	Nil	Nil	Nil	LQ0/3	1000	274
3185	SELF-HEATING LIQUID, CORROSIVE, ORGANIC, N.O.S., PG11	30/500	Nil	Nil	Nil	Nil	LQ0/2	333	274
3185	SELF-HEATING LIQUID, CORROSIVE, ORGANIC, N.O.S., PG111	30/1000	Nil	Nil	Nil	Nil	LQ0/3	1000	274
3186	SELF-HEATING LIQUID, INORGANIC, N.O.S., PG11	30/500	Nil	Nil	Nil	Nil	LQ0/2	333	274
3186	SELF-HEATING LIQUID, INORGANIC, N.O.S., PG111	30/1000	Nil	Nil	Nil	Nil	LQ0/3	1000	274
3187	SELF-HEATING LIQUID, TOXIC, INORGANIC, N.O.S., PG11	30/500	Nil	Nil	Nil	Nil	LQ0/2	333	274
3187	SELF-HEATING LIQUID, TOXIC, INORGANIC, N.O.S., PG111	30/1000	Nil	Nil	Nil	Nil	LQ0/3	1000	274
3188	SELF-HEATING LIQUID, CORROSIVE, INORGANIC, N.O.S., PG11	30/500	Nil	Nil	Nil	Nil	LQ0/2	333	274
3188	SELF-HEATING LIQUID, CORROSIVE, INORGANIC, N.O.S., PG111	30/1000	Nil	Nil	Nil	Nil	LQ0/3	1000	274
3189	METAL POWDER, SELF-HEATING, N.O.S., PG11	30/500	Nil	Nil	Nil	Nil	LQ0/2	333	274, 555

UN	Substance	Excepted Quantities	LQ Packages Receptacle Size	LQ Packages Package Gross	LQ Shrink Wrapped Trays Receptacle Size	LQ Shrink Wrapped Trays Package Gross	Limited Quantity Value/Transport Category	Max Load	Special Provisions
3189	METAL POWDER, SELF-HEATING, N.O.S., PG111	30/1000	Nil	Nil	Nil	Nil	LQ0/3	1000	274, 555
3190	SELF-HEATING SOLID, INORGANIC, N.O.S., PG11	30/500	Nil	Nil	Nil	Nil	LQ0/2	333	274
3190	SELF-HEATING SOLID, INORGANIC, N.O.S., PG111	30/1000	Nil	Nil	Nil	Nil	LQ0/3	1000	274
3191	SELF-HEATING SOLID, TOXIC, INORGANIC, N.O.S., PG11	30/500	Nil	Nil	Nil	Nil	LQ0/2	333	274
3191	SELF-HEATING SOLID, TOXIC, INORGANIC, N.O.S., PG111	30/1000	Nil	Nil	Nil	Nil	LQ0/3	1000	274
3192	SELF HEATING SOLID, CORROSIVE, INORGANIC, N.O.S., PG11	30/500	Nil	Nil	Nil	Nil	LQ0/2	333	274
3192	SELF HEATING SOLID, CORROSIVE, INORGANIC, N.O.S., PG111	30/1000	Nil	Nil	Nil	Nil	LQ0/3	1000	274
3194	PYROPHORIC LIQUID, INORGANIC, N.O.S.	Nil	Nil	Nil	Nil	Nil	LQ0/0	Nil	274
3200	PYROPHORIC SOLID, INORGANIC, N.O.S.	Nil	Nil	Nil	Nil	Nil	LQ0/0	Nil	274
3205	ALKALINE EARTH METAL ALCOHOLATES, N.O.S., PG11	30/500	Nil	Nil	Nil	Nil	LQ0/2	333	183, 274
3205	ALKALINE EARTH METAL ALCOHOLATES, N.O.S., PG111	30/1000	Nil	Nil	Nil	Nil	LQ0/3	1000	183, 274

3206	ALKALI METAL ALCOHOLATES, SELF-HEATING, CORROSIVE, N.O.S., PG11	30/500	Nil	Nil	Nil	Nil	LQ0/2	333	182, 274
3206	ALKALI METAL ALCOHOLATES, SELF-HEATING, CORROSIVE, N.O.S., PG111	30/1000	Nil	Nil	Nil	Nil	LQ0/3	1000	182, 274
3208	METALLIC SUBSTANCE, WATER-REACTIVE, N.O.S., PG1	Nil	Nil	Nil	Nil	Nil	LQ0/1	20	274, 557
3208	METALLIC SUBSTANCE, WATER-REACTIVE, N.O.S., PG11	30/500	500 g	30 kg	500 g	20 kg	LQ11/2	333	274, 557
3208	METALLIC SUBSTANCE, WATER-REACTIVE, N.O.S., PG111	30/1000	1 kg	30 kg	1 kg	20 kg	LQ12/3	1000	274, 557
3209	METALLIC SUBSTANCE, WATER-REACTIVE, SELF-HEATING, N.O.S., PG1	Nil	Nil	Nil	Nil	Nil	LQ0/1	20	274, 558
3209	METALLIC SUBSTANCE, WATER-REACTIVE, SELF-HEATING, N.O.S., PG11	30/500	500 g	30 kg	500 g	20 kg	LQ11/2	333	274, 558
3209	METALLIC SUBSTANCE, WATER-REACTIVE, SELF-HEATING, N.O.S., PG111	30/1000	1 kg	30 kg	1 kg	20 kg	LQ12/3	1000	274, 558
3210	CHLORATES, INORGANIC, AQUEOUS SOLUTION, N.O.S., PG11	30/500	500 ml	30 kg	500 ml	20 kg	LQ10/2	333	274, 558
3210	CHLORATES, INORGANIC, AQUEOUS SOLUTION, N.O.S., PG111	30/1000	1 litre	30 kg	1 litre	20 kg	LQ13/3	1000	274, 605
3211	PERCHLORATES, INORGANIC, AQUEOUS SOLUTION, N.O.S., PG11	30/500	500 ml	30 kg	500 ml	20 kg	LQ10/2	333	274
3211	PERCHLORATES, INORGANIC, AQUEOUS SOLUTION, N.O.S., PG111	30/1000	1 litre	30 kg	1 litre	20 kg	LQ13/3	1000	274
3212	HYPOCHLORITES, INORGANIC, N.O.S.	30/500	500 g	30 kg	500 g	20 kg	LQ11/2	333	274, 559

UN	Substance	Excepted Quantities	LQ Packages Receptacle Size	LQ Packages Gross Package	LQ Shrink Wrapped Trays Receptacle Size	LQ Shrink Wrapped Trays Gross Package	Limited Quantity Value/Transport Category	Max Load	Special Provisions
3213	BROMATES, INORGANIC, AQUEOUS, SOLUTION, N.O.S., PG11	30/500	500 ml	30 kg	500 ml	20 kg	LQ10/2	333	274, 604
3213	BROMATES, INORGANIC, AQUEOUS, SOLUTION, N.O.S., PG111	30/1000	1 litre	30 kg	1 litre	20 kg	LQ13/3	1000	274, 604
3214	PERMANGANATES, INORGANIC, AQUEOUS SOLUTION, N.O.S.	30/500	500 ml	30 kg	500 ml	20 kg	LQ10/2	333	274, 608
3215	PERSULPHATES, INORGANIC, N.O.S.	30/1000	1 kg	30 kg	1 kg	20 kg	LQ12/3	1000	274
3216	PERSULPHATES, INORGANIC, AQUEOUS SOLUTION, N.O.S.	30/1000	1 litre	30 kg	1 litre	20 kg	LQ13/3	1000	274
3218	NITRATES, INORGANIC, AQUEOUS SOLUTION, N.O.S., PG11	30/500	500 ml	30 kg	500 ml	20 kg	LQ10/2	333	270, 274
3218	NITRATES, INORGANIC, AQUEOUS SOLUTION, N.O.S., PG111	30/1000	1 litre	30 kg	1 litre	20 kg	LQ13/3	1000	270, 274, 511
3219	NITRITES, INORGANIC, AQUEOUS SOLUTION, N.O.S., PG11	30/500	500 ml	30 kg	500 ml	20 kg	LQ10/2	333	103, 274
3219	NITRITES, INORGANIC, AQUEOUS SOLUTION, N.O.S., PG111	30/1000	1 litre	30 kg	1 litre	20 kg	LQ13/3	1000	103, 274
3220	PENTAFLUOROETHANE (REFRIGERANT GAS R125)	30/1000	120 ml	30 kg	120 ml	20 kg	LQ1/3	1000	
3221	SELF-REACTIVE LIQUID TYPE B	Nil	25 ml	30 kg	25 ml	20 kg	LQ14/1	20	181, 194, 274

	Name								
3222	SELF-REACTIVE SOLID TYPE B	Nil	100 g	30 kg	100 g	20 kg	LQ15/1	20	181, 194, 274
3223	SELF-REACTIVE LIQUID TYPE C	Nil	25 ml	30 kg	25 ml	20 kg	LQ14/1	20	194, 274
3224	SELF-REACTIVE SOLID TYPE C	Nil	100 g	30 kg	100 g	20 kg	LQ15/1	20	194, 274
3225	SELF-REACTIVE LIQUID TYPE D	Nil	125 ml	30 kg	125 ml	20 kg	LQ16/2	333	194, 274
3226	SELF-REACTIVE SOLID TYPE D	Nil	500 g	30 kg	500 g	20 kg	LQ11/2	333	194, 274
3227	SELF-REACTIVE LIQUID TYPE E	Nil	125 ml	30 kg	125 ml	20 kg	LQ16/2	333	194, 274
3228	SELF-REACTIVE SOLID TYPE E	Nil	500 g	30 kg	500 g	20 kg	LQ11/2	333	194, 274
3229	SELF-REACTIVE LIQUID TYPE F	Nil	125 ml	30 kg	125 ml	20 kg	LQ16/2	333	194, 274
3230	SELF-REACTIVE SOLID TYPE F	Nil	500 g	30 kg	500 g	20 kg	LQ11/2	333	194, 274
3231	SELF-REACTIVE LIQUID TYPE B, TEMPERATURE CONTROLLED	Nil	Nil	Nil	Nil	Nil	LQ0/1	20	181, 194, 274
3232	SELF-REACTIVE SOLID TYPE B, TEMPERATURE CONTROLLED	Nil	Nil	Nil	Nil	Nil	LQ0/1	20	181, 194, 274
3233	SELF-REACTIVE LIQUID TYPE C, TEMPERATURE CONTROLLED	Nil	Nil	Nil	Nil	Nil	LQ0/1	20	194, 274
3234	SELF-REACTIVE SOLID TYPE C, TEMPERATURE CONTROLLED	Nil	Nil	Nil	Nil	Nil	LQ0/1	20	194, 274
3235	SELF-REACTIVE LIQUID TYPE D, TEMPERATURE CONTROLLED	Nil	Nil	Nil	Nil	Nil	LQ0/1	20	194, 274
3236	SELF-REACTIVE SOLID TYPE D, TEMPERATURE CONTROLLED	Nil	Nil	Nil	Nil	Nil	LQ0/1	20	194, 274
3237	SELF-REACTIVE LIQUID TYPE E, TEMPERATURE CONTROLLED	Nil	Nil	Nil	Nil	Nil	LQ0/1	20	194, 274

UN	Substance	Excepted Quantities	LQ Packages		LQ Shrink Wrapped Trays		Limited Quantity Value/Transport Category	Max Load	Special Provisions
			Receptacle Size	Package Gross	Receptacle Size	Package Gross			
3238	SELF-REACTIVE SOLID TYPE E, TEMPERATURE CONTROLLED	Nil	Nil	Nil	Nil	Nil	LQ0/1	20	194, 274
3239	SELF-REACTIVE LIQUID TYPE F, TEMPERATURE CONTROLLED	Nil	Nil	Nil	Nil	Nil	LQ0/1	20	194, 274
3240	SELF-REACTIVE SOLID TYPE F, TEMPERATURE CONTROLLED	Nil	Nil	Nil	Nil	Nil	LQ0/1	20	194, 274
3241	2-BROMO-2-NITROPROPANE-1,3-DIOL	30/1000	Nil	Nil	Nil	Nil	LQ0/3	1000	638
3242	AZODICARBONAMIDE	30/500	1 kg	4 kg	500 g	4 kg	LQ0/2	333	215, 638
3243	SOLIDS CONTAINING TOXIC LIQUID, N.O.S.	1/500	1 kg	4 kg	500 g	4 kg	LQ18/2	333	217, 274
3244	SOLIDS CONTAINING CORROSIVE LIQUID, N.O.S.	30/500	3 kg	30 kg	1 kg	20 kg	LQ23/2	333	218, 274
3245	GENETICALLY MODIFIED MICRO-ORGANISMS	Nil	Nil	Nil	Nil	Nil	LQ0/2	333	219, 637
3246	METHANESULPHONYL CHLORIDE	1/300	Nil	Nil	Nil	Nil	LQ0/1	20	
3247	SODIUM PEROXOBORATE, ANHYDROUS	30/500	500 g	30 kg	500 g	20 kg	LQ11/2	333	
3248	MEDICINE, LIQUID, FLAMMABLE, TOXIC, N.O.S., PG11	30/500	Nil	Nil	Nil	Nil	LQ0/2	333	220, 221, 274, 601
3248	MEDICINE, LIQUID, FLAMMABLE, TOXIC, N.O.S., PG111	30/1000	5 litres	30 kg	5 litres	20 kg	LQ7/3	1000	220, 221, 274, 601

UN	Name								
3249	MEDICINE, SOLID, TOXIC, N.O.S., PG11	1/500	1 kg	4 kg	500 g	4 kg	LQ18/2	333	221, 274, 601
3249	MEDICINE, SOLID, TOXIC, N.O.S., PG111	30/1000	6 kg	30 kg	3 kg	20 kg	LQ9/2	333	221, 274, 601
3250	CHLOROACETIC ACID, MOLTEN	Nil	Nil	Nil	Nil	Nil	LQ0/0	Nil	
3251	ISOSORBIDE-5-MONONITRATE	30/1000	Nil	Nil	Nil	Nil	LQ0/3	1000	226, 638
3252	DIFLUOROMETHANE (REFRIGERANT GAS R32)	Nil	Nil	Nil	Nil	Nil	LQ0/2	333	
3253	DISODIUM TRIOXOSILICATE	30/1000	6 kg	30 kg	2 kg	20 kg	LQ24/3	1000	
3254	TRIBUTYLPHOSPHANE	Nil	Nil	Nil	Nil	Nil	LQ0/0	Nil	
3255	TERT-BUTYL HYPOCHLORITE	Carriage	Prohibited	–	–	Carriage			
3256	ELEVATED TEMPERATURE LIQUID, FLAMMMABLE, N.O.S., WITH FLASH POINT ABOVE 61 °C, AT OR ABOVE ITS FLASH POINT	Nil	Nil	Nil	Nil	Nil	LQ0/3	1000	274, 560
3257	ELEVATED TEMPERATURE LIQUID, N.O.S., AT OR ABOVE 100 °C AND BELOW ITS FLASH POINT (INCLUDING MOLTEN METALS, MOLTEN SALTS ETC)	Nil	Nil	Nil	Nil	Nil	LQ0/3	1000	274, 580, 643
3258	ELEVATED TEMPERATURE SOLID, N.O.S., AT OR ABOVE 240 °C	Nil	Nil	Nil	Nil	Nil	LQ0/3	1000	274, 580, 643
3259	AMINES, SOLID, CORROSIVE, N.O.S. OR POLYAMINES, SOLID, CORROSIVE, N.O.S., PG1	Nil	Nil	Nil	Nil	Nil	LQ0/1	20	274
3259	AMINES, SOLID, CORROSIVE, N.O.S. OR POLYAMINES, SOLID, CORROSIVE, N.O.S., PG11	30/500	3 kg	30 kg	1 kg	20 kg	LQ23/2	333	274

UN	Substance	Excepted Quantities	LQ Packages		LQ Shrink Wrapped Trays		Limited Quantity Value/Transport Category	Max Load	Special Provisions
			Receptacle Size	Package Gross	Receptacle Size	Package Gross			
3259	AMINES, SOLID, CORROSIVE, N.O.S. OR POLYAMINES, SOLID, CORROSIVE, N.O.S., PG111	30/1000	6 kg	30 kg	2 kg	20 kg	LQ24/3	1000	274
3260	CORROSIVE SOLID, ACIDIC, INORGANIC, N.O.S., PG1	Nil	Nil	Nil	Nil	Nil	LQ0/1	20	274
3260	CORROSIVE SOLID, ACIDIC, INORGANIC, N.O.S., PG11	30/500	3 kg	30 kg	1 kg	20 kg	LQ23/2	333	274
3260	CORROSIVE SOLID, ACIDIC, INORGANIC, N.O.S., PG111	30/1000	6 kg	30 kg	2 kg	20 kg	LQ24/3	1000	274
3261	CORROSIVE SOLID, ACIDIC, ORGANIC, N.O.S., PG1	Nil	Nil	Nil	Nil	Nil	LQ0/1	20	274
3261	CORROSIVE SOLID, ACIDIC, ORGANIC, N.O.S., PG11	30/500	3 kg	30 kg	1 kg	20 kg	LQ23/2	333	274
3261	CORROSIVE SOLID, ACIDIC, ORGANIC, N.O.S., PG111	30/1000	6 kg	30 kg	2 kg	20 kg	LQ24/3	1000	274
3262	CORROSIVE SOLID, BASIC, INORGANIC, N.O.S., PG1	Nil	Nil	Nil	Nil	Nil	LQ0/1	20	274
3262	CORROSIVE SOLID, BASIC, INORGANIC, N.O.S., PG11	30/500	3 kg	30 kg	1 kg	20 kg	LQ23/2	333	274
3262	CORROSIVE SOLID, BASIC, INORGANIC, N.O.S., PG111	30/1000	6 kg	30 kg	2 kg	20 kg	LQ24/3	1000	274

3263	CORROSIVE SOLID, BASIC, ORGANIC, N.O.S., PG1	Nil	Nil	Nil	Nil	Nil	LQ0/1	20	274
3263	CORROSIVE SOLID, BASIC, ORGANIC, N.O.S., PG11	30/500	3 kg	30 kg	1 kg	20 kg	LQ23/2	333	274
3263	CORROSIVE SOLID, BASIC, ORGANIC, N.O.S., PG111	30/1000	6 kg	30 kg	2 kg	20 kg	LQ24/3	1000	274
3264	CORROSIVE LIQUID, ACIDIC, INORGANIC, N.O.S., PG1	Nil	Nil	Nil	Nil	Nil	LQ0/1	20	274
3264	CORROSIVE LIQUID, ACIDIC, INORGANIC, N.O.S., PG11	30/500	1 litre	30 kg	500 ml	20 kg	LQ22/2	333	274
3264	CORROSIVE LIQUID, ACIDIC, INORGANIC, N.O.S., PG111	30/1000	5 litres	30 kg	5 litres	20 kg	LQ7/3	1000	274
3265	CORROSIVE LIQUID, ACIDIC, ORGANIC, N.O.S., PG1	Nil	Nil	Nil	Nil	Nil	LQ0/1	20	274
3265	CORROSIVE LIQUID, ACIDIC, ORGANIC, N.O.S., PG11	30/500	1 litre	30 kg	500 ml	20 kg	LQ22/2	333	274
3265	CORROSIVE LIQUID, ACIDIC, ORGANIC, N.O.S., PG111	30/1000	5 litres	30 kg	5 litres	20 kg	LQ7/3	1000	274
3266	CORROSIVE LIQUID, BASIC, INORGANIC, N.O.S., PG1	Nil	Nil	Nil	Nil	Nil	LQ0/1	20	274
3266	CORROSIVE LIQUID, BASIC, INORGANIC, N.O.S., PG11	30/500	1 litre	30 kg	500 ml	20 kg	LQ22/2	333	274
3266	CORROSIVE LIQUID, BASIC, INORGANIC, N.O.S., PG111	30/1000	5 litres	30 kg	5 litres	20 kg	LQ7/3	1000	274
3267	CORROSIVE LIQUID, BASIC, ORGANIC, N.O.S., PG1	Nil	Nil	Nil	Nil	Nil	LQ0/1	20	274

UN	Substance	Excepted Quantities	LQ Packages Receptacle Size	LQ Packages Package Gross	LQ Shrink Wrapped Trays Receptacle Size	LQ Shrink Wrapped Trays Package Gross	Limited Quantity Value/Transport Category	Max Load	Special Provisions
3267	CORROSIVE LIQUID, BASIC, ORGANIC, N.O.S., PG11	30/500	1 litre	30 kg	500 ml	20 kg	LQ22/2	333	274
3267	CORROSIVE LIQUID, BASIC, ORGANIC, N.O.S., PG111	30/1000	5 litres	30 kg	5 litres	20 kg	LQ7/3	1000	274
3268	AIR BAG INFLATORS OR AIR BAG MODULES OR SEAT-BELT PRETENSIONERS	Nil	Nil	Nil	Nil	Nil	LQ0/4	Unlimited	280, 289
3269	POLYESTER RESIN KIT, PG11	Nil	5 litres	30 kg	1 litre	20 kg	LQ6/2	333	236, 340
3269	POLYESTER RESIN KIT, PG111	Nil	5 litres	30 kg	5 litres	20 kg	LQ7/3	1000	236, 340
3270	NITROCELLULOSE MEMBRANE FILTERS	30/500	3 kg	30 kg	500 g	20 kg	LQ8/2	333	237, 286
3271	ETHERS, N.O.S., PG11	30/500	3 litres	30 kg	1 litre	20 kg	LQ4/2	333	274
3271	ETHERS, N.O.S., PG111	30/1000	5 litres	30 kg	5 litres	20 kg	LQ7/3	1000	274
3272	ESTERS, N.O.S., PG11	30/500	3 litres	30 kg	1 litre	20 kg	LQ4/2	333	274, 601
3272	ESTERS, N.O.S., PG111	30/1000	5 litres	30 kg	5 litres	20 kg	LQ7/3	1000	274, 601
3273	NITRILES, FLAMMABLE, TOXIC, N.O.S., PG1	Nil	Nil	Nil	Nil	Nil	LQ0/1	20	274
3273	NITRILES, FLAMMABLE, TOXIC, N.O.S., PG11	30/500	Nil	Nil	Nil	Nil	LQ0/2	333	274
3274	ALCOHOLATES SOLUTION, N.O.S., IN ALCOHOL	30/500	3 litres	30 kg	1 litre	20 kg	LQ4/2	333	274
3275	NITRILES, TOXIC, FLAMMABLE, N.O.S., PG1	1/300	Nil	Nil	Nil	Nil	LQ0/1	20	274, 315

UN	Name								
3275	NITRILES, TOXIC, FLAMMABLE, N.O.S., PG11	1/500	500 ml	2 litres	100 ml	2 litres	LQ17/2	333	274
3276	NITRILES, TOXIC, N.O.S., PG1	1/300	Nil	Nil	Nil	Nil	LQ0/1	20	274, 315
3276	NITRILES, TOXIC, N.O.S., PG11	1/500	500 ml	2 litre	100 ml	2 litres	LQ17/2	333	274
3277	CHLOROFORMATES, TOXIC, CORROSIVE, N.O.S.	1/500	500 ml	2 litres	100 ml	2 litres	LQ17/2	333	274, 561
3278	ORGANOPHOSPHORUS COMPOUND, TOXIC, N.O.S., LIQUID, PG1	1/300	Nil	Nil	Nil	Nil	LQ0/1	20	274, 43, 315
3278	ORGANOPHOSPHORUS COMPOUND, TOXIC, N.O.S., LIQUID, PG11	1/500	500 ml	2 litres	100 ml	2 litres	LQ17/2	333	274, 43,
3278	ORGANOPHOSPHORUS COMPOUND, TOXIC, N.O.S., LIQUID, PG111	30/1000	5 litres	30 kg	5 litres	20 kg	LQ7/2	333	274, 43
3279	ORGANOPHOSPHORUS COMPOUND, TOXIC, FLAMMABLE, N.O.S., PG1	1/300	Nil	Nil	Nil	Nil	LQ0/1	20	274, 43, 315
3279	ORGANOPHOSPHORUS COMPOUND, TOXIC, FLAMMABLE, N.O.S., PG11	LQ17	500 ml	2 litres	100 ml	2 litres	LQ17/2	333	274, 43
3280	ORGANOARSENIC COMPOUND, N.O.S., LIQUID, PG1	1/300	Nil	Nil	Nil	Nil	LQ0/1	20	274, 315
3280	ORGANOARSENIC COMPOUND, N.O.S., LIQUID, PG11	1/500	500 ml	2 litres	100 ml	2 litres	LQ17/2	333	274
3280	ORGANOARSENIC COMPOUND, N.O.S., LIQUID, PG111	30/1000	5 litres	30 kg	5 litres	20 kg	LQ7/2	333	274
3281	METAL CARBONYLS, N.O.S., LIQUID, PG1	1/300	Nil	Nil	Nil	Nil	LQ0/1	20	274, 315, 562
3281	METAL CARBONYLS, N.O.S., LIQUID, PG11	1/500	500 ml	2 litres	100 ml	2 litres	LQ17/2	333	274, 562

UN	Substance	Excepted Quantities	LQ Packages		LQ Shrink Wrapped Trays		Limited Quantity Value/Transport Category	Max Load	Special Provisions
			Receptacle Size	Package Gross	Receptacle Size	Package Gross			
3281	METAL CARBONYLS, N.O.S., SOLID, PG111	30/1000	5 litres	30 kg	5 litres	20 kg	LQ7/2	333	274, 562
3282	ORGANOMETALLIC COMPOUND, TOXIC, N.O.S., LIQUID, PG1	1/300	Nil	Nil	Nil	Nil	LQ0/1	20	274, 562
3282	ORGANOMETALLIC COMPOUND, TOXIC, N.O.S., LIQUID, PG11	1/500	500 ml	2 litres	100 ml	2 litres	LQ17/2	333	274, 562
3282	ORGANOMETALLIC COMPOUND, TOXIC, N.O.S., LIQUID, PG111	30/1000	5 litres	30 kg	5 litres	20 kg	LQ7/2	333	274, 562
3283	SELENIUM COMPOUND, N.O.S., PG1	1/300	Nil	Nil	Nil	Nil	LQ0/1	20	274, 563
3283	SELENIUM COMPOUND, N.O.S., PG11	1/500	1 kg	4 kg	500 g	4 kg	LQ18/2	333	274, 563
3283	SELENIUM COMPOUND, N.O.S., PG111	30/1000	6 kg	30 kg	3 kg	20 kg	LQ9/2	333	274, 563
3284	TELLURIUM COMPOUND, N.O.S., PG1	1/300	Nil	Nil	Nil	Nil	LQ0/1	20	274
3284	TELLURIUM COMPOUND, N.O.S., PG11	1/500	1 kg	4 kg	500 g	4 kg	LQ18/2	333	274
3285	VANADIUM COMPOUND, N.O.S., PG1	1/300	Nil	Nil	Nil	Nil	LQ0/2	333	274, 564
3285	VANADIUM COMPOUND, N.O.S., PG11	1/500	1 kg	4 kg	500 g	4 kg	LQ18/2	333	274, 564
3285	VANADIUM COMPOUND, N.O.S., PG111	30/1000	6 kg	30 kg	3 kg	20 kg	LQ9/2	333	274, 564
3286	FLAMMABLE LIQUID, TOXIC, CORROSIVE, N.O.S., PG1	Nil	Nil	Nil	Nil	Nil	LQ0/1	20	274
3286	FLAMMABLE LIQUID, TOXIC, CORROSIVE, N.O.S., PG11	30/500	Nil	Nil	Nil	Nil	LQ0/2	333	274

UN	Name						LQ		
3287	TOXIC LIQUID, INORGANIC, N.O.S., PG1	1/300	Nil	Nil	Nil	Nil	LQ0/1	20	274, 315
3287	TOXIC LIQUID, INORGANIC, N.O.S., PG11	1/500	500 ml	2 litres	100 ml	2 litres	LQ17/2	333	274
3287	TOXIC LIQUID, INORGANIC, N.O.S., PG111	30/1000	5 litres	30 kg	5 litres	20 kg	LQ7/2	333	274
3288	TOXIC SOLID, INORGANIC, N.O.S., PG1	1/300	Nil	Nil	Nil	Nil	LQ0/1	20	274
3288	TOXIC SOLID, INORGANIC, N.O.S., PG 11	1/500	1 kg	4 kg	500 g	4 kg	LQ18/2	333	274
3288	TOXIC SOLID, INORGANIC, N.O.S., PG111	30/1000	6 kg	30 kg	3 kg	20 kg	LQ9/2	333	274
3289	TOXIC LIQUID, CORROSIVE, INORGANIC, N.O.S., PG1	1/300	Nil	Nil	Nil	Nil	LQ0/1	20	274, 315
3289	TOXIC LIQUID, CORROSIVE, INORGANIC, N.O.S., PG11	1/500	500 ml	2 litres	100 ml	2 litres	LQ17/2	333	274
3290	TOXIC SOLID, CORROSIVE, INORGANIC, N.O.S., PG1	1/300	Nil	Nil	Nil	Nil	LQ0/1	20	274
3290	TOXIC SOLID, CORROSIVE, INORGANIC, N.O.S., PG11	1/500	1 kg	4 kg	500 g	4 kg	LQ18/2	333	274
3291	CLINICAL WASTE, UNSPECIFIED, N.O.S. OR (BIO) MEDICAL WASTE, N.O.S. OR REGULATED MEDICAL WASTE, N.O.S.	Nil	Nil	Nil	Nil	Nil	LQ0/2	333	565
3292	BATTERIES, CONTAINING SODIUM OR CELLS, CONTAINING SODIUM	Nil	Nil	Nil	Nil	Nil	LQ0/2	333	239, 295
3293	HYDRAZINE, AQUEOUS SOLUTION WITH NOT MORE THAN 37% HYDRAZINE, BY MASS	30/1000	5 litre	30 kg	5 litre	20 kg	LQ7/2	333	566
3294	HYDROGEN CYANIDE, SOLUTION IN ALCOHOL WITH NOT MORE THAN 45% HYDROGEN CYANIDE	1/500	Nil	Nil	Nil	Nil	LQ0/0	Nil	610

UN	Substance	Excepted Quantities	LQ Packages		LQ Shrink Wrapped Trays		Limited Quantity Value/Transport Category	Max Load	Special Provisions
			Receptacle Size	Gross Package	Receptacle Size	Gross Package			
3295	HYDROCARBONS, LIQUID, N.O.S., PG1	30/300	500 ml	1 litre	Not	Allowed	LQ3/1	20	649
3295	HYDROCARBONS, LIQUID, N.O.S., PG11	30/500	3 litres	30 kg	1 litre	20 kg	LQ4/2	333	640D, 649
3295	HYDROCARBONS, LIQUID, N.O.S., PG111	30/1000	5 litres	30 kg	5 litres	20 kg	LQ7/3	1000	
3296	HEPTAFLUOROPROPANE (REFRIGERANT GAS R227)	30/1000	120 ml	30 kg	120 ml	20 kg	LQ1/3	1000	
3297	ETHYLENE OXIDE AND CHLOROTETRAFLUOROETHANE MIXTURE, WITH NOT MORE THAN 8.8% ETHYLENE OXIDE	30/1000	120 ml	30 kg	120 ml	20 kg	LQ1/3	1000	
3298	ETHYLENE OXIDE AND PENTAFLUOROETHANE MIXTURE, WITH NOT MORE THAN 7.9% ETHYLENE OXIDE	30/1000	120 ml	30 kg	120 ml	20 kg	LQ1/3	1000	
3299	ETHYLENE OXIDE AND TETRAFLUOROETHANE MIXTURE, WITH NOT MORE THAN 5.6% ETHYLENE OXIDE	30/1000	120 ml	30 kg	120 ml	20 kg	LQ1/3	1000	
3300	ETHYLENE OXIDE AND CARBON DIOXIDE MIXTURE, WITH MORE THAN 87% ETHYLENE OXIDE	Nil	Nil	Nil	Nil	Nil	LQ0/1	20	
3301	CORROSIVE LIQUID, SELF-HEATING, N.O.S., PG1	Nil	Nil	Nil	Nil	Nil	LQ0/1	20	274
3301	CORROSIVE LIQUID, SELF-HEATING, N.O.S., PG11	30/500	1 litre	30 kg	500 ml	20 kg	LQ22/2	333	274

UN No	Name	1/500	500 ml	2 litres	100 ml	2 litres	LQ17/2	333	
3302	2-DIMETHYLAMINOETHYL ACRYLATE								
3303	COMPRESSED GAS, TOXIC, OXIDISING, N.O.S.	Nil	Nil	Nil	Nil	Nil	LQ0/1	20	274
3304	COMPRESSED GAS, TOXIC, CORROSIVE, N.O.S.	Nil	Nil	Nil	Nil	Nil	LQ0/1	20	274
3305	COMPRESSED GAS, TOXIC, FLAMMABLE, CORROSIVE, N.O.S.	Nil	Nil	Nil	Nil	Nil	LQ0/1	20	274
3306	COMPRESSED GAS, TOXIC, OXIDISING, CORROSIVE, N.O.S.	Nil	Nil	Nil	Nil	Nil	LQ0/1	20	274
3307	LIQUEFIED GAS, TOXIC, OXIDISING, N.O.S.	Nil	Nil	Nil	Nil	Nil	LQ0/1	20	274
3308	LIQUEFIED GAS, TOXIC, CORROSIVE, N.O.S.	Nil	Nil	Nil	Nil	Nil	LQ0/1	20	274
3309	LIQUEFIED GAS, TOXIC, FLAMMABLE, CORROSIVE, N.O.S.	Nil	Nil	Nil	Nil	Nil	LQ0/1	20	274
3310	LIQUEFIED GAS, TOXIC, OXIDISING, CORROSIVE, N.O.S.	Nil	Nil	Nil	Nil	Nil	LQ0/1	20	274
3311	GAS, REFRIGERATED LIQUID, OXIDISING, N.O.S.	Nil	Nil	Nil	Nil	Nil	LQ0/3	1000	274
3312	GAS, REFRIGERATED LIQUID, FLAMMABLE, N.O.S.	Nil	Nil	Nil	Nil	Nil	LQ0/2	333	274
3313	ORGANIC PIGMENTS SELF-HEATING, PG11	30/500	Nil	Nil	Nil	Nil	LQ0/2	333	
3313	ORGANIC PIGMENTS SELF-HEATING, PG111	30/1000	Nil	Nil	Nil	Nil	LQ0/3	1000	
3314	PLASTICS MOULDING COMPOUND IN DOUGH, SHEET OR EXTRUDED ROPE FORM EVOLVING FLAMMABLE VAPOUR	30/1000	6 kg	30 kg	6 kg	20 kg	LQ27/3	1000	207, 633

UN	Substance	Excepted Quantities	LQ Packages		LQ Shrink Wrapped Trays		Limited Quantity Value/Transport Category	Max Load	Special Provisions
			Receptacle Size	Gross Package	Receptacle Size	Gross Package			
3315	CHEMICAL SAMPLE, TOXIC, LIQUID OR SOLID	1/300	Nil	Nil	Nil	Nil	LQ0/1	20	250
3316	CHEMICAL KIT or FIRST AID KIT, PG11	Nil	Nil	Nil	Nil	Nil	LQ0/2	333	251, 340
3316	CHEMICAL KIT or FIRST AID KIT, PG111	Nil	Nil	Nil	Nil	Nil	LQ0/3	1000	251, 340
3317	2-AMINO-4,6-DINITROPHENOL, WETTED WITH NOT LESS THAN 20% WATER BY MASS	Nil	Nil	Nil	Nil	Nil	LQ0/1	20	
3318	AMMONIA SOLUTION, RELATIVE DENSITY LESS THAN 0.880 AT 15 °C IN WATER, WITH MORE THAN 50% AMMONIA	Nil	Nil	Nil	Nil	Nil	LQ0/1	20	23
3319	NITROGLYCERIN MIXTURE DESENSITISED, SOLID, N.O.S., WITH MORE THAN 2% BUT NOT MORE THAN 10% NITROGLYCERIN, BY MASS	Nil	Nil	Nil	Nil	Nil	LQ0/2	333	272, 274
3320	SODIUM BOROHYDRIDE AND SODIUM HYDROXIDE SOLUTION, PG11	30/500	1 litre	30 kg	500 ml	20 kg	LQ22/2	333	
3320	SODIUM BOROHYDRIDE AND SODIUM HYDROXIDE SOLUTION, PG111	30/1000	5 litres	30 kg	5 litres	20 kg	LQ7/3	1000	
3321	RADIOACTIVE MATERIAL, LOW SPECIFIC ACTIVITY (LSA-II), NON FISSILE OR FISSILE-EXCEPTED	Nil	Nil	Nil	Nil	Nil	LQ0/0	Nil	172, 317, 325, 336

3322	RADIOACTIVE MATERIAL, LOW SPECIFIC ACTIVITY (LSA-III), NON FISSILE OR FISSILE-EXCEPTED	Nil	Nil	Nil	Nil	Nil	Nil	LQ0/0	Nil	172, 317, 325, 336
3323	RADIOACTIVE MATERIAL, TYPE C PACKAGE, NON FISSILE OR FISSILE-EXCEPTED	Nil	Nil	Nil	Nil	Nil	Nil	LQ0/0	Nil	172, 317
3324	RADIOACTIVE MATERIAL, LOW SPECIFIC ACTIVITY (LSA-II), FISSILE	Nil	Nil	Nil	Nil	Nil	Nil	LQ0/0	Nil	172, 326, 336
3325	RADIOACTIVE MATERIAL, LOW SPECIFIC ACTIVITY (LSA-III), FISSILE	Nil	Nil	Nil	Nil	Nil	Nil	LQ0/0	Nil	172, 326, 336
3326	RADIOACTIVE MATERIAL, SURFACE CONTAMINATED OBJECTS (SCO-I or SCO-II), FISSILE	Nil	Nil	Nil	Nil	Nil	Nil	LQ0/0	Nil	172, 336
3327	RADIOACTIVE MATERIAL, TYPE A PACKAGE, FISSILE, non special form	Nil	Nil	Nil	Nil	Nil	Nil	LQ0/0	Nil	172, 326
3328	RADIOACTIVE MATERIAL, TYPE B (U) PACKAGE, FISSILE	Nil	Nil	Nil	Nil	Nil	Nil	LQ0/0	Nil	172, 337
3329	RADIOACTIVE MATERIAL, TYPE B (M) PACKAGE, FISSILE	Nil	Nil	Nil	Nil	Nil	Nil	LQ0/0	Nil	172, 337
3330	RADIOACTIVE MATERIAL, TYPE C PACKAGE, FISSILE	Nil	Nil	Nil	Nil	Nil	Nil	LQ0/0	Nil	172
3331	RADIOACTIVE MATERIAL, TRANSPORTED UNDER SPECIAL ARRANGEMENTS, FISSILE	Nil	Nil	Nil	Nil	Nil	Nil	LQ0/0	Nil	172
3332	RADIOACTIVE MATERIAL, TYPE A PACKAGE, SPECIAL FORM, NON-FISSILE OR FISSILE EXCEPTED	Nil	Nil	Nil	Nil	Nil	Nil	LQ0/0	Nil	172, 317
3333	RADIOACTIVE MATERIAL, TYPE A PACKAGE, SPECIAL FORM, FISSILE	Nil	Nil	Nil	Nil	Nil	Nil	LQ0/0	Nil	172

UN	Substance	Excepted Quantities	LQ Packages Receptacle Size	LQ Packages Package Gross	LQ Shrink Wrapped Trays Receptacle Size	LQ Shrink Wrapped Trays Package Gross	Limited Quantity Value/Transport Category	Max Load	Special Provisions
3334	AVIATION REGULATED LIQUID, N.O.S.	Not	Subject	To ADR	–	–	Not Subject	to	ADR
3335	AVIATION REGULATED SOLID, N.O.S.	Not	Subject	To ADR	–	–	Not Subject	to	ADR
3336	MERCAPTANS, LIQUID, FLAMMABLE, N.O.S. or MERCAPTANS MIXTURE, LIQUID, FLAMMABLE, N.O.S., PG1	30/300	500 ml	30 kg	Not	Allowed	LQ3/1	20	274
3336	MERCAPTANS, LIQUID, FLAMMABLE, N.O.S. or MERCAPTANS MIXTURE, LIQUID, FLAMMABLE, N.O.S., PG11	30/500	3 litres	30 kg	1 litre	20 kg	LQ4/2	333	274, 640C-D
3336	MERCAPTANS, LIQUID, FLAMMABLE, N.O.S. or MERCAPTANS MIXTURE, LIQUID, FLAMMABLE, N.O.S., PG111	30/1000	5 litres	30 kg	5 litres	20 kg	LQ7/3	1000	274
3337	REFRIGERANT GAS R404A	30/1000	120 ml	30 kg	120 ml	20 kg	LQ1/3	1000	
3338	REFRIGERANT GAS R407A	30/1000	120 ml	30 kg	120 ml	20 kg	LQ1/3	1000	
3339	REFRIGERANT GAS R407B	30/1000	120 ml	30 kg	120 ml	20 kg	LQ1/3	1000	
3340	REFRIGERANT GAS R407C	30/1000	120 ml	30 kg	120 ml	20 kg	LQ1/3	1000	
3341	THIOUREA DIOXIDE, PG11	30/500	Nil	Nil	Nil	Nil	LQ0/2	333	
3341	THIOUREA DIOXIDE, PG111	30/1000	Nil	Nil	Nil	Nil	LQ0/3	1000	
3342	XANTHATES, PG11	30/500	Nil	Nil	Nil	Nil	LQ0/2	333	

UN	Name						LQ	1000	Special
3342	XANTHATES, PG111	30/1000	Nil	Nil	Nil	Nil	LQ0/3	1000	
3343	NITROGLYCERIN MIXTURE, DESENSITISED, LIQUID, FLAMMABLE, N.O.S. WITH NOT MORE THAN 30% NITROGLYCERIN BY MASS	Nil	Nil	Nil	Nil	Nil	LQ0/0	Nil	274, 278
3344	PENTAERYTHRITE TETRANITRATE MIXTURE, DESENSITISED, SOLID, N.O.S. WITH MORE THAN 10% BUT NOT MORE THAN 20% PETN BY MASS	Nil	Nil	Nil	Nil	Nil	LQ0/2	333	272, 274
3345	PHENOXYACETIC ACID DERIVATIVE PESTICIDE, SOLID, TOXIC, PG1	1/300	Nil	Nil	Nil	Nil	LQ0/1	20	61, 274, 648
3345	PHENOXYACETIC ACID DERIVATIVE PESTICIDE, SOLID, TOXIC PG11	1/500	1 kg	4 kg	500 g	4 kg	LQ18/2	333	61, 274, 648
3345	PHENOXYACETIC ACID DERIVATIVE PESTICIDE, SOLID, TOXIC PG111	30/1000	6 kg	30 kg	3 kg	20 kg	LQ9/2	333	61, 274, 648
3346	PHENOXYACETIC ACID DERIVATIVE PESTICIDE, LIQUID, FLAMMABLE, TOXIC, PG1	Nil	500 ml	1 litres	Not	Allowed	LQ3/1	20	61, 274
3346	PHENOXYACETIC ACID DERIVATIVE PESTICIDE, LIQUID, FLAMMABLE, TOXIC, PG11	30/500	3 litre	30 kg	1 litre	20 kg	LQ4/2	333	61, 274
3347	PHENOXYACETIC ACID DERIVATIVE PESTICIDE, LIQUID, TOXIC, FLAMMABLE, PG1	1/300	Nil	Nil	Nil	Nil	LQ0/1	20	61, 274
3347	PHENOXYACETIC ACID DERIVATIVE PESTICIDE, LIQUID, TOXIC, FLAMMABLE, PG11	1/500	500 ml	2 litres	100 ml	2 litres	LQ17/2	333	61, 274

UN	Substance	Excepted Quantities	LQ Packages		LQ Shrink Wrapped Trays		Limited Quantity Value/Transport Category	Max Load	Special Provisions
			Receptacle Size	Package Gross	Receptacle Size	Package Gross			
3347	PHENOXYACETIC ACID DERIVATIVE PESTICIDE, LIQUID, TOXIC, FLAMMABLE, PG111	30/1000	5 litres	30 kg	5 litres	20 kg	LQ7/2	333	61, 274
3348	PHENOXYACETIC ACID DERIVATIVE PESTICIDE, LIQUID, TOXIC, PG1	1/300	Nil	Nil	Nil	Nil	LQ0/1	20	61, 274, 648
3348	PHENOXYACETIC ACID DERIVATIVE PESTICIDE, LIQUID, TOXIC, PG11	1/500	500 ml	2 litres	100 ml	2 litres	LQ17/2	333	61, 274, 648
3348	PHENOXYACETIC ACID DERIVATIVE PESTICIDE, LIQUID, TOXIC, PG111	30/1000	5 litres	30 kg	5 litres	20 kg	LQ7/2	333	61, 274, 648
3349	PYRETHROID PESTICIDE, SOLID, TOXIC, PG1	1/300	Nil	Nil	Nil	Nil	LQ0/1	20	61, 274, 648
3349	PYRETHROID PESTICIDE, SOLID, TOXIC, PG11	1/500	1 kg	4 kg	500 g	4 kg	LQ18/2	333	61, 274, 648
3349	PYRETHROID PESTICIDE, SOLID, TOXIC, PG111	30/1000	6 kg	30 kg	3 kg	20 kg	LQ9/2	333	61, 274, 648
3350	PYRETHROID PESTICIDE, LIQUID, FLAMMABLE, TOXIC, PG1	Nil	500 ml	1 litre	Not	Allowed	LQ3/1	20	61, 274
3350	PYRETHROID PESTICIDE, LIQUID, FLAMMABLE, TOXIC, PG11	30/500	3 litres	30 kg	1 litre	20 kg	LQ4/2	333	61, 274
3351	PYRETHROID PESTICIDE, LIQUID, TOXIC, FLAMMABLE, PG1	1/300	Nil	Nil	Nil	Nil	LQ0/1	20	61, 274

UN	Description								
3351	PYRETHROID PESTICIDE, LIQUID, TOXIC, FLAMMABLE, PG11	1/500	500 ml	2 litres	100 ml	2 litres	LQ17/2	333	61, 274
3351	PYRETHROID PESTICIDE, LIQUID, TOXIC, FLAMMABLE, PG111	30/1000	5 litres	30 kg	5 litres	20 kg	LQ7/2	333	61, 274
3352	PYRETHROID PESTICIDE, LIQUID, TOXIC, FLAMMABLE, PG1	1/300	Nil	Nil	Nil	Nil	LQ0/1	20	61, 274, 648
3352	PYRETHROID PESTICIDE, LIQUID, TOXIC, FLAMMABLE, PG11	1/500	500 ml	2 litres	100 ml	2 litres	LQ17/2	333	61, 274, 648
3352	PYRETHROID PESTICIDE, LIQUID, TOXIC, FLAMMABLE, PG111	30/1000	5 litres	30 kg	5 litres	20 kg	LQ7/2	333	61, 274, 648
3354	INSECTICIDE GAS, FLAMMABLE, N.O.S.	Nil	Nil	Nil	Nil	Nil	LQ0/2	333	274
3355	INSECTICIDE GAS, TOXIC, FLAMMABLE, N.O.S.	Nil	Nil	Nil	Nil	Nil	LQ0/1	20	274
3356	OXYGEN GENERATOR, CHEMICAL	Nil	Nil	Nil	Nil	Nil	LQ0/2	333	284
3357	NITROGLYCERIN MIXTURE, DESENSITISED, LIQUID, N.O.S., WITH NOT MORE THAN 30% NITROGLYCERIN, BY MASS	Nil	Nil	Nil	Nil	Nil	LQ0/2	333	274, 288
3358	REFRIGERATING MACHINES, CONTAINING FLAMMABLE, NON-TOXIC, LIQUEFIED GAS	Nil	Nil	Nil	Nil	Nil	LQ0/2	333	291
3359	FUMIGATED UNIT	Not Subject	To ADR	–	–				302
3360	FIBRES, VEGETABLE, DRY	Not Subject	To ADR	–	–	Not Subject	to	ADR	
3361	CHLOROSILANES, TOXIC, CORROSIVE, N.O.S.	1/500	Nil	Nil	Nil	Nil	LQ0/2	333	274
3362	CHLOROSILANES, TOXIC, CORROSIVE, FLAMMABLE, N.O.S.	1/500	Nil	Nil	Nil	Nil	LQ0/2	333	274

UN	Substance	Excepted Quantities	LQ Packages Receptacle Size	LQ Packages Gross Package	LQ Shrink Wrapped Trays Receptacle Size	LQ Shrink Wrapped Trays Gross Package	Limited Quantity Value/Transport Category	Max Load	Special Provisions
3363	DANGEROUS GOODS IN MACHINERY OR DANGEROUS GOODS IN APPARATUS	Not	Subject	To ADR	–	–	Not Subject	to	ADR
3364	TRINITROPHENOL (PICRIC ACID), WETTED, WITH NOT LESS THAN 10% WATER BY MASS	Nil	Nil	Nil	Nil	Nil	LQ0/1	20	
3365	TRINITROCHLOROBENZENE (PICRYL CHLORIDE), WETTED, WITH NOT LESS THAN 10% WATER BY MASS	Nil	Nil	Nil	Nil	Nil	LQ0/1	20	
3366	TRINITROTOLUENE (TNT), WETTED, WITH NOT LESS THAN 10% WATER BY MASS	Nil	Nil	Nil	Nil	Nil	LQ0/1	20	
3367	TRINITROBENZENE, WETTED, WITH NOT LESS THAN 10% WATER BY MASS	Nil	Nil	Nil	Nil	Nil	LQ0/1	20	
3368	TRINITROBENZOIC ACID, WETTED, WITH NOT LESS THAN 10% WATER BY MASS	Nil	Nil	Nil	Nil	Nil	LQ0/1	20	
3369	SODIUM DINITRO-O-CRESOLATE, WETTED, WITH NOT LESS THAN 10% WATER, BY MASS	Nil	Nil	Nil	Nil	Nil	LQ0/1	20	
3370	UREA NITRATE, WETTED, WITH NOT LESS THAN 10% WATER BY MASS	Nil	Nil	Nil	Nil	Nil	LQ0/1	20	
3371	2-METHYLBUTANAL	30/500	3 litres	30 kg	1 litre	20 kg	LQ4/2	333	
3373	DIAGNOSTIC SPECIMENS	Nil	Nil	Nil	Nil	Nil	LQ0/0	Nil	319

UN	Name								
3374	ACETYLENE, SOLVENT FREE	Nil	Nil	Nil	Nil	Nil	LQ0/2	333	
3375	AMMONIUM NITRATE EMULSION OR SUSPENSION OR GEL, INTERMEDIATE FOR BLASTING EXPLOSIVES, LIQUID OR SOLID	30/500	Nil	Nil	Nil	Nil	LQ0/2	333	309
3376	4-NITROPHENYL-HYDRAZINE WITH NOT LESS THAN 30% WATER BY MASS	Nil	Nil	Nil	Nil	Nil	LQ0/1	20	
3377	SODIUM PERBORATE MONOHYDRATE	30/1000	1 kg	30 kg	1 kg	20 kg	LQ12/3	1000	
3378	SODIUM CARBONATE PEROXYHYDRATE, PG11	30/500	500 g	30 kg	500 g	20 kg	LQ11/2	333	
3378	SODIUM CARBONATE PEROXYHYDRATE, PG111	30/1000	1 kg	30 kg	1 kg	20 kg	LQ12/3	1000	
3379	DESENSITISED EXPLOSIVE, LIQUID, N.O.S.	Nil	Nil	Nil	Nil	Nil	LQ0/1	20	274, 311
3380	DESENSITISED EXPLOSIVE, SOLID, N.O.S.	Nil	Nil	Nil	Nil	Nil	LQ0/1	20	274, 311
3381	TOXIC BY INHALATION LIQUID N.O.S., PG1	1/300	Nil	Nil	Nil	Nil	LQ0/1	20	274
3382	TOXIC BY INHALATION LIQUID N.O.S., PG1	1/300	Nil	Nil	Nil	Nil	LQ0/1	20	274
3383	TOXIC BY INHALATION LIQUID, FLAMMABLE, N.O.S., PG1	1/300	Nil	Nil	Nil	Nil	LQ0/1	20	274
3384	TOXIC BY INHALATION LIQUID, FLAMMABLE, N.O.S., PG1	1/300	Nil	Nil	Nil	Nil	LQ0/1	20	274
3385	TOXIC BY INHALATION, LIQUID, WATER-REACTIVE N.O.S., PG1	1/300	Nil	Nil	Nil	Nil	LQ0/1	20	274
3386	TOXIC BY INHALATION, LIQUID, WATER REACTIVE N.O.S., PG1	1/300	Nil	Nil	Nil	Nil	LQ0/1	20	274
3387	TOXIC BY INHALATION, LIQUID, OXIDISING, N.O.S., PG1	1/300	Nil	Nil	Nil	Nil	LQ0/1	20	274

UN	Substance	Excepted Quantities	LQ Packages Receptacle Size	LQ Packages Package Gross	LQ Shrink Wrapped Trays Receptacle Size	LQ Shrink Wrapped Trays Package Gross	Limited Quantity Value/Transport Category	Max Load	Special Provisions
3388	TOXIC BY INHALATION, LIQUID, OXIDISING, N.O.S., PG1	1/300	Nil	Nil	Nil	Nil	LQ0/1	20	274
3389	TOXIC BY INHALATION, LIQUID, CORROSIVE, N.O.S., PG1	1/300	Nil	Nil	Nil	Nil	LQ0/1	20	274
3390	TOXIC BY INHALATION, LIQUID, CORROSIVE, N.O.S., PG1	1/300	Nil	Nil	Nil	Nil	LQ0/1	20	274
3391	ORGANOMETALLIC SUBSTANCE, SOLID, PYROPHORIC, PG1	Nil	Nil	Nil	Nil	Nil	LQ0/0	Nil	274
3392	ORGANOMETALLIC SUBSTANCE, LIQUID, PYROPHORIC, PG1	Nil	Nil	Nil	Nil	Nil	LQ0/0	Nil	274
3393	ORGANOMETALLIC SUBSTANCE, SOLID, PYROPHORIC, WATER REACTIVE, PG1	Nil	Nil	Nil	Nil	Nil	LQ0/0	Nil	274
3394	ORGANOMETALLIC SUBSTANCE, LIQUID, PYROPHORIC, WATER REACTIVE, PG1	Nil	Nil	Nil	Nil	Nil	LQ0/0	Nil	274
3395	ORGANOMETALLIC SUBSTANCE, SOLID, WATER REACTIVE, PG1	Nil	Nil	Nil	Nil	Nil	LQ0/1	20	274
3395	ORGANOMETALLIC SUBSTANCE, SOLID, WATER REACTIVE, PG11	30/500	500 g	30 kg	500 g	20 kg	LQ11/2	333	274
3395	ORGANOMETALLIC SUBSTANCE, SOLID, WATER REACTIVE, PG111	30/1000	1 kg	30 kg	1 kg	20 kg	LQ12/3	1000	274

3396	ORGANOMETALLIC SUBSTANCE, SOLID, WATER REACTIVE, FLAMMABLE, PG1	Nil	Nil	Nil	Nil	Nil	Nil	LQ0/0	Nil	274
3396	ORGANOMETALLIC SUBSTANCE, SOLID, WATER REACTIVE, FLAMMABLE, PG11	30/500	500 g	30 kg	500 g	20 kg	LQ11/0	Nil	274
3396	ORGANOMETALLIC SUBSTANCE, SOLID, WATER REACTIVE, FLAMMABLE, PG111	30/1000	1 kg	30 kg	1 kg	20 kg	LQ12/0	Nil	274
3397	ORGANOMETALLIC SUBSTANCE, SOLID, WATER REACTIVE, SELF HEATING, PG1	Nil	Nil	Nil	Nil	Nil	LQ0/1	20	274
3397	ORGANOMETALLIC SUBSTANCE, SOLID, WATER REACTIVE, SELF HEATING, PG11	30/500	500 g	30 kg	500 g	20 kg	LQ11/2	333	274
3397	ORGANOMETALLIC SUBSTANCE, SOLID, WATER REACTIVE, SELF HEATING, PG111	30/1000	1 kg	30 kg	1 kg	20 kg	LQ12/3	1000	274
3398	ORGANOMETALLIC SUBSTANCE, LIQUID, WATER REACTIVE, PG1	Nil	Nil	Nil	Nil	Nil	LQ0/0	Nil	274
3398	ORGANOMETALLIC SUBSTANCE, LIQUID, PG11	30/500	500 ml	30 kg	500 ml	20 kg	LQ10/0	Nil	274
3398	ORGANOMETALLIC SUBSTANCE, LIQUID, PG111	30/1000	1 litre	30 kg	1 litre	20 kg	LQ13/0	Nil	274
3399	ORGANOMETALLIC SUBSTANCE, LIQUID, WATER REACTIVE, FLAMMABLE, PG1	Nil	Nil	Nil	Nil	Nil	LQ0/0	Nil	274
3399	ORGANOMETALLIC SUBSTANCE, LIQUID, WATER REACTIVE, FLAMMABLE, PG11	30/500	500 ml	30 kg	500 ml	20 kg	LQ10/0	Nil	274
3399	ORGANOMETALLIC SUBSTANCE, LIQUID, WATER REACTIVE, FLAMMABLE, PG111	30/1000	1 litre	30 kg	1 litre	20 kg	LQ13/0	Nil	274
3400	ORGANOMETALLIC SUBSTANCE, SOLID, SELF HEATING, PG11	30/500	1 kg	4 kg	500 g	4 kg	LQ18/2	333	274

UN	Substance	Excepted Quantities	LQ Packages Receptacle Size	LQ Packages Package Gross	LQ Shrink Wrapped Trays Receptacle Size	LQ Shrink Wrapped Trays Package Gross	Limited Quantity Value/Transport Category	Max Load	Special Provisions
3400	ORGANOMETALLIC SUBSTANCE, SOLID, SELF HEATING, PG111	30/1000	500 g	30 kg	500 g	20 kg	LQ11/3	1000	274
3401	ALKALI METAL, AMALGAM, SOLID	Nil	Nil	Nil	Nil	Nil	LQ0/1	20	182, 274
3402	ALKALINE EARTH METAL, AMALGAM, SOLID	Nil	Nil	Nil	Nil	Nil	LQ0/1	20	183, 506, 506
3403	POTASSIUM METAL ALLOYS, SOLID	Nil	Nil	Nil	Nil	Nil	LQ0/1	20	
3404	POTASSIUM SODIUM ALLOYS, SOLID	Nil	Nill	Nil	Nil	Nil	LQ0/1	20	
3405	BARIUM CHLORATE SOLUTION, PG11	30/500	500 ml	30 kg	500 ml	20 kg	LQ10/2	333	
3405	BARIUM CHLORATE SOLUTION, PG111	30/1000	1 litre	30 kg	1 litre	20 kg	LQ13/3	1000	
3406	BARIUM PERCHLORATE SOLUTION, PG11	30/500	500 ml	30 kg	500 ml	20 kg	LQ10/2	333	
3406	BARIUM PERCHLORATE SOLUTION, PG111	30/1000	1 litre	30 kg	1 litre	20 kg	LQ13/3	1000	
3407	CHLORATE AND MAGNESIUM CHLORIDE MIXTURE SOLUTION, PG11	30/500	500 ml	30 kg	500 ml	20 kg	LQ10/2	333	
3407	CHLORATE AND MAGNESIUM CHLORIDE MIXTURE SOLUTION, PG111	30/1000	1 litre	30 kg	1 litre	20 kg	LQ13/3	1000	
3408	LEAD PERCHLORATE SOLUTION, PG11	30/500	500 ml	30 kg	500 ml	20 kg	LQ10/2	333	
3408	LEAD PERCHLORATE SOLUTION, PG111	30/1000	1 litre	30 kg	1 litre	20 kg	LQ13/3	1000	
3409	CHLORONITROBENZENES, LIQUID	1/500	500 ml	2 litres	100 ml	2 litres	LQ17/2	333	279

UN	Name								
3410	4-CHLORO-O-TOLUIDINE HYDROCHLORIDE SOLUTION	30/1000	5 kg	30 kg	5 kg	20 kg	LQ7/2	333	
3411	BETA-NAPHTHYLAMINE SOLUTION, PG11	1/500	500 ml	2 litres	100 ml	2 litres	LQ17/2	333	
3411	BETA-NAPHTHYLAMINE SOLUTION, PG111	30/1000	5 kg	30 kg	5 kg	20 kg	LQ7/2	333	
3412	FORMIC ACID, PG11	30/500	1 litre	30 kg	500 ml	20 kg	LQ22/2	333	
3412	FORMIC ACID, PG111	30/1000	5 litres	30 kg	5 litres	20 kg	LQ7/3	1000	
3413	POTASSIUM CYANIDE SOLUTION, PG1	1/300	Nil	Nil	Nil	Nil	LQ0/1	20	
3413	POTASSIUM CYANIDE SOLUTION, PG11	1/500	500 ml	2 litres	100 ml	2 litres	LQ17/2	333	
3413	POTASSIUM CYANIDE SOLUTION, PG111	30/1000	5 litres	30 kg	5 litres	20 kg	LQ7/2	333	
3414	SODIUM CYANIDE SOLUTION, PG1	1/300	Nil	Nil	Nil	Nil	LQ0/1	20	
3414	SODIUM CYANIDE SOLUTION, PG11	1/500	500 ml	2 litres	100 ml	2 litres	LQ17/2	333	
3414	SODIUM CYANIDE SOLUTION, PG111	30/1000	5 litres	30 kg	5 litres	20 kg	LQ7/2	333	
3415	SODIUM FLUORIDE SOLUTION	30/1000	5 litres	30 kg	5 litres	20 kg	LQ7/2	333	
3416	CHLOROACETO-PHENONE, LIQUID	1/500	500 ml	2 litres	100 ml	2 litres	LQ17/2	333	
3417	XYLYL BROMIDE, SOLID	1/500	1 kg	4 kg	500 g	4 kg	LQ18/2	333	
3418	2,4-TOLUYLENEDIAMINE SOLUTION	30/1000	5 litres	30 kg	5 litres	20 kg	LQ7/2	333	
3419	BORON TRIFLUORIDE ACETIC ACID COMPLEX, SOLID	30/500	3 kg	30 kg	1 kg	20 kg	LQ23/2	333	
3420	BORON TRIFLUORIDE PROPIONIC ACID COMPLEX, SOLID	30/500	3 kg	30 kg	1 kg	20 kg	LQ23/2	333	
3421	POTASSIUM HYDROGENDIFLUORIDE SOLUTION, PG11	30/500	1 litre	30 kg	500 ml	20 kg	LQ22/2	333	

UN	Substance	Excepted Quantities	LQ Packages		LQ Shrink Wrapped Trays		Limited Quantity Value/Transport Category	Max Load	Special Provisions
			Receptacle Size	Package Gross	Receptacle Size	Package Gross			
3421	POTASSIUM HYDROGENDIFLUORIDE SOLUTION, PG111	30/1000	5 litres	30 kg	5 litres	20 kg	LQ7/3	1000	
3422	POTASSIUM FLUORIDE SOLUTION	30/1000	5 litres	30 kg	5 litres	20 kg	LQ7/2	333	
3423	TETRAMETHYL - AMMONIUM HYDROXIDE, SOLID	30/500	6 kg	30 kg	2 kg	20 kg	LQ24/2	333	
3424	AMMONIUM DINITROL-O-CRESOLATE SOLUTION, PG11	1/500	500 ml	2 litres	100 ml	2 litres	LQ17/2	333	
3424	AMMONIUM DINITROL-O-CRESOLATE SOLUTION, PG111	30/1000	5 litres	30 kg	5 litres	20 kg	LQ7/2	333	
3425	BROMOACETIC ACID, SOLID	30/500	3 kg	30 kg	1 kg	20 kg	LQ23/2	333	
3426	ACRYLAMIDE SOLUTION	30/1000	5 litres	30 kg	5 litres	20 kg	LQ7/2	333	
3427	CHLOROBENZYL CHLORIDES, SOLID	30/1000	6 kg	30 kg	3 kg	20 kg	LQ9/2	333	
3428	3-CHLORO-4-METHYLPHENYL ISOCYANATE, SOLID	1/500	1 kg	4 kg	500 g	4 kg	LQ18/2	333	
3429	CHLOROTOLUIDINES, LIQUID	30/1000	5 litres	30 kg	5 litres	20 kg	LQ7/2	333	
3430	XYLENOLS, LIQUID	1/500	500 ml	2 litres	100 ml	2 litres	LQ17/2	333	
3431	NITROBENZO-TRIFLUORIDES, SOLID	1/500	1 kg	4 kg	500 g	4 kg	LQ18/2	333	
3432	POLYCHLORINATED BIPHENYLS, SOLID	30/500	1 kg	30 kg	1 kg	20 kg	LQ25/0	Nil	305

UN	Name								
3434	NITROCRESOLS, LIQUID	30/1000	5 litres	30 kg	5 litres	20 kg	LQ7/2	333	
3436	HEXAFLUORACETONE HYDRATE, SOLID	1/500	1 kg	4 kg	500 g	4 kg	LQ18/2	333	
3437	CHLOROCRESOLS, SOLID	1/500	1 kg	4 kg	500 g	4 kg	LQ18/2	333	
3438	ALPHA-METHYLBENZYL ALCOHOL, SOLID	30/1000	6 kg	30 kg	3 kg	20 kg	LQ9/2	333	
3439	NITRILES, TOXIC, SOLID, N.O.S., PG1	1/300	Nil	Nil	Nil	Nil	LQ0/1	20	274
3439	NITRILES, TOXIC, SOLID, N.O.S., PG11	1/500	1 kg	4 kg	500 g	4 kg	LQ18/2	333	274
3439	NITRILES, TOXIC, SOLID, N.O.S., PG111	30/1000	6 kg	30 kg	3 kg	20 kg	LQ9/2	333	274
3440	SELENIUM COMPOUND, LIQUID N.O.S., PG1	1/300	Nil	Nil	Nil	Nil	LQ0/1	20	563, 274
3440	SELENIUM COMPOUND, LIQUID N.O.S., PG11	1/500	500 ml	2 litres	100 ml	2 litres	LQ17/2	333	563, 274
3440	SELENIUM COMPOUND, LIQUID N.O.S., PG111	30/1000	5 litres	30 kg	5 litres	20 kg	LQ7/2	333	563, 274
3441	CHLORODINITROL-BENZINES, SOLID	1/500	1 kg	4 kg	500 g	4 kg	LQ18/2	333	279
3442	DICHLOROANILINES, SOLID	1/500	1 kg	4 kg	500 g	4 kg	LQ18/2	333	279
3443	DINITROBENZINES, SOLID	1/500	1 kg	4 kg	500 g	4 kg	LQ18/2	333	
3444	NICOTINE HYDROCHLORIDE, SOLID	1/500	1 kg	4 kg	500 g	4 kg	LQ18/2	333	43
3445	NICOTINE SULPHATE, SOLID	1/500	1 kg	4 kg	500 g	4 kg	LQ18/2	333	
3446	NITROTOLUENES, SOLID	1/500	1 kg	4 kg	500 g	4 kg	LQ18/2	333	
3447	NITROXYLENES, SOLID	1/500	1 kg	4 kg	500 g	4 kg	LQ18/2	333	
3448	TEAR GAS SUBSTANCE, SOLID, N.O.S., PG1	1/300	Nil	Nil	Nil	Nil	LQ0/1	20	274

UN	Substance	Excepted Quantities	LQ Packages		LQ Shrink Wrapped Trays		Limited Quantity Value/Transport Category	Max Load	Special Provisions
			Receptacle Size	Gross Package	Receptacle Size	Gross Package			
3448	TEAR GAS SUBSTANCE SOLID N.O.S., PG11	1/500	1 kg	4 kg	500 g	4 kg	LQ18/2	333	274
3449	BROMOBENZYL CYANATES , SOLID	1/300	Nil	Nil	Nil	Nil	LQ0/1	20	138
3450	DIPHENYCHLORO-ARSINE, SOLID	1/300	Nil	Nil	Nil	Nil	LQ0/1	20	
3451	TOLUIDINES, SOLID	1/500	1 kg	4 kg	500 g	4 kg	LQ18/2	333	279
3452	XYLIDINES, SOLID	1/500	1 kg	4 kg	500 g	4 kg	LQ18/2	333	
3453	PHOSPHORIC ACID, SOLID	30/1000	6 kg	30 kg	2 kg	20 kg	LQ24/3	1000	
3454	DINITROTULUENES, SOLID	1/500	1 kg	4 kg	500 g	4 kg	LQ18/2	333	
3455	CRESOLS, SOLID	1/500	1 kg	4 kg	500 g	4 kg	LQ18/2	333	
3456	NITROSYLSULPHURIC ACID, SOLID	30/500	3 kg	30 kg	1 kg	20 kg	LQ23/2	333	
3457	CHLORONITROTOLUENES, SOLID	30/1000	6 kg	30 kg	3 kg	20 kg	LQ9/2	333	
3458	NITROANISOLES, SOLID	30/1000	6 kg	30 kg	3 kg	20 kg	LQ9/2	333	279
3459	NITROBROMOBENZENES, SOLID	30/1000	6 kg	30 kg	3 kg	20 kg	LQ9/2	333	
3460	N-ETHYLBENZYL-TOLUIDINES, SOLID	30/1000	6 kg	30 kg	3 kg	20 kg	LQ9/2	333	
3462	TOXINS, EXTRACTED FROM LIVING SOURCES, SOLID, N.O.S., PG1	1/300	Nil	Nil	Nil	Nil	LQ0/1	20	210, 274

UN	Name								
3462	TOXINS, EXTRACTED FROM LIVING SOURCES, SOLID, N.O.S., PG11	1/500	1 kg	4 kg	500 g	4 kg	LQ18/2	333	210, 274
3462	TOXINS, EXTRACTED FROM LIVING SOURCES, SOLID, N.O.S., PG111	30/1000	6 kg	30 kg	3 kg	20 kg	LQ9/2	333	210, 274
3463	PROPIONIC ACID	30/500	1 litre	30 kg	500 ml	20 kg	LQ22/2	333	
3464	ORGANOPHOSPHORUS COMPOUND, TOXIC, SOLID, N.O.S., PG1	1/300	Nil	Nil	Nil	Nil	LQ0/1	20	43, 274
3464	ORGANOPHOSPHORUS COMPOUND, TOXIC, SOLID, N.O.S., PG11	1/500	1 kg	4 kg	500 g	4 kg	LQ18/2	333	43, 274
3464	ORGANOPHOSPHORUS COMPOUND, TOXIC, SOLID, N.O.S., PG111	30/1000	6 kg	30 kg	3 kg	20 kg	LQ9/2	333	43, 274
3465	ORGANOARSENIC COMPOUND, SOLID, N.O.S., PG1	1/300	Nil	Nil	Nil	Nil	LQ0/1	20	274
3465	ORGANOARSENIC COMPOUND, SOLID, N.O.S., PG11	1/500	1 kg	4 kg	500 g	4 kg	LQ18/2	333	274
3465	ORGANOARSENIC COMPOUND ,SOLID, N.O.S., PG111	30/1000	6 kg	30 kg	3 kg	20 kg	LQ9/2	333	274
3466	METAL CARBONYLS, SOLID, N.O.S., PG1	1/300	Nil	Nil	Nil	Nil	LQ0/1	20	274, 562
3466	METAL CARBONYLS, SOLID, N.O.S., PG11	1/500	1 kg	4 kg	500 g	4 kg	LQ18/2	333	274, 562
3466	METAL CARBONYLS, SOLID, N.O.S., PG111	30/1000	6 kg	30 kg	3 kg	20 kg	LQ9/2	333	274, 562
3467	ORGANOMETALLIC COMPOUND, TOXIC, SOLID, N.O.S., PG1	1/300	Nil	Nil	Nil	Nil	LQ0/1	20	274, 562
3467	ORGANOMETALLIC COMPOUND, TOXIC, SOLID, N.O.S., PG11	1/500	1 kg	4 kg	500 g	4 kg	LQ18/2	333	274, 562

UN	Substance	Excepted Quantities	LQ Packages		LQ Shrink Wrapped Trays		Limited Quantity Value/Transport Category	Max Load	Special Provisions
			Receptacle Size	Package Gross	Receptacle Size	Package Gross			
3467	ORGANOMETALLIC COMPOUND, TOXIC, SOLID, N.O.S. PG111	30/1000	6 kg	30 kg	3 kg	20 kg	LQ9/2	333	274, 562
3468	HYDROGEN IN A METAL HYDRIDE STORAGE SYSTEM	Nil	Nil	Nil	Nil	Nil	LQ0/2	333	321
3469	PAINT, FLAMMABLE, CORROSIVE, PG1 (INCLUDING PAINT, LACQUER, ENAMEL, STAIN, SHELLAC, VARNISH, POLISH, LIQUID FILLER AND LIQUID LACQUER BASE) OR PAINT RELATED MATERIAL, FLAMMABLE, CORROSIVE (INCLUDING PAINT THINNING AND REDUCING COMPOUND)	Nil	500 ml	1 litre	Not	Allowed	LQ3/1	20	163
3469	PAINT, FLAMMABLE, CORROSIVE, PG11 (INCLUDING PAINT, LACQUER, ENAMEL, STAIN, SHELLAC, VARNISH, POLISH, LIQUID FILLER AND LIQUID LACQUER BASE) OR PAINT RELATED MATERIAL, FLAMMABLE, CORROSIVE (INCLUDING PAINT THINNING AND REDUCING COMPOUND)	30/500	3 litres	30 kg	1 litre	20 kg	LQ4/2	333	163
3469	PAINT, FLAMMABLE, CORROSIVE, PG111 (INCLUDING PAINT, LACQUER, ENAMEL, STAIN, SHELLAC, VARNISH, POLISH, LIQUID FILLER AND LIQUID LACQUER BASE) OR PAINT RELATED MATERIAL, FLAMMABLE, CORROSIVE (INCLUDING PAINT THINNING AND REDUCING COMPOUND)	30/1000	5 litres	30 kg	5 litres	20 kg	LQ7/3	1000	163

UN No.	Name								
3470	PAINT, CORROSIVE, FLAMMABLE (INCLUDING PAINT, LACQUER, ENAMEL, STAIN, SHELLAC, VARNISH, POLISH, LIQUID FILLER AND LIQUID LACQUER BASE) OR PAINT RELATED MATERIAL, FLAMMABLE, CORROSIVE (INCLUDING PAINT THINNING AND REDUCING COMPOUND)	30/500	1 litre	30 kg	500 ml	20 kg	LQ22/2	333	163
3471	HYDROGENDIFLUORIDES SOLUTION N.O.S., PG11	30/500	1 litre	30 kg	500 ml	20 kg	LQ22/2	333	
3471	HYDROGENDIFLUORIDES SOLUTION N.O.S., PG111	30/1000	5 litres	30 kg	5 litres	20 kg	LQ7/3	1000	
3472	CROTONIC ACID LIQUID	30/1000	5 litres	30 kg	5 litres	20 kg	LQ7/3	1000	
3473	FUEL CELL CARTRIDGES CONTAINING FLAMMABLE LIQUIDS	Nil	1 litre	30 kg	1 litre	20 kg	LQ13/3	1000	328
3474	1-HYDROXYLBENZOTRIAZOLE, ANHYDROUS, WETTED	Nil	Nil	Nil	Nil	Nil	LQ0/1	20	
3475	ETHANOL & GASOLINE MIXTURE OR ETHANOL AND MOTORSPIRIT MIXTURE OR ETHANOL AND PETROL MIXTURE	30/500	3 kg	30 kg	1 kg	20 kg	LQ4/2	333	333
3476	FUEL CELL CARTRIDGES OR FUEL CELL CARTRIDGES CONTAINED IN EQUIPMENT OR FUEL CELL CARTRIDGES PACKED WITH EQUIPMENT	Nil	500 ml/kg	30 kg	500 kg/ml	20 kg	LQ10/11/3	1000	328, 324
3477	FUEL CELL CARTRIDGES OR FUEL CELL CARTRIDGES CONTAINED IN EQUIPMENT OR FUEL CELL CARTRIDGES PACKED WITH EQUIPMENT CONTAINING CORROSIVE SUBSTANCES	Nil	1 kg/litre	30 kg	1 kg/litre	20 kg	LQ12/13/3	1000	328, 324

UN	Substance	Excepted Quantities	LQ Packages		LQ Shrink Wrapped Trays		Limited Quantity Value/Transport Category	Max Load	Special Provisions
			Receptacle Size	Package Gross	Receptacle Size	Package Gross			
3478	FUEL CELL CARTRIDGES OR FUEL CELL CARTRIDGES CONTAINED IN EQUIPMENT OR FUEL CELL CARTRIDGES PACKED WITH EQUIPMENT CONTAINING LIQUEFIED FLAMMABLE GAS	Nil	120 ml	30 kg	120 ml	20 kg	LQ1/2	333	328, 324
3479	FUEL CELL CARTRIDGES OR FUEL CELL CARTRIDGES CONTAINED IN EQUIPMENT OR FUEL CELL CARTRIDGES PACKED WITH EQUIPMENT CONTAINING HYDROGEN IN METAL HYDRIDE	Nil	120 ml	30 kg	120 ml	20 kg	LQ1/2	333	328, 339
3480	LITHIUM BATTERIES	Nil	Nil	Nil	Nil	Nil	LQ0/2	333	188, 230, 310, 636
3481	LITHIUM BATTERIES CONTAINED IN EQUIPMENT OR LITHIUM ION BATTERIES PACKED WITH EQUIPMENT	Nil	Nil	Nil	Nil	Nil	LQ0/2	333	188, 230, 636